# the GILLARD PROJECT

Michael Cooney has served as speechwriter to Prime Minister Julia Gillard, policy director to federal Labor leaders Kim Beazley and Mark Latham, and was the founding policy director of the progressive think tank Per Capita. He is now executive director of the Chifley Research Centre, the official think tank of the Australian Labor Party.

'The essential task of great speechwriters is to not be themselves. Rather they must eloquently channel their principal's authentic voice into words that hope to inform and inspire. In this book, Michael Cooney has thrown off that restriction. This is Michael's voice and a book only he could write. No one else could combine the perspective that comes from spending years in a windowless room in the prime minister's office with the cultural wealth accumulated through a lifetime of devouring great literature. No one else could make you smile, nod in agreement, furrow your brow in disagreement and then, at the most unexpected moments, offer you an ode to Labor's spirit.'

JULIA GILLARD

# the GILLARD PROJECT

*Michael Cooney*

VIKING
*an imprint of*
PENGUIN BOOKS

VIKING

UK | USA | Canada | Ireland | Australia
India | New Zealand | South Africa | China

Penguin Books is part of the Penguin Random House group of companies whose addresses can be found at global.penguinrandomhouse.com.

First published by Penguin Group (Australia), 2015

2 4 6 8 10 9 7 5 3 1

Text copyright Michael Cooney © 2015

The moral right of the author has been asserted.

All rights reserved. Without limiting the rights under copyright reserved above, no part of this publication may be reproduced, stored in or introduced into a retrieval system, or transmitted, in any form or by any means (electronic, mechanical, photocopying, recording or otherwise), without the prior written permission of both the copyright owner and the above publisher of this book.

Cover and text design by Laura Thomas © Penguin Group (Australia)
Cover photograph by Carla Gottgens/Bloomberg via Getty Images
Typeset in Adobe Garamond
Colour separation by Splitting Image Colour Studio, Clayton, Victoria
Printed and bound in Australia by Griffin Press, an accredited ISO AS/NZS 14001 Environmental Management Systems printer.

National Library of Australia
Cataloguing-in-Publication data:

Cooney, Michael
The Gillard project / Michael Cooney
9780670078141 (paperback)
Gillard, Julia – Oratory
Australian Labor Party
Political leadership – Australia
Australia – Politics and government – 2001–
324.220994

ISBN 9780670078141

penguin.com.au

# Contents

*Preface*      I

**Part One: The Crown in the Bush**
1. Thanks, PM      11
2. That First Fine, Careless Rapture      20
3. Permission to Perform      41

INTERLUDE: *The Staff Life*      54

**Part Two: Sufficient to Have Stood, Though Free to Fall**
4. Pivot      77
5. Delivery and Decision      99
6. The Shadow of the Past      116
7. We Are Us      127

INTERLUDE: *The Movement*      143

**Part Three: Raining Stones**
8. The Sleep of Reason      163
9. Basest Things      183
10. I Will Not      194
11. The World at Our Feet      204

INTERLUDE: *The Shy Child*      223

**Part Four: Small Hammers**
12. Now or Never      241
13. The Last Grand Days      257
14. Drafting the B Speech      272

*Endnotes*      290
*Acknowledgements*      299
*Index*      303

*To the Australians who served, suffered
and died in Afghanistan*

# Preface

*Writing a speech for the president of the United States is like playing tennis with a gigantic tennis racket.*

ELEANOR DRAKE, FICTIONAL SPEECHWRITER<br>FOR GEORGE BUSH IN *DEATH OF A PRESIDENT*

This book is about lot of things, but at its simplest, it is about what I found out while I was writing speeches for a Labor prime minister. This is not a diary of disillusion; I have tried not to 'work the wound'. While I learned things – about Labor, about my mates, about Julia Gillard – I didn't fundamentally change my mind. What did Hugh Gaitskell (in the 1950s the leader of UK Labour) write, while still an undergraduate activist, of the General Strike in 1926? He would not 'desert his side just because it had miscalculated its means'.

But yes, I learned a lot about some people and things I love.

I learned about the Australian Labor Party. I've always wanted to believe that we are a 'normal' political party; that while we have a different plan for the nation from the Liberal Party and its predecessors, our relationship with the system of politics is essentially analogous to theirs. I think this was because I wanted to believe that Labor's task, winning and governing to progress, was easier than some said.

In this, at least, I don't think I was right.

Labor is more different, and different in more ways, than I ever understood. It's obvious our structures and theory of self are different – we have our own ecclesiology; no one 'rats' on the Liberals – but in government I learned that Labor is actually a different kind of *thing*. The difference between Labor and other parties is ontological. We have to understand that, and to understand it, we have to write it down.

If Labor had not already been 'collective memory in action' before the great Labor historian and speechwriter Graham Freudenberg coined the phrase, the power of those words would certainly have made us so since. In the same way, Labor people only universally became 'true believers' after the playwright and Labor speechwriter Bob Ellis brought the phrase from the mass to a mass audience, with the 1980s ABC miniseries of the same name, and in turn to Paul Keating's election night speech of 1993. These are phrases that have done so much to identify and define Labor's role as a 'grand old party' in Australian politics. We are more than that though; we are a 'party of initiative'. And we operate in a system made up mostly of 'parties of resistance'. Things begin in Labor, they begin with and through Labor, in a system with so many incentives to stop things happening; we're not just a cause, we cause things. And that's hard. That's why, more than the other parties, Labor needs its golden legends and it needs its soldiers' songs; our night chants, 'impatient for the coming fight/ and as we wait the morning's light'; because the struggle of a party of initiative is a different and difficult thing.

But we need references as well as reflections; war diaries as well as war poems. Ontology isn't enough. There are operational lessons to be learned. The next Labor government will have to fight harder for change than the last one, just as we had to fight harder than the one before us. If consensus and charisma were ever enough, God knows they aren't enough now. This why unity matters for Labor; this is also why not biting off more than we can chew matters. Not just because the business of government is complex, though it is; not just because the means for communicating progress are fragmented, though that's true too; but because Labor is opposed. We meet opposition – not only in politics, but in society at large. This has been chronic, and by 2013 it was acute as well – Labor was opposed by a business community dominated and distorted by a handful of big firms who were more conservative and politicised than since before the Second World War; by a media mogul as political as any in our history, with more individual power than any in our history; but above all by a conservative political movement in the country and a conservative coalition in the Parliament whose leadership was dominated by conservative prejudice and vested-interest politics as any we have known.

We know we are the party of initiative in Australian life, but far too often we forget theirs is a party of resistance. And we forget that they will fight.

You can't reflect on the Gillard story without reflecting on that, and Labor can't apply the lessons of the Gillard story to our party without understanding our particular enemy and its contemporary strengths.

I learned about my party and I also learned a lot about my mates. I'm so proud of the men and women I have known and worked with on Labor staff during the past two decades – and none more so than the staff of the Gillard government and the staff of the Gillard Prime Minister's Office. I want you to know about them. Various and bright and humble and Labor – and tired, always so tired, and badly used and brave; they deserve better than they get in the papers. The staff who said they wanted their names in a book laughed because they didn't really mean it; the staff who said they didn't want their names in a book looked right at me when they told me. I haven't forgotten.

So it's a story about my party and my mates – and it's a story about my boss.

Labor is different; Labor prime ministers are different. A leader of a party of resistance can hold the pass for a time and be considered a success. The work of a leader of a party of initiative can ultimately never be complete. It will always be true that you could have done more. So Labor prime ministers have only three final stories: death, failure or defeat.

When former prime minister Keating told the newly former prime minister Gillard, 'We all get taken out in a box, love,' I believe this is what he was talking about. It ends; the only question is how and when, and how much you do before it does. And maybe – a little – how you wear it.

In his most famous speech, Chifley said the leadership of Labor was 'a man-killing job'; he and John Curtin still lie in state in the King's Hall of our minds. The collapse and resignation of Andrew Fisher – a man so strong he forced the fusion of the anti-Labor forces in Australia – remains a kind of death. This is the true state of Labor grace: heroic virtue and final perseverance. Few truly seek it.

Failure – loss at one's own hand – is never far from mind. Our poor sainted prime minister Jimmy Scullin failed in the face of the worst that the global economic crisis of 1931 could send; his counsel was so precious to Curtin and Chifley in the crises of the 1940s, and I like to think he interceded for us in government in the crisis of 2008. His prayers were answered, at least for a while. Kevin Rudd failed too – failed to stand for the Labor leadership when challenged in 2010; failed to challenge for the Labor leadership in 2012; failed to restore respect for the Labor Party when elected in the ballot Prime Minister Gillard offered him that day in 2013. A gifted politician and a person of achievement, but a Labor failure.

Our first great man and first prime minister, the cryptic Chris Watson, exceeds all categories still; his comrade Billy Hughes chose life outside the movement.

For the remaining few who escape death or failure, all that is left is the certainty of defeat. Stay in office as long as you can – have no doubt, longevity matters – make as many big changes as you can before you're overcome or undermined by capital and conservatism, or the strains of conflict bring you down through the entropy within; then retire to inspire the next generation to fight on: no Labor prime minister can do more. Had Chifley lived to enjoy retirement from parliamentary life, that's how we'd see him today. That's what Gough Whitlam, Bob Hawke and Paul Keating each did.

When then opposition leader Tony Abbott warned his party room against Julia Gillard's life-force in 2012, predicting she wouldn't 'lie down and die', his natural phrase-making lifted a routine warning against complacency into an expression of genuine insight. We wore that line like a medal, with the PM herself repeating it to huge applause at party conferences and union events. No matter what occurred, she would not fail, and she would not die. That's Julia Gillard's story: she knew she would be defeated one day, but she had a project, and every day she had, she spent to get it done.

There's been a lot said about how Julia Gillard became prime minister, and less said about what she did while she was there; I don't believe her record needs a defender, but perhaps it could do with an explainer. So this is not only what I learned about Julia Gillard as a person, but about her as a prime minister. It's about the things she did and planned to do – what I call the Gillard project.

Above all, Julia Gillard governed as a 'great nation progressive'. She led a big country and saw the possibilities and obligations of this: for a virtuous cycle of national modernisation where our progressive role in the world reinforces our economic strength now, and where we use that strength to underpin policy modernisation at home that in turn strengthens our economy and society for the future. In her words in early 2013, an Australia 'strong and fair but also smart'. That's why, in the time she had, she managed the economy in the interests of ordinary Australians, and kept creating jobs, in the most difficult and complex circumstances. She made national progress, modernising our social safety net by launching DisabilityCare, the national disability insurance scheme; renewing our factories of opportunity by improving our schools; strengthening the US alliance and the relationship with China. She put a price on carbon when no one else could or would.

'If we want things to stay as they are, things will have to change' – di Lampedusa's lament for the passing of old Sicily – rings heavily in my mind. To stay fair, to preserve our national character, much about national policy urgently has to update and change. National modernisation under conditions of national fairness as a project – the work of a great nation progressive – was not completed by 2013; but it contains the essential elements of what is required for Australia today.

And okay. There's no point pretending this is not a story about me. I worked as Julia Gillard's speechwriter for almost three years, and followed in her camp from Canberra to Washington and Beijing, via Phillip Street and Rooty Hill. It was a comedy of manners, it was a comedy of errors, it was a tragedy, it was a bunch of stuff that happened; it was a calvary and a triumph. There were days of despair but I never lost hope.

That is what I most want to tell you; this is the 'message in a bottle' from the island of my mind: it was worth it.

Whether you read this book starting by searching for your name in the index a few hours after it is published, or whether you pull this book off a bookshelf in a beach house in forty years' time, what I want you to know is that in these thousand days, she was a good prime minister, we did good things, politics mattered, the Labor Party was the only way for Australia to become its best future self – and all of that is still true today.

In this respect, it's very much my story, and it's certainly mine in another sense: I don't speak for everyone, and I don't tell everything. Legitimately in staff work, and in life, there are some confidences to protect and some responsibilities to respect; always in life, there are some things better left unsaid. In *Walden*, Henry David Thoreau wrote, 'You will pardon some obscurities, for there are more secrets in my trade than in most men's, and yet not voluntarily kept, but inseparable from its very nature. I would gladly tell all that I know about it, and never paint *No Admittance* on my gate.'

But I'll tell you as much as makes sense and as much as I can.

PART ONE

# THE CROWN IN THE BUSH

# 1.
# Thanks, PM

*In the plants and mines in the west and the north I've seen the great Australian cultural tradition of informality that rejects the sort of snobbishness and expectations of obsequiousness that infect other societies.*

*'Oi, Julia, give us a wave.' They don't talk like that to the president of France. And I love it.*

PRIME MINISTER JULIA GILLARD

On the good days, I noticed the comedy of manners more than the comedy of errors. One of the good days was 11 February 2011 and I remember it well.

That was the day of the Mick Young Scholarship Trust's annual dinner at the Four Seasons in Sydney – a good Labor function in honour of a great Labor man – and I'd written part of the speech the Labor prime minister was due to give.

Julia Gillard had spent the afternoon with some of her staff, me included, catching up on paperwork and holding meetings in the then-Commonwealth Parliamentary Offices in Phillip Street in Sydney's CBD. At that time, what we called 'the Sydney CPO' was a strange place, where the shade of John Howard was always present. The prime minister's suite, like a number of ministerial suites on the floor above it, was still fitted out in the chesterfields and chestnut, droll-but-they're-not-joking retro style the former PM had made a point of in his first term fifteen years before. Indeed the whole space remained largely untouched since the mid-nineties. Since 2007 Labor's Prime Minister's Office (PMO) staffs had principally used it as a visiting venue – only a relative handful of advisers had been permanently based there.

On a quiet day it felt a bit like the Melbourne Club in *On the Beach*. There were dozens of empty desks, more than one room no one ever entered and more than one door no one ever opened, and corridors where the lights were rarely on. This day, with Gillard in the office, there was a consciously still but active and purposeful atmosphere, which made the place feel even quieter, albeit more inhabited; a bit like an examination hall during a big test.

Now, just before the car was to take the boss to Kirribilli so she could change for dinner and come back across the bridge to the event, I was going to have to break this methodical silence. The press secretaries in our Canberra office were having a little panic about a line – one of my lines – in the speech. I'd resisted removing it and this had been agreed on condition that I 'represent' their concerns to the boss. The transaction was pretty much to make sure that if it went bad, it was either her fault or my fault, but not their fault.

This was all wrong. They'd had the draft for a week, of course, and of course now it was almost literally physically too late to take a line out (in fact, there was barely time to say to her, 'We haven't taken a line out'), so of course it was now they had rung. The prime minister was walking out of the building at the moment I got off the phone, and she was leaving with the police but no staff, so there wasn't even anyone I could text or phone saying 'stop!' And I certainly couldn't wait to ring her in the car: that really would be too late.

If (God forbid) she actually said, 'Oh hell, Cooney, the press secs are right – what have you done to me!' I'd have to horror-rush this change as it was; sometimes you can just pull a line from a speech, but when it's a sharp expression of the point of a whole section, cutting a line can leave the entire speech high and dry. You can't just 'edit' the moral out of a story and I actually wasn't sure what the solution would look like in that event.

Finally, if this went bad, my plans for getting a beer in before the dinner were definitively spannered.

You don't run around a prime minister's office, and I defy anyone (even a press secretary) to enjoy a conversation of substance with a prime minister, no matter how brief, while short of breath. So I sort of trotted up the corridor, and when I got to about five metres behind her she was at the door. I wasn't going to have to shout, but I was going to have to raise my voice to get her attention.

And before I could do that, I was going to have decide what to call her. Good Lord.

So, I'd first met Julia Gillard nine years earlier. We'd been pretty close, particularly in the period where I was future Labor leader Mark Latham's closest adviser and she was his closest colleague. I hesitate to say any MP I first met when I was a staffer is a 'mate', but we'd socialised, and certainly I called her Julia. The Labor leaders I'd worked with for years were always known by their first names – Simon, Mark, Kim.

But PMs are different. People who'd worked in the Rudd PMO or had only worked for Gillard since she took office tended to refer to her as 'the PM', and think of her that way as well. By contrast I'd come in after the election, a few months before this moment; in fact until now, I hadn't had to think about what I was going to call her. (In meetings a boss typically speaks first.) But here, I was definitely going to have to be the one to use a title or a name. In the half-seconds that this *Seinfeld*-in-the-PMO monologue ran through my brain, her hands were reaching to push on the door. 'Oi' just wasn't going to cut it.

'Julia!'

She stopped and turned around. I caught up with her and said, 'The press secs wanted to be sure you were happy with the "cunning and courage" line in the speech for tonight – it's a reflection on Faulkner's party reform speech from last year. You got that reference, right?'

She looked at me straight and said, 'Yep, that's fine. Okay? Gotta go.' But the cops looked at me funny.

I totally should have said 'PM'.

—

I was standing in that doorway with Prime Minister Julia Gillard as an experienced leader's office adviser, with ten years' staff work under my belt, fifteen years as a party activist and thirty-eight years of living in Canberra, boy and man, with my nose pressed against the window of national politics. In a thousand ways it was just more staff work; I was in my own battalion, my own footy club, and it was everything I knew how to do.

And in a thousand ways it was changed utterly – it wasn't just politics, it was 'the PMO'; my battalion had been sent to a whole new front, and the footy club had made the finals for the first time in a long time, and I had no idea what I was in for.

So much more would change by the next time I called the prime minister 'Julia'. Polluters would have to pay a price for carbon, schools would have a national plan for improvement and a funding model to back it, there would be a national disability insurance scheme – and a levy to fund it, forever. Australia would have risen past a declining Spain to become the twelfth-largest economy in the world, there'd be US marines training out of Darwin and a new deal with China. Australians would have hundreds of thousands of new jobs.

Labor would have made enough mistakes to fill a book. Some people would say, and possibly even mean, that this was the worst government in Australia's history – very kind to Lyons and Hughes and Bruce, and as for Menzies in 1940, well, you would forget, wouldn't you – and measured public opinion would suggest that for periods, we were the least popular government on record.

There would even be the suggestion that Labor's advice wasn't always perfect and Labor's speeches weren't always that great. Hard to believe.

And Australian politics would go so mad that Germaine Greer would look like a chauvinist, I'd look like a feminist literary critic, and Tony Abbott would look like a prime minister for a while.

—

Prime Minister Gillard had two speechwriters, my mate Carl Green and me. I was a better adviser, Carl was a better writer; I knew more about Labor in Canberra, he knew more about Labor in office; he was a lot more lyrical and I was a little more demotic. Carl certainly wasn't proud, and I certainly wasn't perfect, so if you think we didn't get everything right, I promise you're not alone.

In Carl's past, he'd also advised on the arts; and he had grand, rarely shared stories about people like Bob Ellis and Graham Freudenberg and even David Malouf. In my past, I'd been a policy director; mine were stories of the *apparat*, about professionals like David Epstein and Mike Kaiser and Geoff Walsh. Carl and I were both melancholics, but I had more spleen. We sat next to each other in a quiet windowless room within a larger windowless room within a big windowless suite about sixty or seventy paces from the PM's desk for most of the three years Julia Gillard was prime minister. (Don Watson had a better office.) I typed too loudly; but we saw it through together to the last day.

We'd usually find our writing jobs in our diary, when a Microsoft Outlook notification bobbed up, two or three weeks out from the date. I would wander the PM's office asking senior staff whose idea the speech was and what the political objective was. If that failed I came back to the windowless room, talked about how hopeless the diary process was, and then started again. First question was always: who writes the first draft? Carl's and my distinct tempers and talents meant it wasn't hard to break up the writing jobs between us. Big do for Chinese New Year – Carl. Big National Press Club on economy – Cooney. National apology for forced adoption – Carl. Introduction of carbon price legislation – Cooney. ANZAC Day – usually Carl. Afghanistan – usually Cooney. Land rights – Carl. Closing the Gap – Cooney. Gough – Carl. Obama – Cooney. ('We are us', Labor national conference 2011 – Cooney. But don't let me spoil that story yet.)

First draft in hand, we would set off to find policy staff to talk to about the issues; and then we'd submit the draft to the PM on the Friday before the speech was due to be delivered, via the personal staff who managed her 'pack', a weekly folder of documents for review. (This had the effect of making her guess who'd written the draft when she made notes or gave us feedback, which of course we could have fixed by marking the drafts, but it was a fun guessing game.)

Over time we trained the senior staff (and the boss and ourselves, I suppose) into getting us time with the PM before we started drafting major speeches, rather than once we had thousands of words on paper. Major speeches – conference and congresses and press clubs – also went through exhaustive processes of circulation to ministers for written comment and meetings where staff and officials would go through the statements of policy and claims of fact in drafts, and debate the politics as well. But the vast bulk of routine speeches – including big speeches that weren't politically complex – began in this way, on a blank page on the screens in the windowless room, with the PM then reading a draft on the weekend before they were to be delivered and sending back notes in writing or by email on Sunday or Monday morning.

God, I loved working on speeches on the weekend. It was the actual best thing in my life at the time.

While ordinarily one or the other of us took the speech, we had rare crossover topics, and Mick Young was one of them: campaign director to Whitlam, leader of the house for Hawke, mate to Beazley, mentor to Swan, dead at fifty-nine in 1996 when maybe we needed him most. Carl's first draft was great, but it came back from the PM with a note saying it needed a little bit more grunt, basically, so I lobbed in to add some pragmatic politics – and for the end, we worked up some partisan red meat:

> Reg Withers, a tough Tory, used to say there's two sides in Australian politics; there has been since the First Fleet, since the first bloke in a red coat put his boot in the backside of the first bloke with arrows on his suit.
>
> I don't think Mick would have argued with that.
>
> And Michael Jerome Young was never on the red coats' side.
>
> He knew that politics is a fight between us and them, a fight where we can never accept a false choice between cunning and courage. Because our courage gives us our great goal and our cunning gets us there.

'Cunning and courage' was the line that the press secretaries wet their pants about; it was a reflection on, and a rebuttal of, a widely reported speech calling for changes to Labor party rules that then minister for defence John Faulkner had given late the previous year, saying that our party was 'struggling with the perception we are very long on cunning, and very short on courage'.

So as usual, we knocked something up in the windowless room; as usual, we fixed it up when the PM told us what she wanted; and as usual, we had a big poo fight with someone on staff about some detail right at the end, swore at them on the phone and then kissed and made up afterwards (we relatively rarely actually kissed).

And for once it worked.

It didn't hurt that the dinner was barely two hundred metres from where Governor Phillip drew the first frontier in the politics of the new, white Australia, along the creek that would become the Tank Stream – when he put the red coats' barracks up the hill to the east and the quarters for the blokes with arrows on their suits over to the west. It also didn't hurt that the PM had been happy with my line and so I didn't have to rewrite, and instead I'd been able to sneak in those beers before dinner at Hart's in the Rocks with our beloved economic adviser Amit Singh.

Or that I ran into my old mate from the Australian National University, Jim Chalmers, now Wayne Swan's chief of staff, at the function. We hung out at the side near the drinks servery and cracked gags about the crowd. This was a good Labor audience, put together by some great progressive business people like Ray Wilson of Plenary in Sydney, but talking to each other still beat talking to 'other people'.

Or that when I did go to my table, the comedian for the night was seated next to me. Fiona O'Loughlin is never not funny, and her stand-up routine that evening destroyed me; I made people stare. When she got back to the table we bonded over both having heaps of kids and the fact I had laughed at all the bits the Sydney people didn't get.

Or that I found myself sitting directly across the table from Bob Hawke. Carl's lines about Mick's life and values made him cry and ask Bart Cummings, on his right, for a hanky. My lines about Mick fighting to make Labor understand the way Australians were living in the new middle class and the new suburbs made him grab MP Craig Emerson, on his left, by the arm and say, 'That's right, that's right.'

Some days later we even received a beautiful note from the Young family.

—

I was the only staff member returning to Canberra that night. After the dinner I followed the PM out to the airport and flew back in the VIP plane with her and partner Tim Mathieson. We got on the plane and she called out to me to come up and join them in the front cabin, which was nice. Her first question? 'So how many beers did you and Amit have time to get in before dinner?'

Whatever else Julia Gillard was, she was remorseless. She loved doing stuff like that. And I *had* laughed pretty loud during O'Loughlin's routine.

I parried by comparing Bob and Bart's bouffant hairdos, then Tim rescued me, wondering aloud about the leaks on the carbon pricing negotiations and who could be behind it and why. I said lightly that it could always be Godwin Grech again; you could never be completely sure.

No one looked convinced.

I thought I'd change the subject and tell a story about staff hanky-panky – for as long as I'd known Gillard, a reliable topic to pique her interest – and got to the end before realising that the punchline was a girl saying, 'If you like it so much, put a ring on it.' To these two. On the plane they invited me on to, in the cabin they invited me in to. Oh, yeah. Champagne Cooney. Gosh, are we descending? I better go back to my seat and put my folder away.

But I hadn't learned nothing. We landed, the PM's car came on to the tarmac to the foot of the steps, and as the PM left the plane she called out, 'Thanks, Cooney! See you on Monday.' She was pretty hard to offend.

And I called back, 'Thanks, PM.'

There's a first time for everything.

# 2.
# That First Fine, careless Rapture

*Can I say to the Australian people: there will be some days I delight you, there may be some days I disappoint you. On every day I will be working my absolute hardest for you.*

PRIME MINISTER JULIA GILLARD

On Monday 28 June 2010 the prime minister began her week with a morning visit to Riverside Plaza, Queanbeyan.

It's a main-street shopping mall in a town of forty thousand people with a chemist and a travel agent, a Coles and a Gloria Jean's. And a newsagent, where the PM was on the cover of *Woman's Day* and *New Idea*. The mall is in the NSW seat of Eden-Monaro, then held for Labor by the decorated former army officer Mike Kelly. It remains the only seat to have gone with the government of the day at every election since 1972. That may change.

Five days earlier, on the night of Wednesday 23 June, Deputy Prime Minister Gillard had told Prime Minister Rudd he had lost her confidence and asked him for a leadership ballot of the Labor caucus, one in which she intended to stand. On the morning of Thursday 24 June, Kevin Rudd failed to nominate for the Labor leadership and resigned the prime ministership. Julia Gillard was elected unopposed.

On Friday 25 June, the *Illawarra Mercury*'s front page read *Julia reignites Labor's chances* and showed her in the likeness of the Redheads matchbox character. The day after Gillard toured Riverside, Newspoll would show a seven-point lift in Labor's primary vote. It was working. And the work had begun.

In a certain sense, the Rudd government committed suicide that June. The task for the new Gillard government was to defy the same despair: 'within the limits of nihilism . . . to find the means to proceed beyond nihilism'. For this prime minister, existence preceded essence: now she had 'to live and to create, in the very midst of the desert'.

Her first full week as prime minister would be spent preparing. There would be a four-hour cabinet meeting. Briefings and meetings on the Resource Super Profits Tax – the 'mining tax' that had done so much to damage the Rudd government – and on asylum-seeker policy. A phone call with US president Barack Obama and a visit and picture with Jeff Bleich, the US ambassador to Australia, along with calls to David Cameron of the UK, Paul Harper of Canada, John Key of New Zealand, Susilo Bambang Yudhoyono of Indonesia and Najib Razak of Malaysia. There was time to speak on the phone with Joel Klein, the reformist head of New York City's schools under Mayor Michael Bloomberg. She would read, think and write.

The PM would appear on *A Current Affair*, *Today Tonight* and *The 7.30 Report* and be interviewed for Channel Ten's news and by Laurie Oakes on *Weekend Today*. There'd be a tour of regional seats, meeting premiers, visiting mines, bushfire recovery areas and schools. Plus five and a half hours on a Saturday shooting a *Women's Weekly* cover.

She would also soon attend military funerals in the Northern Territory and two states. On Saturday, Private Timothy Aplin, Private Benjamin Chuck and Private Scott Palmer arrived home from Afghanistan. The previous Monday, an American Black Hawk helicopter carrying them into action in Eastern Shah Wali Kot crashed and burned. Aplin and Palmer were killed instantly; Chuck died of his wounds within the hour. In that action, their 2nd Commando

Regiment won the first battle honour awarded to an Australian unit since Vietnam. That day, Private Nathan Bewes of 6 Battalion RAR still had a few weeks to live; an improvised explosive device would kill him on 9 July. Julia Gillard's prime ministership would be one during which Australia was at war.

What looks like a whirlwind of policy and politics reflected her priorities as she took office. Pull the group together; fix the outstanding problems; don't forget education. Strange to say, it also reflected her determination to pursue a measured pace in this period. She remained mostly in Canberra. She was yet to conduct radio interviews with the big city talk-radio hosts – they would come later in this week. Governing was the priority, 'back on track' were the *mots de jour*, and that meant meeting decision-makers and making decisions, not running around getting photos taken; except when it meant getting photographs taken of sitting in rooms getting decisions made. It wasn't a complicated plan – she would govern, and look like it; and it was all of a piece with what I had thought a well-worked statement on the day she took office. Then the new PM had said she 'believed that a good government was losing its way'; that she had 'a responsibility to step up, to take control and to make sure that this government got back on track'; and that she would govern for 'people who play by the rules, set their alarms early, get their kids off to school, stand by their neighbours and love their country'.

You'd be amazed how many people do not set their alarms early and really resent this line. Well, maybe you wouldn't be. I was.

On that day, the PM had also nominated a problem-solving agenda, a commitment to resolve the issues which the Rudd government could not – to 're-prosecute the case for a carbon price at home and abroad', seeking consensus and acting as economic conditions improved; and to gain agreement through negotiation with the mining industry on the Resource Super Profits Tax. She did not nominate asylum-seeker policy as a problem to solve – indeed, questions from the press gallery on the day pointed out this omission, and when she responded to those, she did so in boilerplate – but over coming days and in subsequent interviews this came to be seen as the third problem the new PM had pledged to fix.

Fix carbon, fix mining, fix boats.

Fix policy problems. Fix the government.

But you still need some pictures, if only to prove you can do them well, and so Riverside would be a rare occasion for what Paul Keating once called going 'through some shopping centres, tripping over TV crews' cords'. Queanbeyan may be a country town in a marginal regional seat, but it is also barely fifteen minutes' drive from Parliament House, so campaigning there has a Potemkin-village-with-real-people feel. The camera guys know where to stand – they've been there often enough before. It's a grand community. The people and place are really authentic, and as politically acute as a New Hampshire diner waitress. Still, that Monday, the PM was thronged by grocery buyers – vital median voters. People thrilled to her. She was intent on self-deprecation and played up her 'first ranga' status harder than her 'first female' achievement; no ginger child was safe. But many people were especially excited to see the first woman to serve as prime minister. Older women looked over their shoulders, mums smiled, little girls grinned.

They weren't the only ones there. The tobacconist at Riverside made his anger at increased cigarette excises so obvious that he was removed from the centre. He was right to be concerned about what lay ahead for him. Outside the shops on Crawford Street, Phil Coorey for the *Sydney Morning Herald* found a bloke in a VB cap with something to say. He was a 'birther', evidently influenced by the tenacious conspiracy theories disputing President Obama's birthplace of Hawaii and questioning his constitutional eligibility to hold presidential office in the United States. 'Vic Bitter' told Coorey, 'She's not a real Australian; she was born in Wales. You have to be Australian-born to be prime minister.' The globalisation of the paranoid style and nativist anxiety hadn't slowed down.

For this picture-oriented event, the PM also wore a new coat, a painterly print. Years later she would joke at a staff party that this was 'the coat that divided the nation'. In fact, it united the nation. Seen in person, it's a striking and stylish piece, rather Flinders Lane. On TV it looks like it has been left out in a storm. Men are told to choose their ties for television carefully, as the wrong pattern or texture can phase or bleed on screen; a coat is a hundred times bigger than a tie. It was a shocker. Ten days later, in the weekend News Limited tabloids, a Melbourne-based 'image consultant' told reporter Paul Toohey, 'It honestly looked like a cheap motel bedspread,' and recommended a five-figure sum for a prime-ministerial clothing allowance like that of the governor-general, under the prominent picture headline *Gillard's technicolour scream-coat*. Toohey didn't win a Walkley for the piece, but he also didn't make every Australian editor think, 'I never want to commission a piece about clothes in the news pages again.'

Three women hung out the doors of the Go Figure gym calling, 'Bye, Julia!' as she left.

Once back at Parliament House, the PM announced the first Gillard ministry: a modest reshuffle, emphasising stability and continuity. She would tell the press conference in her courtyard that her own former portfolios would be filled by Simon Crean ('a very safe pair of hands'). Trade would be added to Stephen Smith's responsibilities in foreign affairs ('a strong and safe pair of hands'). Tony Burke (hands unspecified) was to have his portfolio of population renamed sustainable population. Lindsay Tanner had announced he would not seek re-election to the parliament; he would remain finance minister to the election. Kevin Rudd would seek re-election for the seat of Griffith, and the PM announced that were he elected and the government returned, she would 'welcome him into the cabinet, in a senior position' – an undertaking she would be forced to repeat in the campaign.

In 1985, the late Democratic governor of New York State, Mario Cuomo, famously told the students of Yale University, 'We campaign in poetry, but when we're elected we're forced to govern in prose.' Even in these first days, Gillard was more Janet Malcolm than Sylvia Plath. The PM also looked scripted at times – as if she was trying to remember her lines. Days into the prime ministership, this was basically because at times she *was* trying to remember her lines. Her decisions and remarks were sound: they reflected her view of needs of the government first; they were well executed. Some of it was clever, some of it was wise; much of it worked at the time and all of it seemed like the best option at the time. (If you put a better idea in writing that week, do let me know.) But no, of course it wasn't enough. It wasn't frank enough, which, in turn, implied that the PM didn't trust the people's capacity to understand or accept the reality of what had happened to the government they had elected, and licensing them to withhold their trust from her. Maybe it wasn't ambitious enough either; maybe problem solving wasn't enough, especially when the problem she said she'd come to fix was the government itself.

But there'd be time for a Gillard-centred, values-rich agenda in the future.

First, fix – fix, fix, fix.

—

I wanted to come back.

Since Kim Beazley's defeat in December 2006, or more precisely since Kevin Rudd's accession to the Labor leadership that day, I had been away from staff work for the federal parliamentary Labor Party. I was never a Kevin Rudd person; and after five years alongside first Mark Latham and then Beazley, three of them as policy director to the federal leader, I had earned a break.

During 2006, David Hetherington, a gifted policy and financial analyst, and a triallist for Australia's 1992 Olympic swimming team, had returned from the Institute of Public Policy Research in London to found Per Capita, a new independent progressive think tank. From the moment we met up at the Rose of Australia Hotel in Erskineville early in 2007, we were destined to work together. (He'd picked a pub for a meeting; we had the same birthday; and as far as we knew we were the only two progressive think-tank types in Australia who were passionate about rugby.) Two years as his policy director – he in Sydney, me in Melbourne – gave me two years of thinking and writing, and learning a bit about boards and fundraising and Melbourne. There was a lot of AFL footy and small bars, and I had time to finish reading some cherished big books as well. Per Capita built an unparalleled network of Labor thinkers and advisers in this, the early Rudd period – a nascent 'ideas faction' which remains a vital asset to Labor in the opposition years of today.

But I was born by a river. Weston Creek in Canberra's southern suburbs was always home. At the end of 2008 my great mate Andrew Barr was re-elected to the ACT Legislative Assembly and retained the portfolios of education and planning in Jon Stanhope's territory Labor government. If you get a chance to work with a reformer in office, you take it, and Andrew Barr is a reformer for the ages. When you tell a mate, 'Call if you need me,' and he calls – you better come. And on your first day back, if you walk from your old school to the press club and the dry spring afternoon makes your eyes prick with near tears of recognition and relief, it's time to stay home.

There were good days in my four years out of national politics. Helping David arrange a Per Capita policy exchange in Canberra addressed by then acting PM Gillard and Andrew Barr, and wearing two hats as Per Capita's Gillard-greeter and Barr's chief of staff – that was one of them. And my old colleague from Kim Beazley's office, Tim Dixon, now writing speeches for Kevin Rudd, sometimes needed a joke or a quote or just a fresh pair of eyes for a speech for his PM; sometimes other mates on staff would need some advice. I always had time.

But the bad days were all a bit Siegfried Sassoon: in 1917, recuperating in Kent from his mental and physical wounds, Sassoon was still close enough to the front to hear the guns across the Channel. When Robert Graves visited, Sassoon would say in his agony he didn't know whether to write a letter to *The Times* condemning the war or to rush back to France and die with his battalion. Obviously, I would rather have been working in the federal government. I wanted to make a difference; I wanted to serve the Labor Party; I wanted to be with my mates. But my service with Latham and Beazley had left me with plenty of baggage; Rudd wouldn't have me. Fair enough; I probably wouldn't have him.

When Julia Gillard became PM, that changed. Nonetheless, as much as I'd have liked to, I didn't walk out of a dinner party to head to the building on the night of 23 June like Walter Pidgeon in *Mrs. Miniver*, jumping in his little boat to head to Dunkirk. I had things to finish in the ACT, and the new Gillard PMO had a lot of cooks on the broth. But from June on, we started discussing a few options. The election would also be really, really soon, and my mates had a fair bit to fix at work. In a series of speeches and decisions over twenty-three days, the PM would seek to complete the Labor Party's expression of its 'no' to Kevin Rudd's broken government, and to commence an affirmative expression of the government she and Labor sought to become. Some politicians attempt 'listening tours' – for Julia Gillard, an attempt at a 'fixing tour' was about to begin – starting with refugees.

On Tuesday 6 July 2010, the PM addressed the Lowy Institute in Sydney in an effort to fix the asylum seeker and population debates, which had become so entangled that year. Eight months earlier, on 18 October 2009, the Australian Customs vessel MV *Oceanic Viking*, acting at the request of Indonesian authorities, had rescued seventy-eight Sri Lankan asylum seekers whose boat had foundered in Indonesian waters. When the *Oceanic Viking* reached port at the Indonesian island of Bintan, an eight-week stand-off followed – the asylum seekers refusing to disembark and the government of Australia refusing to take them to Australia and process their claims as refugees. The liberal commentator Robert Manne would later describe the Rudd government's asylum-seeker policy – measures like children out of detention and an end to temporary protection visas – as 'new humanitarianism . . . free-riding on the "success" of the Howard government's inhumanity'. In October 2009, the free ride was already over.

The same week, the secretary of the Treasury, Ken Henry, had given a speech in Brisbane forecasting a 60 per cent increase in the Australian population by 2050, with seven million people to be living in Sydney by that time. Prime Minister Rudd responded in a *7.30 Report* interview that night, which had mostly concerned asylum seekers, notoriously answering, 'Well, first of all, let me just say: I actually believe in a big Australia.' This had been intended as a business-friendly bromide. By January 2010, when the same ABC current affairs flagship was running a four-part *Population Debate* series, it was operating more like pseudoephedrine. Whatever any of us thought Australia's optimal population is or should be, by July, the debate was completely out of control and political necessity demanded we swallow our pride and use different language to express our view.

So at Lowy, in a speech titled 'Moving Australia Forward', the PM put her foot down. She made three essential points. First, no 'big Australia' – rejecting the language that Australia 'hurtle' towards a 'big population' and instead articulating support for 'sustainable' population growth. Second, a regional approach to processing refugees: discussions had begin with President Ramos Horta about a regional processing centre in Timor Leste. Third, Australians deserved something better than what she called an 'incendiary' and 'appalling' debate – no more labelling the general community as 'rednecks' and no more slogan-driven policy like 'turn the boats around'.

Fix population, fix refugees. Next?

The PM flew west, and on Friday 9 July addressed a business breakfast in Perth, under the title 'Western Australia: Going Forward Together'. She devoted the first few minutes to explaining away the negative reaction of Timor Leste prime minister Gusmao to the announcement of her regional processing centre proposal.

Then she turned to the business of the day: 'certainty for the future of the mining industry'.

Whatever one thought the ideal or even preferable policy design, this also just had to be settled. So, she conceded, yes, the original design of the Resource Super Profits Tax had 'created uncertainty'; yes, her government had shifted from the Rudd government's position, through a 'calm, methodical and analytical approach'; that was how a 'breakthrough agreement' had been reached; some would 'still have their criticisms' but we had 'struck the right balance'. Quintessential Gillard language in this period – she governed in prose. Heads of agreement had been signed, a Policy Transition Group would be getting down to work, legislation would come into the Parliament in 2011. But the PM restated simply that the government had 'secured an agreement that moves Australia forward'. Mining – surely fixed ...

This attempt at a fixing tour was also an expedition into the heart of Australian politics: the personality of the leader and the plan for the economy. So en route to Perth, Gillard had visited Adelaide for the first time as prime minister, spending Sunday at home with her parents before giving a speech to the Per Capita circle the next day to introduce herself. (Title? 'Moving Forward Together'.)

A prime minister is a person of genuine interest in the way no other politician really is. This female prime minister was a novel person in multiple respects, and she'd come to the role in unique circumstances and with a relatively lower profile than the multi-decade public figures like Hawke, Keating and Howard, or the hyper-media-exposed Rudd. So she particularly needed to introduce herself; and this isn't just a political necessity, it's also appropriate in a democracy. People are both right to want to know what the prime minister is 'like' and rational to judge and vote on 'personality' in its fullest sense: a prime minister is a leader and you're choosing him or her not just to deliver proposed plans but to make decisions in circumstances you can't predict. In many ways, personality is the most important thing.

So she had to talk about herself; and for me, at least, the speech the PM gave that day read as a fascinating effort I often returned to as a source in the following years.

Gillard introduced herself as the loyal daughter of migrants who were denied higher education but who delivered higher education to her and in turn showed her its 'transformative power'; their 'shy child' who through their nurture had found 'the sense of self to face the world with confidence'. She spoke of a mother who scrubbed pots in a Salvation Army aged care home; a father who worked nightshift as a psychiatric nurse and quoted poetry at the dinner table. Seven years earlier I had read (and lent her) Jonathan Rose's book *The Intellectual Life of the British Working Classes*; this speech made me think of the chapter on the Welsh miners' libraries. I heard Luke Kelly singing 'School Days Over'; I pictured John Gillard in his youth, borrowing Gibbon from a workingman's club, walking home past the gates of a new national school.

Gillard introduced her personal characteristics and public values in terms she would repeat many times. Education and hard work; activism and optimism. And another theme she would return to – one she'd already struck so strongly at the Lowy Institute – that Australians are 'better than the cynics would believe us to be'. For Gillard, both the professional race-baiters and the vocational anti-racists underestimated Australians; for Gillard, the Australian people were mostly right, most of the time, and certainly better than many activists on all sides believed. More united, more generous, and, even in their scepticism, more wise.

If Adelaide was personality, Canberra was purpose. In some ways there's only one National Press Club speech – 'the politics of the economy today' – and so on 15 July she spoke on the purpose and process of economic policy: why, and how, to create jobs. (Yes. 'Moving Forward to a Stronger and Fairer Economy'.) First, a fiscal breastplate: the existing commitment to surplus in 2013–14 and a new promise of zero net spending in the campaign to come. Second, a clear statement that the weak global economy meant the Australian economy faced a specific contemporary risk, and that this was not the time to risk Australian jobs with a conservative leader who had got the big economic calls wrong over the previous two years. Third, a new economic policy agenda, for a new kind of micro-economic reform from that of the 1980s and 1990s. It would touch new sectors like health and education, and applying 'market design' principles to combine public and private resources, rather than applying a simple preference for market allocation and private capital to an ever greater sphere in society.

This was strong where it needed to be, reassuring on fiscal policy but putting that reassurance in a progressive Labor framework that argued for stimulus, temporary and targeted. It was partisan where it needed to be, sharpening the differences with the Liberal approach to the GFC; and it was fresh where it needed to be as well, asserting development from, not just continuity with, past Labor approaches in government in decades past. A fitting conclusion to the fixing tour.

Oh, there was a big fix yet unmade: a solution on carbon awaited the campaign proper.

But the next day was Friday: a morning in northern Tasmania, an afternoon in Melbourne's west, a three-hour hair appointment in Albert Road – some things you just have to make time for if you're going to call an election the next day. There was a big press conference to prepare for in Canberra. The fixing tour was over and the campaign was about to begin.

—

These speeches – some disappointing, some delightful – still weren't my work. I'd had long experience of the difference between helpful advice and 'helpful advice', and was doing my best to erase the scare quotes in my case. So when it suited Dixon, I'd read some drafts and made some suggestions; and when it suited me, I was peppering a variety of mates inside with chatty, positive emails.

But that Friday night – three weeks into the Gillard prime ministership, on the eve of the formal campaign – I fired in my only really negative input of the period.

> I am still worried about taking a great, crucial, central winning theme for us, forward not back, and killing it with nauseating repetition. Even worse than turning people off, you can take our most powerful argument and trivialise it, make a joke of it. Stop actually literally calling the speeches 'Moving forward to . . .' and instead release them under a title which is a sentence or fragment from the speech . . . I mean, who reads the title of the speech – only the loser *Oz* journalist who is going to start the drumbeat of stories about your lines and themes.
>
> I just think a bit of finesse here, just some deftness of touch, can get the message across without losing any clarity or resonance, and without some stupid process story reminding people that even WE think we spent too much time thinking about message discipline over the last two years.

You're rarely completely right in politics; you're almost never *proved* completely right. I've written emails in my time I'd hate to read four years down the track and which I'd be mad to put in a book. This wasn't one of them.

—

On the Saturday morning, 17 July's Newspoll recorded a primary vote lead for Labor of 42 to 38, and a two-party preferred lead of 55 to 45. Julia Gillard had a thirty-point lead over Tony Abbott as preferred prime minister. That was the day Gillard stood in the courtyard of her office, in front of two Australian flags, in a fitted jacket the colour of the federation star, and opened the election campaign. It was classic Gillard: do the right thing, speak for party, listen to political advice, work from press brief, get line up, get job done. Fix fix fix. Prose prose prose.

> Today I seek a mandate from the Australian people to move Australia forward.

Canberra in winter isn't mostly fog and ice: it's mostly a cold light, from a highland winter sun which shows everything and warms nothing.

The next day the *Sunday Herald-Sun*, Australia's largest-selling newspaper, reported that Gillard used the phrase 'moving forward' twenty-four times in a prepared statement of just under fifteen hundred words – and eighteen times in the questions that followed. The broadcast news had played the 'moving forward' mantra on loop: satire as news. Nonetheless, that press conference was the start of an election campaign that didn't result in a change of government. And that matters more than any emotion you or I may have felt about political style that afternoon, even if that emotion was 'wanting to put a chair through a television' (I presume the Germans have a word for that).

The most useful record of the course of the five weeks of campaigning and the seventeen days of negotiation that followed comes in Barrie Cassidy's *Party Thieves*, and the most influential interpretation of their meaning can be found in George Megalogenis's Quarterly Essay *Trivial Pursuit*. Taken together, their view isn't an encouraging one: that two parties which in 2009 were led by 'party thieves', anti-traditionalists in Rudd and Turnbull, returned to type in the election year; that the election first of Abbott and then Gillard was a resumption of the contest proper between Liberal and Labor in Australia. But then, that the electoral contest between these two leaders was a failure of our politics to make the contest between Labor and Liberal a contest of ideas – it was a 'trivial pursuit'.

It's an interesting explanation of how the campaign looked and felt, but I don't think it goes quite far enough to explain the actual result, Julia Gillard's victory, and what that meant over time. Do what I did: read every word in those essays, but draw your own conclusions about what happened and what it all meant. Mine are these.

First: Julia Gillard won the 2010 election. Perhaps with the passage of the years, this will not need saying as much as it did between 2010 and 2013. But in those years it was a remarkably contested point. Julia Gillard won the popular two-party preferred vote in August 2010 by a touch over thirty thousand votes, something John Howard, for instance, failed to do when he was re-elected in 1998. This margin was narrow but not in dispute. And the parliamentary majority she earned was just as narrow, but just as durable and clear.

Second: whenever Labor was united in 2010, Labor was in front. This was true in the spectacular first third of the campaign, when Labor pressure brought an explosion for the Liberal side on industrial relations and dramatic exposures of Joe Hockey's weaknesses as an economic spokesman. This was just as true in the final two weeks of the campaign, when the worst of the leaks against the PM and the sideshow created by Mark Latham's assignment as a reporter for *60 Minutes* had passed. It was in equal parts a reflection on Gillard's underestimated abilities in a formal campaign – the only one she led – and a reflection on Labor's prospects as an Australian party. As Megalogenis wrote in the Quarterly Essay, 'Australia still leans Centre-Left on the issues, even in the bush.'

Third: when Labor argued the issues, Labor surged. Two weeks from election day, the PM threw the switch to policy and got the public argument back on the economy and families, things that matter, by promising a budget surplus. It worked. She even got back to an argument about the future – and not by saying 'forward' a thousand times an hour, but by talking about the implementation of the national broadband network (NBN) and e-health and e-learning, especially in the formal campaign launch at the start of that vital last week and a half. This was backed by tough decisions in private, including an unheralded campaign shake-up: one of her senior policy staff, Ian Davidoff, went up to the campaign plane to sort out the travelling policy operation; Ryan Batchelor, later the PM's policy director, came in from Jenny Macklin's office and took over policy in the Sydney headquarters to back him up.

So the '*Seinfeld* election – an election about nothing' line was wrong again in 2010. (It's even wrong about *Seinfeld*. It takes obstinate credulity to believe Larry David's self-mocking joke if you've watched even one hyperkinetic episode of surely the most densely plotted and event-filled comedy in television history.) Indeed it was precisely because it was about something that Labor won.

To give you just one example – the 2010 election was about the proposed NBN. This was nation-building infrastructure with a great resonance in the Australian legend, and a demonstrated place in the future of society and the economy. Talking about what broadband could do in schools and health clinics allowed us to demonstrate the direct connection between modern economic infrastructure and modern health and education services. It also allowed us to show that our ideas for reform in health and investment in education were also policies which would grow the economy and create jobs. And the contrast with the Liberals, who in 2010 still said broadband was a white elephant they would rip out of the ground (okay, they didn't really mix the metaphor as directly as that), was political gold.

At last, in the desperate final push of the campaign itself, a 'Gillard project' had begun to emerge.

Fourth: it's no accident Julia Gillard didn't just win the election campaign but also won the negotiations to form a government that followed – it says something about her as a person and as PM. Both major party leaders had the chance to win the support of the independents and minor parties. The popular vote had given Gillard a mandate, but she needed to confirm her majority. No one was better placed to do this than the PM herself.

Small things helped – in the case of the experienced independent parliamentarians, Julia Gillard had an established relationship of respect; she always treats people properly, even in private. In meetings, she isn't inclined to 'perform' – she's not very inclined to perform in public for that matter – so in those conversations, she naturally did what was most important: she listened and thought and responded on substance. Her policy project itself also appealed to the regional independents; again, broadband was key. But above all it was her character that would secure the support of the cross-bench.

I remember watching on TV in my loungeroom in Canberra with admiration and delight when she went to the footy during the 2010 election campaign, and ran onto the ground to embrace Barry Hall, who kicked seven goals in a winning Bulldogs side, and sang the song with the sons of the west in the winning rooms. The Western Bulldogs chief executive Campbell Rose told a plainly sceptical *Australian* newspaper journalist, who wanted to know if all this was 'real', that he didn't know if you could ever know a real politician, whether Liberal or Labor, but he did know that Gillard was a 'rusted-on Bulldogs member and supporter'.

The aspects of her personality, rusted-on, which the people who know her personally all admire, are precisely what won her the confidence of the cross-bench. Gillard is surely the most resilient Australian civilian who ever lived. She is as game as Ned Kelly and as proud as Mary MacKillop and as mentally tough as Steve Waugh. Add to that, she combines personal resilience with political purpose; she has character to burn, and she needed it all in the negotiations over those seventeen days.

By contrast, the private scrutiny on her political opponent told. Tony Abbott flippantly and cynically told Tony Windsor, the independent member for New England, 'The only thing I wouldn't do is sell my arse – but I'd have to give serious thought to it,' and recklessly offered Andrew Wilkie, the independent member for Denison, a billion dollars for the Royal Hobart Hospital. They were unforgiving. The renewed public scrutiny in this period on the plans of the opposition was just as devastating: independent costings released after the election but during the negotiations revealed funding shortfalls that proved fatal to their credibility. (The Coalition's election-year accountants were subsequently professionally sanctioned for their role in this.)

So on 7 September, Julia Gillard was commissioned as prime minister for the second time that year. Even during the negotiations to form government, the war in Afghanistan was never far from mind: Trooper Jason Brown's funeral was at Queen of Peace Church in Normanhurst in Sydney; Private Grant Kirby at St Peter Chanel's in Brisbane, both during the negotiations. Now, Gillard's first public duty in office was a duty of war; to attend Private Tomas Dale's funeral in Adelaide on 8 September. Two days after that, she was back in Brisbane, in Ashgrove, for Lance Corporal Jared McKinney's funeral. The two men had been killed in incidents separated by four days and two kilometres.

—

A week later, while I was spending my final days in territory politics, the second Gillard ministry was formed. Minister Barr and I had travelled to Shanghai on a long-planned trade mission with various representatives of higher education. Even from our distance, we could see long-term implications and short-term wrinkles in the ministry.

In the biggest decisions, Penny Wong had gone to finance and Greg Combet had been promoted to climate change. Penny was a coordinator who could count, and Greg, like Penny before him, was a serious person who knew the stakes and what was going on. But throughout the campaign, with Lindsay Tanner's effective retirement, the assistant treasurer Chris Bowen had carried much of the load of the fiscal and costings argument, even debating the opposition finance spokesman Andrew Robb; he had surely expected the finance role. Instead, Chris, who'd been sympathetic to Rudd but was still the senior minister from the NSW Labor Right, got what had become the hardest job in a Labor government: the ministry for immigration. It wasn't smart and it probably wasn't fair either. The other big decision was not to act: long-serving front-benchers Simon Crean, Martin Ferguson and Robert McClelland remained in the cabinet. This was no 'generation next' reset. And of course, the new foreign minister was Kevin Rudd.

The immediate wrinkles included the omission of a titled minister or parliamentary secretary for women or for multicultural affairs, and the division of the education portfolio between two cabinet ministers, neither formally titled 'higher education'. This was particularly odd given the PM's own record levels of new investment and her ambitious reforms in the sector. There would be complaints about those symbolic exclusions – obviously the functions were retained, but what did it mean that the names were not? – but what was obvious to Andrew and me in the hotel foyer in Shanghai was that the vice-chancellors were going off like tops. Higher education now fell to Chris Evans, the minister for 'jobs and skills'. It was pretty hilarious, these uni blokes arcing up about the mercantile impression given about their sector while they were on a sales trip to the Far East ('Madam, I am not in *trade*!').

Andrew and I escaped for lunch high above the Bund; adversity's last sweet use. He asked me what I thought had gone on with the reshuffle – were the portfolios forgotten? Were they deliberately omitted? Which was worse? – and I said, 'How does this sound: "Yeah, I'm not sure, mate, I'm just a speechwriter so I'm not really in that loop – I'm a creative now, I don't have a decision-making role."'

We laughed. He agreed the line would come in handy from time to time.

At last, on the night the PM gave the Light on the Hill address in Bathurst on 18 September, my old mate Tim Dixon ended the discussions about when I'd return and in what role. Tim, speechwriter to Beazley and Rudd (and Graves to my Sassoon), had carried on with

Gillard for the transition. In the Comcar after the dinner, he told the PM that he was done, but that they both knew who he should hand over to. Tim gave me a ring that Saturday night; I was at a mate's in Wangaratta recovering from Collingwood's preliminary final win in Melbourne the night before. I'd start the Monday after the AFL grand final, in nine days. I drove back to Canberra the next day with Bruce Springsteen absolutely blaring.

That week, I gave 'outside comments' on a draft PM speech for the last time, for Gillard's grand final breakfast remarks. After the hung parliament, it seemed to me it was pretty obvious what the main joke should be, so I dropped it in an email, along with some other stuff that wasn't all used.

> One thing I do know is this. Please – please – we cannot have a draw. Our nation just couldn't bear it.

(The finest moment of my career as a volunteer.) Next week, I'd be the one desperately seeking comment and inspiration from mates. Getting a line up in the speech was nearly as exciting as getting tickets to the game; I was heading back to Melbourne for the second time in a week, to see my Magpies meet their fate.

At the Melbourne Cricket Ground I was a guest of the AFL and the Greater Western Sydney football club's board – the GWS chair Tony Shepherd (later Tony Abbott's commission of audit chair) wasn't scandalised at the ACT government's expenditure on sport – and before the game I found a moment to say hello to the new boss, nearby at the top table. We'd come a long way since going to the 2003 grand final together.

There was a footy match, too. Jenny Macklin, the minister for families, community services and Indigenous affairs, heard me barracking, ten rows behind her, at pretty much the first decent contest between Nick Maxwell and St Kilda's Steven Baker; she recognised my voice, turned round and gave me the most wonderful, unforgettable,

Mum eyeroll. (A year later, the AFL's CEO Andrew Demetriou told me that my performance that afternoon would be worth a chapter in his memoirs – and when I said, 'Oh, "Mad fans I have sat near"?' he said, 'No no, just you, just that day.' He wasn't kidding. But our song says 'as all barrackers should' for a reason, and I'm not going to say I wasn't proud. Punters paid his bills.) I got a hug from Jenny at half-time and she said, 'It's good to have you back.'

I said, 'I'll see you Monday.'

—

The bottom line on the winter election of 2010 is that it was a very Gillard outcome. She had snatched victory from the jaws of defeat from the jaws of victory. It was Labor's Miracle of the Marne: a chaotic and flawed campaign by the parliamentary party as a whole, but also one in which a brilliant leader-led recovery and a heroic seat-by-seat defence by the much-criticised state machines saved government in incredible circumstances.

She had survived. Now to govern.

It was a draw on grand final day and the workingman's club still won the premiership. That would be the story of 2010.

# 3.
# Permission to perform

*We have outlived the shade of our founding and yet we remain young.*

PRIME MINISTER JULIA GILLARD

In the Whitlam government of 1972–75, essence preceded existence: the leader had come to office with the Program, his plan for Australia, worked out over the years of opposition – now to govern. But Labor was opposed: in office, he was often frustrated by the parties of resistance in the upper house. In the 1975 Chifley Memorial Lecture, he grappled with the issue of his time.

> So the debate about the meaning of the mandate has centred on the question of whether in 1972 and again in 1974 the Australian Labor Party was given only a general mandate to govern or a specific mandate to implement each part of its program. Is the mandate merely general or is it specific?
>
> Is it a grant of 'permission to preside' or a 'command to perform'?

For Gillard, the negotiations to secure confidence in the government provided a neat inversion of Whitlam's famous phrase: she earned permission to perform. She saw her moment and took her chance – it was an opportunity available to no prime minister since Fraser, who controlled both House and Senate for years, and she didn't miss it. On 21 August, Gillard had won a remarkable election victory. And by 7 September, she had done something even more remarkable – secured an effective working majority in both houses for the Gillard project, which had only begun to emerge.

This did more than guarantee confidence in the government for the purpose of its budgets, significant though that would be in a time of huge economic risk and huge domestic controversy about macroeconomic settings, especially the purpose of fiscal policy. This also brought with it parliamentary support for the Gillard project, in broadband and in health and education – changes opposed by important interests with strong public and parliamentary voices, changes which it is hard to imagine could have passed our Parliament without this negotiated support. Ironically, a majority government without such agreements might have failed in the Senate where the Gillard minority government was able to succeed.

The first proof of that parliamentary support was for the NBN – more specifically, for the trust-busting legislation to structurally separate Telstra's wholesale and retail operations that was part of the plan. This change – one which Gillard would later call 'a real "white whale" which has escaped many a reformer's harpoon in the past' and indeed one which as treasurer Paul Keating could not persuade the Hawke cabinet to deliver even back when the company was still publicly owned – would soon pass the Senate and then finally make it through the House in a dramatic Monday sitting on 29 November 2010, over the opposition of the opposition but with the support of the cross-bench, fully four days after the scheduled rising of the Parliament for the year.

The parliamentary agreements brought important implications

for Labor's plans in health. Much of the government's hospital funding agenda would not require legislation, but could be done through funding and via agreement with the territories and states. But the private health insurance rebate – introduced by the Howard government in 1999; over time one of the most expensive and most inefficient programs of high-income welfare ever introduced in Australia; for almost its whole thirteen-year life, generally considered the paradigm of a bad policy unable to be changed because of political weakness in the face of vested interest – was in law; changing it would take the Parliament's support. So when in February 2012 the Parliament finally means-tested the rebate, it did so despite Liberal opposition, with cross-bench support. Cross-bench support which in practice had been secured by September 2010.

Above all else though, these discussions with the independent MPs and with the minor parties created the opportunity to act on climate change. It might be the last.

—

Gillard had won from the parliament permission to perform as a prime minister and now had an emerging project to deliver as well. The miracle of the 2010 election win set the stage for an even greater miracle – a chance to redeem the carbon price failures of 2009. In the campaign she had ruled out a carbon tax, but kept the door open to emissions trading. An interview with Ten News brought the grab 'there will be no carbon tax under the government I lead' which became infamous, followed by the less memorable statement that she would lead a debate for a consensus for a cap on carbon pollution; in an interview with *The Australian* on election eve the PM said, 'I don't rule out the possibility of legislating a carbon pollution reduction scheme, a market-based mechanism. I rule out a carbon tax.'

The government's minority in the House created the need to negotiate with the minor parties there, and this created a new context in which to negotiate with the Greens in the Senate. There was plenty of ground to make up.

Global warming is not so much an environmental problem with economic consequences as an economic problem with environmental consequences – and in turn it is one which demands an economic solution. The best way to decouple emissions growth from economic growth in Australia is to do it through responsible, modern economics and as a project of the political middle ground. That was the most likely way to secure an enduring change – and it was also the most likely way of securing the right kind of change.

So from when Prime Minister John Howard announced that a re-elected Coalition government would introduce emissions trading, Labor's goal was to deliver climate action with conservative support. Successive Liberal leaders Howard, Brendan Nelson and Malcolm Turnbull had known the Australian public believed the climate was changing as a result of human activity. They had worked to keep their libertarians, contrarians, coal clients and nut jobs under control with distractions from nuclear power to carbon capture and storage, while trying to respond to public opinion and achieve their idea of the best economic outcome: a least-cost-first, efficiently allocated mechanism for cutting emissions.

By 2009, however, the changing dynamic on the conservative side of the Parliament created a new deadline and one no one could precisely measure in advance: an emissions trading scheme had to be voted on by the Parliament before Malcolm Turnbull fell. The final vote came too late. On the first of December, Turnbull was gone and Tony Abbott was leader. That meant that in the end, the next day, thirty-one Labor senators voted for Prime Minister Rudd's ETS for the second time, and this time so did two Liberals – but not one Green. What is it about the second of December and ramshackle coalitions? Every single Greens party senator sat with Nick Minchin and Barnaby Joyce and voted 'no'.

Prime Minister Rudd missed it by *this* much.

This wasn't irrational of the Greens – in their contest for the vote-switchers on Labor's left, they needed a rejection and renegotiation, proving their case that Labor didn't initially go far enough. That's why their best 2010 election television ad (not the early one, which says 'Your Vote Can Move Australia Forward' – truly) had a simple theme. Moderate-looking actors portraying former Labor voters spoke to camera saying, 'This election I'm voting Green in the Senate to put pressure on Labor to do the right thing and not cave in to powerful interests.'

It's a clever ad – and a brave one, when you've just voted with those powerful interests against a carbon pollution reduction scheme. It is part of the record of politics during the Rudd government – literally, it's in Hansard – that the Greens party was not a partner for progress. Even on its best days, the Greens party is Labor's stoner son-in-law, not Labor's better self, and its best days are not as many as it thinks.

We'd learned a bit about the Greens after 2009 and so now following the 2010 election we had to lock it into a process that would generate action it couldn't oppose. It would not be easy to get the Greens senators to vote for an actually existing emissions trading scheme plan – something they'd never previously done. So on 27 September 2010, following the successful negotiations to ensure support for the government in the House, the prime minister called a press conference to announce what would happen next. She was joined by the climate minister Greg Combet, but also Deputy PM Wayne Swan, Greens party leader Bob Brown and his deputy and presumed successor Christine Milne – locking this in as an economic plan and committing the Greens to the path ahead. The news? The government would form a Multi Party Committee on Climate Change to develop options for the introduction of a carbon price.

We were on the road to redemption.

The PM's outlook was understated: 'The case for a price on carbon is a very simple one'. And it was just a start: the options the committee developed would go to cabinet. She took questions from the News

Limited tabloid journalists about why the committee's deliberations would be private and from *The Australian*'s journalists about what it all meant for coal. It was left to Phil Coorey, of the *Sydney Morning Herald*, to ask the only question that mattered.

'Prime Minister, given you see the committee winding up at the end of next year, is it your intent to seek a mandate at the election after, should we run three years, for a policy to put a price on carbon, whatever that policy is? Will you be taking something to the election?'

The PM replied in prose. 'If you're going to have this work then you've got to have options on the table, not immediately start the usual rule-in, rule-out games.'

Would action await the 'consensus' she had said she would work for in the campaign? No answer today.

It was also my first day at work. I arrived to a mix of 'where the hell have you been?' and 'who the hell are you?', and tried to keep a straight face, but it was hard not to beam. I was back in the building – but I came in through a new door this time. This was my first job in the ministerial wing.

—

October and November brought a new phase for the prime minister. The rapture had passed and so had the first fixes. Now the work of the Gillard government really began. In the cabinet room, across the corridor from the PM's office, budget preparation was underway. The climate change committee's work ground on. The major domestic policy processes – education, health, broadband – were in train. And there were also two big public arguments to nail in this period, on national security and the economy. The first: what the hell was going on in Afghanistan?

Julia Gillard was prime minister in the penultimate and most intense phase of Australia's longest foreign war. Australians first went into Afghanistan in the days following 11 September 2001. The mission: to defeat Al-Qaeda and to destroy the safe haven for terrorism that operated there under the Taliban. In February 2002 Sergeant Andrew Russell was the first Australian military death in action since the Vietnam War. But by then, the Howard government was already focused on the US plans for an invasion of Iraq. By the end of that year, Australia's Afghanistan commitment was paper-thin.

It was late 2005 before we returned to Afghanistan in force, with a special forces task group deployed for twelve months, following a renewed American commitment, and returning to Australia before the 2007 election. Our numbers on the ground grew again during the Rudd government's first year, with about a thousand personnel there; Trooper David Pearce was the second Australian killed there, in October 2007. It still wasn't enough. President Obama's revised international strategy and the surge of thirty thousand US troops announced in December 2009 was in many ways the last roll of the dice and through 2010 we had our largest commitment in place, peaking with more than fifteen hundred Australians in uniform in country.

So there was an important governing purpose to this speech – it would settle contested elements of our Afghanistan policy for years, above all, our approach to 'transition', the term of art employed to describe the phase during which we would hand over combat duties to the Afghan forces themselves. In this, the PM got more advice than assistance from the bureaucracy – every agency worked to relitigate its every interest. Our remarkable international adviser Richard Maude, now the director-general of the Office of National Assessments, would prove a worthy successor to Alan Gyngell in both jobs. In all the drafting and redrafting, Richard owned the details of all the advice. He delivered.

The public debate on the Afghanistan commitment, still hesitant, was growing; you could feel the politicisation creeping in from both extremes. Our blokes were hooking in pretty hard in Uruzgan Province and elsewhere through winter 2010, and that brought with it Australian woundings and deaths. The war retained the support of mainstream progressives but was coming under increasing strain both from older liberal commentators used to the logic of anti-war opinion and from further to the political left, increasingly including the Greens. It wasn't deeply unpopular, but everyone was sick of it and no one really understood it – it was more late Korea than late Vietnam – and so for the media and the public as a whole, the overarching strategy had to be rearticulated. As a new prime minister with an old war on her hands, Julia Gillard had to make clear how, and when, she thought it should end.

So on 19 October, the PM opened her speech in Australia's first parliamentary debate on the war in Afghanistan by giving the House and the people the rationale for our presence there and the basis for her thinking about the future, in the clearest terms available. The purpose – to prevent terrorist attacks launched from there, and to stand by our alliance commitment to the United States. The method – counter-insurgency and security assistance, so that the Afghan state itself, not the international community, could take responsibility to prevent the country being 'a safe haven for terrorists' as it had been before 2001.

These were and remain limited and achievable war aims – not that Afghanistan become the Switzerland of Central Asia, but that the government there could stop jihadists doing what they did before 2001 – and to date, those war aims remain secured. Afghanistan today is not a safe haven for terrorism.

The conservative side of politics in Australia had also begun nibbling around the edges – trying to find grounds to say the Labor government wasn't providing enough support to the troops. Games were played and issues embroidered – ranging from the level of equipment like body armour, to fire support and helicopter support arrangements in Uruzgan Province, to the rules of engagement which were questioned in Parliament, and the military justice system which was savagely attacked by talkback radio hosts. Of course isolated voices of dissent could never be silenced, but the PM had to snap the connection between fringe individual complaints and the mainstream political debate. This wasn't so much a political task as a task to lift the war back out of politics. So through the middle of the speech, those arguments had to be firmly confronted and put down. This largely succeeded – in particular, she smashed any 'rules of engagement' argument right out of the ground – but it would not be until the following year that Tony Abbott would feel the whole force of the folly he had engaged in by playing politics with this war.

This was my first serious parliamentary speech in five years. The PM really only needed me for my interior thesaurus and anthology, but she did need that, because there was another job this speech had to do. She had attended the funerals of eight Australian soldiers in the previous sixteen weeks. As well as speaking for the government to Australians about the war, she had a responsibility to speak for Australians to their families – about those men.

By the time I was writing this speech, it was more than ten years since my kid brother Paul went overseas in uniform for the first time, following our father, Brian, and his father, Frank; Paul would spend a fair bit of time in Afghanistan while I was in the PMO. This speech, like the condolence speeches the PM customarily gave in the house following the deaths of our blokes, was a small thing I could do; 'they also serve'. At midnight the night before the debate I sat in the windowless room with half a dozen different copies of the speech with marked-up comments from officials of various agencies on my desk and a book I'd recently robbed from a friend's bookshelf.

In Peter Coleman's faithful tribute to his friend, *The Heart of James McAuley*, I had found a few brave lines from 'The Ascent of Heracles', and passed them to the PM; she thought they did the job, and told the Parliament: 'When I think of these Australians we have lost in Afghanistan, I think of the Australian poet James McAuley's words: 'I never shrank with fear/But fought the monsters of the lower world/ Clearing a little space, and time, and light/For men to live in peace.'

The House was silent for her, and for them. It was a very fine hour.

The other public argument to close the year was about the government and 'reform'.

When the Rudd government had lost its way, it had lost much of its claim for legitimacy in both the modern Labor succession and the centre of the economic debate. So the PM sought to reclaim credibility in serious policy circles, by arguing that much of her policy agenda should be seen as the next phase of Labor's post-1983 economic practice, consistent with the decisions of that era to create a globalised Australian economy and competitive domestic markets. Her policy project, from the budget and education to broadband and health to the environment, should not be seen simply as spending the benefits of a strong economy on social projects – or even as public investment in things that would make the economy stronger in future – but as containing smart, market-oriented policy changes that reflected genuinely contemporary economic thought.

So at the Queensland Media Club on 12 October, when she spoke about her policies she characterised them in more abstract, economic terms. The return to surplus was cast as 'significant fiscal consolidation'; the education revolution as 'leveraging new investment in human capital'; even environmental policies on climate change and the Murray-Darling could be considered 'restructuring markets' and 'economic reforms'. To the Australian Industry Group in Parliament House a fortnight later on 26 October the PM said, 'decoupling economic growth from growth in emissions is a key micro-reform' and promised to push on not only in the specific pro-market policy mould of the 1980s and 1990s but with the same determination to privilege the general good over any one group of merchants:

> In government, we must walk the reform road every day. One or two big-ticket reforms is not enough. Reform is a seamless robe, which cannot be divided to suit sectional interest.

And she warned against 'rising voices against reform' in the Coalition – hinting at the 'economic Hansonism' of populists like the prominent Nationals senator Barnaby Joyce as a real risk in a finely balanced Parliament. The day of the speech I told her I was worried the line looked like overstatement. It looks like understatement five years down the track. Paul Kelly's Saturday column for *The Australian* called it 'indelible rhetoric . . . words that stick' – but:

> Does Gillard grasp the meaning and impact of such declarations? The problem is obvious: Labor's credentials on economic reform are flawed and the gap between its promise and delivery seems entrenched. Since 2007 Labor's message has been its fidelity to Hawke-Keating pro-market reformism yet this is more a ritualistic slogan reflecting the party's pride in its history than a serious platform for action . . .

I was as keen as anyone to make this argument and press this approach. Hawke and Keating were Labor champions and more prestigious than ever in Australia's broadsheet press; they were touchstones of political success in the national interest. We couldn't literally do what they'd done – anyone could see that if they'd made the Australian economy change, that meant new policies were required, because the economy was now actually different – but it was the vibe of the thing. 'Reform' was the shibboleth; surely all we had to do was to pronounce it right and the columnists would let us across the river. So a week and half later, to a big audience at the Rotary Club of Adelaide on 10 November, the PM insisted that 'the measure of progress is in the years'.

> The task of government is [not] to deliver reforms exclusively in line with the contemporary media cycle. I can only put it this plainly. I do believe I will convince you of my long-term reform credentials. I do not believe I will convince you of my

long-term reform credentials tomorrow. I quite literally, and by definition, cannot. And I am not about to try.

'What do we want? Long-term reform.' – Yes, agreed. 'When do we want it? Before we tape our *Insiders* segment.' – Sorry, ain't gonna happen.

It got a good run on *Insiders*.

—

For Julia Gillard, 2010 ended in Adelaide, at home. She made her customary address on 28 December at the Proclamation Day celebrations at Holdfast Bay in Glenelg commemorating the founding of South Australia in 1836.

I worked on the final version of these remarks on the afternoon of Christmas Eve, on a kitchen bench top where we were house-sitting in Carlton. The kids were out shopping and going to confession. There was a warm breeze. There was beer in the fridge. I was working. God, I was so happy.

I sent the speech through to the PM from my laptop and texted her the familiar message, *Draft on your email*, and logged off. She finished the speech off at home, speaking without her notes but staying pretty close to the planned text.

The ceremony takes place near an Adelaide landmark, the Old Gum Tree, where the free-settler colony of South Australia was proclaimed by Governor Hindmarsh in 1836. It is a eucalypt older than Barcaldine's tree of knowledge and naturally enough today is a remnant of its mature life – it is held up with concrete – and her final address for the year reflected on the paradox:

> I believe those who heard Governor Hindmarsh read the Proclamation here absolutely intended this new society to live longer than this historic tree . . .

... We have outlived the shade of our founding and yet we remain young. Lawson wrote of 'the old dead tree' and 'the young tree green'. The old gum tree may have withered, but our state and our country is still young, still looking forward to the best days to come.

The government and the prime minister ended the year looking forward to the best days, the days to come. So did I. I'll know worse New Year's Eves than that of 2010. I spent it with family down at Dromana. During the day I kept growing my Christmas beard and at night we slow-danced to Stephen Foster's 'Hard Times Come Again No More'.

# INTERLUDE:
# the staff life

*On the human side, few soldiers have had in such measure the supreme soldierly gift of comradeship [as did the Australians]. Whenever they were in a fight, breaking King's regulations, or raiding the Hun trenches, they stuck together.*

*The Battalion was the digger's home, and he was never truly happy, or a really first-class soldier, away from it.*

CONTRIBUTOR TO *ROUND TABLE* MAGAZINE MARCH 1919

There is a story that Jennie Lee refused the UK Ministry for Health from Prime Minister Harold Wilson in 1964, saying it would be 'a wreath for Nye'. I can't claim that within a labour party I would very often have voted with the old Left warrior, or with her life's passion, the founder of the National Health Service Aneurin 'Nye' Bevan – even a populist leader like Wilson would have been a bit to the left of me – but I love the magnificent, labour bitterness in her breast.

Someone once told me that Liberal staff don't use the en suite toilets in the offices in Parliament House; supposedly they use the corridor toilets and leave their boss to the office facility. I don't know if that's true but I hope it is. I don't know anything about staff life in general; what I know about is staff life in the Labor Party.

Labor staff are deeply partisan people: full of belief and ideas and full of the dream of a better politics. It's often hard to improve on Dennis Glover's words and what he wrote in *The Australian* on 22 October 2010 about staff – smashing the 'gross generalisations', 'conspiracy theories', 'cheap assertions' and 'unworthy slurs' they endure – is in this category.

> When the politicians delay or abandon platform promises you can bet the advisers will be the ones most upset, drowning their sorrows in Canberra bars. They have a passion for public service that frequently sees them rise at 5.30am, leave the office at midnight, dash home for the birth of children, and be reduced to walking zombies by the end of a parliamentary sitting fortnight through lack of sleep. If you want to find them at 10pm, they'll be in the basement of Parliament House searching for a still-stocked vending machine for the dinner they were too busy to buy before the dining room closed.

That's the staff, my battalion, and it's made up of all sorts of funny little platoons. There are 'wogs' – their word – and kids, and veterans, and progressives and Laborites, and even public servants. And there are a few of us who are basically lifers.

---

When I worked for the ACT government, I'd had a staff member who was friends with a guy called Damian Kassabgi. He'd been a political adviser to Prime Minister Rudd; now he was a senior policy adviser to Prime Minister Gillard, on the NBN and other infrastructure. Early in my time in the Gillard PMO, I introduced myself and our connection, telling him that if Lorna had said, 'Damian said this funny thing, Damian did that funny thing' one more time I would have screamed; but it was nice to meet him. He said he'd got pretty sick of hearing about me too. He was charismatic, that was for sure; he'd entered primary school with his first language as 'broken English', and had found a genuine knack for words and wit.

Later that day someone I was talking to about this said, 'Damian's from Melbourne, right?' and I laughed before replying, 'I don't actually know, and I've only met him for five minutes, but if he's not a Sydney head office wog, I'll be amazed.' And yes, I soon learned, not only was Damian a good Christian boy from Coptic and Catholic parents from Sydney's south but, some years earlier, he had worked for the NSW ALP. He left the place allergic to the culture in Sussex Street back then. He had come from that platoon, but fought in an entirely different fashion.

The scholarship kids of migrants are a special breed. Their parents come from all over the world. They are interesting: alienated insiders, Indians and Fijian Indians, Maltese and Vietnamese, their academic achievements at public schools unlocking access to all sorts of educational and professional elites. These are tough little suburbanites whose mums locked them in their bedrooms to do homework, and who came out to kick in the doors of the uni SRC. And then when their contemporaries from across the bridge – most of our cities have a bridge like this, or at least a river – had got appalling jobs in professional services, these kids had done the maddest thing of all and gone into politics or public service. Some of them had even taken jobs in Treasury in Canberra, or at the Reserve Bank; and then once they'd got them, had left them to fight for the Labor Party! I loved watching them slice open badly phrased economic advice from officials who had no idea what, or who, they were dealing with.

The immigrant vigour came from all over the world. In late 2011 I sat next to Anthony Albanese's adviser Jessika Loefstedt at the Boxing Day Test and said, 'Hey, did you know Eddie Cowan played cricket in Holland?' And she looked at me and said, 'Hey, did you know I'm Swedish, not Dutch?' Oh, yeah. Getting it done. These policy and political advisers rarely met gallery journalists and were invisible to every furious blogger (and blog commenter) in the country. They are the real human legacy in modern Labor of the multiculturalism of the

1970s and the economic opening to the world in the 1980s. They are some of the best Australians I know.

Not all staff are young; and being young isn't such a crime; but one of the most important platoons in Labor is the kids.

Because Kevin Rudd did have a fairly young group of senior staff, a cliché that young staff were running riot took hold early in the Rudd government and proved hard to shake. I thought it was very odd how many experienced commentators wrote about it as if it were a new thing. There's something really unflattering about resentful newspaper columns about young staff running the country when written by middle-aged people who can't think of a worse word than immature or a better word than grown-up. I wouldn't want to make my disquiet at my own ageing, or participation in intergenerational rivalry, quite so obvious. Anyway, how old do they think political adviser Geoff Walsh was when he was working for Bob Hawke in the 1980s? Or private secretaries like John Menadue with Whitlam in the 1960s, or John Burton with Doc Evatt in the 1940s?

In fact, for what it's worth, my observation is that during our six years and two terms, the youngest chief of staff Labor had in government – Alister Jordan – and the youngest communications director we had in government – Lachlan Harris – were also the best performed in those roles. One reason for this was their strength of character; another, that they were very experienced. Each of them did the job for years. In the decade and a half since 1 January 2001, federal Labor has had eight leaderships and six leaders. Labor's leader's office has had at least twelve chiefs of staff, eight comms directors and a similar turnover in other key appointments, like director of policy and senior political adviser. For a very long time, most of these jobs have been done by people learning the ropes. That's been a much bigger problem for Labor's political capacity than these jobs being done by people of any particular age.

What's more, the younger staff mostly fill what are functionally relatively junior roles. They do an immense amount of travel; many spend half the year in Canberra and half on the road with their boss. No one more than the staff I knew is forced to make Yeats's choice between 'perfection of the life or of the work'. I saw thirty- and forty-something advisers come and go, leaving with tearful speeches, broken by the hours, the travel, the pressure of having this job and a family, the fear of never having a family . . . even as they lived 'the night's remorse'; many of the ones who arrived when they were still kids just stayed. Some of them are still there.

The ancient Irish fighting legends collected by Lady Gregory a hundred or more years ago tell us that when Ulster was besieged by the Queen of Munster's 'cattle raid of the north', all the men of Ulster's red hand were bewitched by the enemy, and only the champion Cuchulain stood in the ford to fight in water and his own blood; then it was the boy-troop who came down to him to help, and to go to their slaughter. No one ever resents young people in politics when they'll stay out all night putting up posters before election day. It seems like it's only a problem when they get confident enough to tell you what to do.

I loved the kids. The year after the Loefstedt Blunder I sat next to Catherine King's adviser Jessica Weereratne at the Melbourne Sri Lanka Test and asked her what she was reading over the break. 'Oh! *The Catcher in the Rye*,' she said brightly. I'm sure my poker face failed me; God I'm old, I thought. 'That's magnificent,' I said. 'What's it like?' Actually the big Salinger bio was out then and the movie was coming; really, this reading reflected the influence of American higher education, not the influence of the high-school reading list.

Even Labor's youngest staff, those who are most taken with America, aren't usually all that wound up with that American TV show about politics though.

At Victorian ALP conference in May 2011, the PM called Tony Abbott 'the love child of Sarah Palin and Donald Trump'. (No, I can't remember why.) Bernard Keane, on *Crikey*, wrote 'it yet again showed that too many Labor staff, including those at the highest levels, appear to think Australian politics is one big variant of *The West Wing*...' In fairness to Keane, his own anxiety at the repetition of this incredibly trite and familiar assertion about Labor staff being obsessed with Aaron Sorkin's television show peeks out in that little 'yet again'. At least he didn't pretend it was new; but he did seem to think it's true.

How did this 'kids obsessed with *West Wing*' thing become a staple of grumpy old man attacks on Labor staff? I really don't know. It's weird: people like Tony Walker and Tony Wright, journalists who are not always silly, would solemnly say this and seemingly mean it; over time it spread from comments to comment boxes to public conversation. Sophie Morris, again in the generally sensible camp, profiled first-term Labor MPs for the *Saturday Paper* in 2014; noting my mate Jim Chalmers, by then the new member for Rankin, had gone to the National Union of Workers conference and told them Labor's job was to get them ready for the jobs of the future not to protect the jobs of the past. Morris saw the parallel with a *West Wing* incident but seemingly not with the original Clinton 'the muscle jobs aren't coming back' moment in the 1992 primaries that *The West Wing* was echoing. It was a great New Democrat moment, dramatised in *Primary Colors* before it was adapted for TV, and certainly both Chalmers or Sorkin would be able to tell you about it chapter and verse. Chris Kenny in *The Australian* wrote yet another lengthy piece about staff and *The West Wing* when summarising the politics of the year 2014; you could fill a book with these columns. I'm not sure it's staff who are obsessed with *The West Wing* to the exclusion of all other political culture.

And why associate the TV show with young staff, of all people? Plenty of people were super keen on the show when it first aired in Australia – about twelve years before Bernard Keane wrote that article, now more than fifteen years ago. In 2002, Stephen Spencer, then Simon Crean's press secretary, later a journalist at Ten and now back on Labor's staff, and who is the best kind of antithesis of a bright young thing, would save VHS tapes for me if I missed a late Thursday night episode. VHS tapes. That's how old the show is. In 2001, Peter

Hendy, then the defence minister Peter Reith's chief of staff, now the member for Eden-Monaro, who is a rather different antithesis of a bright young thing, was sitting up late watching an episode of *The West Wing* when the first news came through of the attacks on the World Trade Center.

Press gallery journalists often think all advisers are young press secretaries obsessed with TV and trivia and the short term and with no great interest in policy or political conviction. Maybe. Or maybe chiefs of staff know whose time can be spared on dealing with the press; and maybe those young staff just know their audience. The kids are all right.

I said the Labor staff battalion has many platoons. It's got its veterans too. Remember I said the ones who didn't want to be in a book looked straight at me when they said it? They were mostly veterans.

Summer 2011 brought me back into Malcolm McGregor's orbit for a last happy season. In the 1980s McGregor worked for NSW head office and Bob Carr, and in the 1990s probably should have advised Kim Beazley as well; he went on to do some very interesting journalism before returning to the army in senior thought-leadership roles. We shared interests – rugby, polyphony, politics – and the young Lieutenant McGregor had served with the old 8 Battalion Royal Australian Regiment in Queensland a few years after my father left.

Macca was working on a blog that became a marvellous book, *Indian Summer*, about the memorable Indian Test tour of 2011–12 and we saw a lot of each other around the cricket that year. We heard Rahul Dravid's spellbinding Bradman Oration in the aircraft hall at the Australian War Memorial; saw a face-off between contending future Australian bats, Usman Khawaja and the late Phil Hughes at Manuka Oval; made plans to meet at the tests. We couldn't meet at Melbourne; we were rooted to our seats in different stands by the last great Sachin Tendulkar cameo on Australian soil. The little master played one lofted late cut to the southern boundary that gave my son and me goosebumps – we talk about it every year – and then he was gone.

So in Sydney we had coffee before the day's play and watched the teams practise in the nets. Despite the Beard Fiasco of the previous year — don't worry, I'll get to that story later — I had been invited to lunch in the Sydney Cricket Ground Trust box again. This was the Year of the Grandstand around Australia — the AFL-led redevelopment of Adelaide Oval and the upcoming 2015 one-day cricket world cup was driving a little glut of stadium building — and Gillard government staff were so popular, even Rodney Cavalier would spill a drink on us if we were burning to death. By day, Cavalier was the larger-than-life chairman of the SCG Trust; by night the Southern Highlands private-library-owning hammer of all political appointees. No one has done more to make the cause of party reform a personal crusade against people who work for the party. Yet there he was, slavering over our sports adviser Andrew Downes (not a head office wog admittedly, but certainly a head office boy), inviting him to every day of the Test and thanking him at every lunch that week — and inexplicably not repeating what he'd said in his book about no staffer being permitted to run for office for five years after leaving staff work, and that for many staff, the choice between the two parties was a choice between which employer offered greater advancement.

Then again, Rodney isn't stupid: 'Downesy' had turned up with fifty million dollars for a new SCG grandstand in his jacket pocket and a bit of staff work had gone into getting that done.

This performance was so predictable I grumbled about it in advance, with McGregor over coffee at the nets. ('I don't reckon we'll get a lecture about reform of the election of the SCG Trust . . . if we opened that up you might get Ray Hadley in the chair . . .') But I wasn't too proud to take the lunch, the club red and the shady seat watching Michael Clarke get to three hundred and then to see Sachin Tendulkar bat for the last time. Ah staff, we are a gracious lot.

Then every grumbling, grumpy, bitter word was reproduced in McGregor's book! And more besides. Good God; at least it's a really good read. Published under the credit Malcolm McGregor, the concluding sections tell a story of gender transition. We met for the last time as Michael and Malcolm at Lodge drinks before the PM's XI in 2012; we next had a long coffee at Gus's in Canberra as Michael and Cate. Cate's become a cause célèbre, and her politics are far from fixed or partisan (nor should they be), but for me she also carries the scars, and the respect, of a veteran of the life of Labor staff.

The Labor staff believe in a better politics but they don't all understand a better politics to mean the same thing – there are definite differences. In his book *Recollections of a Bleeding Heart*, speechwriter Don Watson divided Paul Keating's staff into 'pointy heads' and 'bleeding hearts', in part according to their stance on government intervention in the recovery from the 1991 recession. Peg Noonan's memoir of the Reagan White House, *What I Saw at the Revolution*, made a more generally applicable distinction, between the 'Republicans' and the 'conservatives' in the Reagan team. There's something in this. We had 'progressives' and 'Laborites'.

The progressives weren't necessarily to Labor's left by any means. But they had prior intellectual commitments – most often economic or environmental; in some cases, anti-discrimination is a deep commitment – for which Labor was a logical vehicle in politics. The Laborites had a prior organisational commitment. Our thing preceded any one plan; our church before a creed. *Fraternité* preceded *égalité*; mateship preceded the fair go.

Of course, in government, a lot of advisers also had a background in the public service. It's also common for some advisory positions – particularly in policy – to be filled by public servants on extended leave (of years' duration) from their departments; this has been true for many decades. When people tell you that staff have too much influence over government and that this crowds out the advice of the public service, this is one of the many facts they generally fail to explain. The public servants who work as advisers are usually of the independent centre, and they fight against problems and for what makes sense. Over time, they work out that what is a problem and what makes sense can't be divorced from a value-based definition of what makes a good society. It's usually then that they either form a partisan identity or return to the public service. The public servants I worked with who were serving as advisers were central to every success we had; balanced with the right proportion of Labor and progressive advice, they are essential to any good government.

Over time, long-term governments can sometimes come to rely on them too much. At least we solved that problem.

Finally, in the ranks of Labor, there are a few of us who are basically lifers. On election eve 2004, Sandy Rippingale, the mainstay of our national secretariat staff, said to me, 'What are you going to do after we lose?' And I said, 'Oh, stay, I suppose?' And she shrugged and said, 'Yeah, you're a lifer.'

Best compliment ever.

—

I liked the Labor Party when I was seven or eight and Bill Hayden opposed a boycott of the 1980 Moscow Olympic Games; I was just a little boy who thought sport mattered. But I fell in love with the Labor Party when I was eleven and I saw Paul Keating on television for the first time. Through my adolescence, hearing Paul Keating say things like, 'Banking is the artery of the economy and we've had hardening of the arteries for too long in this country', or 'Howard will wear his leadership like a crown of thorns, and in the parliament I'll do everything to crucify him', changed my life. Keating's brawling id, the Catholic literary imagination, that shining ego, making the economy work better by taking it away from the rich and from the right, wearing a better suit than the other side, smashing the liberals and slicing up the old left; it was like seeing Dylan go electric every night on the news. And my God, was he Irish.

I finally joined the Labor Party in 1994, after my daughter was born, when I was almost finished uni, and it was time to live an adult life.

But as a staffer, it was Mark Latham who gave me a start, when he was assistant shadow treasurer, in January 2002. The first press release I wrote was about petrol prices. The first parliamentary speech I wrote was about forestry-managed investment schemes. That's what assistant shadow treasurers do. Eighteen months later he was shadow treasurer; six months after that, on 2 December 2003, he was Labor leader; a generational change in Labor leadership, leaping forward from the sons of Whitlam ministers to a forty-something fresh face, and promising plenty of change to come. I think it was four days later that we caught a plane together from Melbourne to Sydney and read a newspaper from earlier in the week. Mark's face was half the front page, under a headline that read something like *Australian politics remade*. Struth.

That was the entrée to 2004; by October that year the Labor leader would have thanked me first in his election-night concession speech. Mixed feelings. Mark defied political gravity for a long time that year. He remained leader following the election; in December, he went on leave, and so did I.

By the last day of the year I had put aside the basic material for a family holiday – we were going to drive from home in Canberra to the beach at Tootgarook on Port Phillip Bay. To read, a copy of *The Gorton Experiment*, Alan Reid's account of the larrikin leader John Gorton's decline and fall. To listen to, that gloomy Peter Gabriel and Kate Bush 'Don't Give Up' song; plus a compilation of the Band – that month I had finally seen their concert film *The Last Waltz* on pay TV. But first, New Year's Eve on the back deck in Weston Creek. We slow-danced in our bare feet to 'A Change Is Gonna Come'. I didn't believe it. Governing for Labor seemed a lot more than three years away.

And then things really fell apart. On Boxing Day, one of the greatest natural disasters ever struck Asia. The scale of the loss took time to become apparent, even as government aid efforts began. And after a few days, a woman on the Gold Coast wrote a letter to the *Courier-Mail* asking, 'Where is Mark Latham since the tsunami struck? Very strange isn't it.' By the time I was driving south for our swim, the letter had been published and Mark's absence from public comment on the Asian tsunami had become a national issue. (It would be almost ten years before I read a newspaper article by David Marr and others reviewing the end of Mark's leadership which told me that it was pretty much exactly at the moment that we were dancing on that New Year's Eve that she wrote those words.)

The demands for Mark to make a statement about the tsunami had forced him to tell his staff, and through them the media and the public, that he had suffered a recurrence of pancreatitis and was seriously ill, and therefore would not be making a public appearance. A quarter of a million people were dead, a million and a half displaced, across an area a third of the circumference of the globe. Obviously you'd urgently want to know whether this pancreatitis story stacked up – if so, why was he not at home in Campbelltown but had instead been seen in a pool with his kids at Terrigal, and what did all this mean for his future plans?

I drove south from Canberra with my phone turned off. Not my first Labor leadership crisis; but it was my first leader's-office last days.

We stopped at an Apex park in Wangaratta where I switched on my phone, deleted some messages and returned some calls; I will never forget leaning on my car and looking at the Ovens River go past as I did this. I spoke to Mark's chief of staff, George Thompson, and asked what we should do about our own position if Mark resigned. He said wait; he was right. George hides the mind of Le Carré's Smiley behind the face of Dick van Dyke. I kept driving.

My final conversation with Mark as leader came the next day. I wish I could forget leaning on my car in the driveway at my dad's house in Melbourne while we spoke on the phone. I'm proud that we got the best out of each other and I'm glad we parted on good terms.

By that night I had reached Tootgarook. I sat on the beach reading Reid, phone occasionally lighting up with 'chin up' text messages from mates – in any leadership crisis, always the worst sign of all. Talk about the pathetic fallacy: the sun was actually setting. I wouldn't have been surprised to look up and see that someone had written 'hopes expire' in the sky. On my way to mass on Sunday I rang Jenny Macklin, who was now acting leader, and gave her a line from Joyce about the ocean, 'a bowl of bitter tears', to use if she needed something to say on the tsunami at a service she was attending. She used it when Parliament resumed.

I really just wanted an excuse to talk to someone about work.

A few days after that he was gone; I wasn't even able to see Mark's notorious resignation press conference in a pocket park in Glen Alpine in Sydney's south west on TV, much less be there and help. This wasn't defeat, it was failure.

The Labor Party prepared to turn back to Kim Beazley as leader. In ruling out his own leadership ambitions, MP Stephen Smith put it pretty precisely.

> We weren't regarded as a political basket case at six o'clock on 9 October 2004 [when polls closed on election night]. But we've created that impression since. So the response I've had from many of my colleagues is what they're looking for on this occasion is stability and certainty.

You could say that again.

—

Having worked pretty hard on Mark's staff to deny Kim Beazley the leadership in 2003, it was going to be humbling to front up and make myself available. But as Sandy said, I guess I'm a lifer. I hope I thought the team still needed me. I hope I didn't just want to stay in the game.

I had always liked and admired Kim. I knew many of his staff and I'd worked with him on his return to Labor's front bench during 2004; I appreciated his character and shared his faith. (On a memorable later occasion I would see Brian Harradine walk through the wrong door in Parliament House and into a Labor shadow ministry meeting. After he left with apologies, Kim said *sotto voce*, 'What might have been.') I had also shared elements of the critique of Beazley's leadership from 1996 to 2001. Mark quoted me pretty accurately (on this, at least) in his diary, published the year he left the leadership – and I certainly had thought Beazley the wrong man for the time in 2003.

His 'small-target strategy' was exaggerated in hindsight and it still is. Beazley's strategy 1996–2001 wasn't to have no policies, it was to have a few policies which cut through. You probably even remember the name of one of them – Knowledge Nation – which, nearly fifteen years later, is not a bad effort and is something of a sign that we can see the glass half-full. Bad management (at its peak when the former minister and Knowledge Nation taskforce head Barry Jones self-indulgently insisted on a childish and inaccurate diagram in the report) and bad luck conspired. Kim and his people had run a strategy with a lot to recommend it, but it was subject to external shock. And then at the end of 2001, with the *Tampa*, the attacks on Washington and New York, and the commencement of the war in Afghanistan, they got the shocks of our lives.

I was confident Kim would be elected leader, and I wanted to serve. But the shadow minister for health, Julia Gillard, was in the race too. I had a lot of heart for Julia. We'd got on well since I arrived in Mark Latham's office, next door to hers in Parliament House, and had worked really closely together on occasion in the past year. She'd given me generous personal advice in one or two very trying times. I often contributed jokes for her remarks and sometimes gave her proper comment on big speeches. In 2003 we had gone to the AFL grand final together and seen my Magpies thrashed on the scoreboard and embarrassed in the physical contest.

So when she rang and asked me to give her some advice before an interview with the News Limited Saturday papers focused on international policy, I didn't think the conflict of interest was too great. I was still technically employed by Mark, who supported Julia, and I hadn't been asked to advise Kim on his campaign. She knew her mind on the issues so it was really a primer – suggesting frameworks and themes, pointing out terms of art to employ or avoid, encouraging her along paths she was considering. I did this while I was still on holiday down south, in a long phone conversation. When the article did appear, it was a picture story, comparing Gillard to a number of 'female world leaders' – including Condoleezza Rice, pictured in a somewhat notorious outfit featuring long black boots. It's fair to say some of the finer points of my brief – distinctions between speaking about an international system and the international society, or the defence of Australia and defending Australia's interests – were lost.

For the Fairfax Sunday papers, she was interviewed in the kitchen at her Altona home. She'd just got back from overseas. The picture that appeared the next day, of Gillard seated in her unrenovated kitchen with an empty 'fruit bowl' on her kitchen table, was widely greeted as a sign of a single career woman out of touch with middle Australia.

After a weekend on the phones, Julia withdrew. Kim would be elected leader unopposed. It was back to business as usual, and it felt like time for it too, as much as my heart wanted to stand for change and tomorrow.

I flew back to Canberra to meet George Thompson at the end of January and then the night before the caucus met to elect Kim leader, he and I briefed Kim in Jenny Macklin's office. The first thing was that Mark's resignation, which had taken immediate effect, meant that most staff had only a few more days of employment left. We explained that while we didn't want to rush Kim, he would in fact have to move on some staffing decisions within days. Kim said he'd like to do that, as he had a few people whom he'd be obviously asking to move on. Then he leaned back and stretched, turned his head away from us and sort of yawned out, 'Present company excepted, of course, fellas.' George and I left the room, looked at each other, laughed and shook hands.

The two years that followed as policy director to Kim were as professionally and personally fulfilling as any I've known in politics or life. They ended with defeat by Kevin Rudd in a leadership ballot on the morning of 4 December 2006. A short time after the result was declared, we were told Kim's brother David had died in Perth. In the office, as the news sunk in (or didn't), Kim's chief of staff gave a magnificent farewell speech to our boss. Then, wondering aloud how his father would survive, Kim went to the airport and left Canberra that afternoon. He's since returned many times to visit this city where you can live the life of the mind; I think he loves it nearly as much as I do.

With Kevin and Julia in the leadership and our work for Kim done, we packed the leader's office up, set our email out-of-office messages to Captain Oates, and went to lunch at the Sukothai in Yarralumla before question time began. It was a sentimental choice, one of Kim's old favourites, and a practical one, as they didn't mind if we brought our own cases of beer. I'd first dined with Kim in the same place eight years earlier. In answer to the question, 'What do you think of Abbott?' he'd introduced me to the word *flâneur*. This day his staff toasted and laughed and stole each other's phones and set each other up.

Lunch turned into afternoon and evening drinks at the Kingston Hotel: *tout* Canberra, full of historic significance. It is the site of the actual 'faceless men's bar', the room from which Calwell and Whitlam were notoriously excluded while the Labor federal conference made vital decisions in 1963; I also had my buck's night there. (Canberra doesn't have many pubs.) This was an otherwise quiet Monday night and in the front bar, someone was overheard saying, 'God, that group is drunk.' Our press sec's wife shouted at her, 'They've all just lost their jobs!' I was sitting on a pool table telling jokes when someone came up to me and asked how I was. I said, 'I just tried so hard,' and started crying my head off. It was great. At least we knew we did something we cared about.

The next day Kim's senior staff all still woke up early as usual. We didn't have a morning press briefing any more, so we decided to drive to the Royal Adelaide Hotel at Moruya on the south coast of New South Wales. We took commiseratory calls on the road and picked up new old books on the way and had a contemplative beer (press secretary Colin Campbell had a glass of wine – *very eccentric*) under a touch football perpetual trophy that is better witnessed than described. Back in Canberra on Wednesday we went to the movies at lunchtime to see *Borat*, then home to watch television in the afternoon as Australia ran down the Poms in the Adelaide Test: 'funemployment'. By the following week, Kim was back in town for our office Christmas party. We had a long dinner with the big fella and stayed out long after. The octave of the feast finished the following weekend in our chief of staff's backyard, a barbecue for his fortieth birthday. It was the kind of Canberra backyard I'd been barbecuing in since I was a child. On a December evening, we stayed late enough that his kids had to be sent inside to find 'guest jumpers'.

That week of December 2006 I drove out of the 'reps car park' on the east side of Parliament House with a car full of boxed files and a head full of misery. We'd tried to do things differently with Mark, we'd been in touch and interesting, and failed; we'd tried to do things smart with Kim, we'd been professional and functional, and been beaten. In the previous week I had lost a set of car keys and my best jacket on a cab rank and had gained a four-day hangover. I had a copy of *The Aeneid* and a copy of the memoir of Ulysses S Grant to keep me going over summer; we were going to drive the kids to Queensland this time, and stop at the Big Banana on the way.

It would be four years of exile and adversity's sweet uses before I was advising a Labor leader again. By that time, the Labor leader would be the Australian prime minister, and the Labor staff life would be the life of government staff.

—

How many Labor staff did it take to change a lightbulb in the Gillard government? That's right, you don't know. You don't know, because you weren't there.

Sorry. That isn't really directed towards you. But there are many unattractive elements to Australian politics, and just one of them is the public disrespect for Labor's staff.

What strikes me most about this culture of complaint is it's gutless. If you generalise and criticise politicians, public servants, military officers, business leaders, union leaders – and God only help you if you have a crack at journalists – then the self-appointed deans of their informal colleges will be well into the fray. The eminent retirees, leading current figures, young up and comers – get ready to have to defend your view against any and all contrary ideas. It won't happen if you have a crack at Labor staff. Whether you're a former head of the public service, or a former state minister, or a head of the Business Council of Australia – whoever you are – there's one speech you can give and one column you can file that will earn you absolutely no public pain whatsoever. It's about as brave as bagging rugby (union) on the back page of the *Daily Telegraph*. Why? Because serving staff don't do media and can't talk back.

So a little bit of all this is talking back, on their behalf.

---

Staff life comes back to me in flashes of memory, like details of a drunken night.

In 2002, my first year as an adviser, a sombre dinner in Kingston with staff who had been to the funeral of their admired friend Tracey Aubin, Kim Beazley's former media adviser, who had died by suicide aged thirty-nine.

The mad December day later that same year when my boss Latham and the journalist Misha Schubert dared me to gatecrash John Howard's press gallery Christmas drinks at the Lodge – and I got as far as a handshake and a conversation with the PM about Eliot

Cohen's book *Supreme Command* before the hysterical laughter of *The Australian*'s Matt Price alerted Howard's press secretary Tony O'Leary to my presence. Afterwards, champagne to toast the triumph with Nick Sherry's policy adviser Amber Saggers and Carmen Lawrence's press secretary Jo Fox.

In my period of exile from the staff life seeing Tim Dixon, then Kevin Rudd's speechwriter, arrive in a cab from the airport for a drink (an airport where the PM had just gone 'wheels up') and skip lightly across the street to my office in Carlton – and then making the poor man walk past every bar between Cardigan Street and Meyers Place with his tongue hanging out like a dog. I wasn't working on staff; I had all the time in the world.

After one of my first and better arguments about a speech draft with Ian Davidoff, slipping him a copy of Yeats's 'Remorse for Intemperate Speech':

> . . . though in each
> Fine manners, liberal speech,
> Turn hatred into sport,
> Nothing said or done can reach
> My fanatic heart,
> Out of Ireland have we come.
> Great hatred, little room,
> Maimed us at the start.
> I carry from my mother's womb
> A fanatic heart.

Crossing the road in Byron Bay the day before my mates Jim Chalmers and Gillard press secretary Laura Anderson got married there; seeing Senator Penny Wong pointing at me and saying, 'Look – hacks!', before realising she was pointing to a *hat*stand in a chemist behind me and talking baby talk with her child.

Former international adviser Richard Maude walking into a coffee shop in Canberra to find me writing this very page of this very chapter; you couldn't make it up. Then a moment of droll uncertainty – handshake or hug.

Farewelling one of the great Labor veterans Jack Lake from our office; welcoming his (younger) contemporary Tracey Robinson back into a PMO. Staff who were colleagues and predecessors – people who went to Keating government reunions and formed a connection both with the staff past and with our own post-PMO future.

Years when we could only 'tear our pleasures with rough strife/ through the iron gates of life'. Barbecues where we danced on tables; dinners where we argued; bars where we cried.

One Friday in those Gillard years, after a(nother) leadership week, I encountered something that, of everything I've ever read, had most urgently to be shared with the greatest number of staff mates. It was a letter in the *London Review of Books*. I read it in an airport lounge and I emailed it to everyone I could think of. It was morning and it still almost made me cry right there.

> The drift of Gideon Lewis-Kraus's piece about the Spanish Civil War is that it was 'one wake-up call after another', in which the untrained, poorly armed volunteers had their optimism shattered by the reality of battle. The tone is one of disillusionment.
>
> The Loyalist side of the Spanish Civil War was my first 'cause', at age ten or 11, because my favourite cousin, Coleman (Charlie) Persily, fought on various fronts with the Abraham Lincoln Brigade. Over the years I've spoken to Cousin Charlie and other American 'Lincolnistas' and found their youthful commitment unchanged.
>
> Maybe it's old guys putting a romantic gloss on a bad experience.
>
> Or maybe, even in the face of the Loyalists' ugly factionalism and incompetent leadership, they believed in the Republic despite everything.

I found these ageing guys full of piss, vinegar and militant optimism.

Happy to have survived, happy to have been there.

Despite everything. That is what staff work was like.

## PART TWO

# SUFFICIENT TO HAVE STOOD, THOUGH FREE TO FALL

# 4.
# Pivot

*And 'The Blackbird' broke the silence as you whistled it so sweet, and in Brendan Behan's footsteps I danced up and down the street.*

THE POGUES, 'THOUSANDS ARE SAILING'

Just before lunchtime on Saturday 5 March 2011, the PM boarded a RAAF 737 Boeing Business Jet (BBJ) to travel to Washington.

The BBJ is a great way to travel around Australia and not quite so great a way to travel around the world. Up front, the PM has a cabin of her own with four seats – two facing forwards, two back – and a table that can ease down for coffee or a briefing, and ease up for a meal or to work on a document. There's a separate forward bathroom and the seats in the cabin lay down flat to make proper beds.

The second cabin has ten business-class-style seats – three facing backwards and three forwards across two tables; then another four facing forwards with no table to work on. Then there's a bulkhead and two cupboards for jackets and bags, then through to another sixteen forward-facing seats laid out in a business-class configuration.

Thirty hours and one or even two refuelling stops is a hell of a long time for three lucky people to spend flying backwards – but on the upside, at least those backward-facing seats lay down flat for sleep. Only three of the forward-facing ones do. If you don't need a heavy roller driven up and down your back after writing a four-thousand-word speech on a laptop which is actually on your lap, and then 'sleeping' upright, you've got more core strength than me. Once it's up high, the plane is either soporifically stuffy and hot, or toe-snappingly cold, and it really is sometimes both, so that your head dozes and your feet freeze. You have to hope the most senior person in your cabin doesn't have weird blood pressure or they'll make the crew turn the thermostat down (or up) at precisely the wrong moment and then everyone goes to hell. I loved it.

You knew it mattered. The thrill of looking out the window of that jet while writing a speech for my prime minister never went away. I wish I were on it right now.

A great deal of work for a major overseas visit is done on that plane en route. There's little else to do on a flight like that: in March 2011 the BBJ still didn't have inflight internet connections and a voice call to the plane only came via satellite phone. The policy staff and officials at home and in country would have done a mountain of preparation, and the PM would have had a chance to read a telephone-directory-sized briefing pack, but this is her best chance to ask serious questions of the most senior officials, who travel on a trip like this. So with them, the PM would work through the whole program in outline: discuss the purpose of every meeting; review all the unresolved issues for decision; update the advice from our diplomats in country; and go through the planned media announcements and picture opportunities – especially complex on the US east coast, where the deadlines and the date line conspire to force you to preview most announcements in their final and public form eighteen hours in advance, which really feels like an eternity.

All that would happen in a meeting in the second cabin that would begin as soon as the seatbelt sign was off and the boss had eaten, and could go for hours. The PM would come back down the plane, carrying her notes and a cup of green tea. She'd take one of the proper seats from her chief of staff, the RAAF crew would bring out a few little two-foot-high camp chairs to put in the aisles, and the departmental secretaries and chiefs of staff and national security advisers and press secs would start to play musical chairs.

I could never work out what this ritual reminded me of more: actress Glenda Jackson as Elizabeth I arriving at privy council for the first time, and all these blokes having to shuffle down one seat; or the card games I played in caravans on the NSW south coast when I was a kid.

The little green camp chairs ended up closest to the PM and you looked active sitting on them, so they were prime spots – but you couldn't weigh much more than ninety kilos and you'd be semi-crouching for two hours or more. Plus it's really hard to make a thoughtful cradle with your fingers on your chest when your knees touch your chin because you're sitting on a twenty-four-inch-high folding chair. To me, the choice of who sat on the little folding chairs in the aisles of the PM's plane next to the big seats with arms always illustrated Walter Bagehot's classic separation of the English constitution into two: the efficient part and the dignified part.

A staffer took the camp chair.

One of the traditional pieces of advice to advisers is to work out if your boss is a reader-commenter or a listener-questioner and, in turn, to work out whether to brief them for big issues on paper or face-to-face. Most can do both, but all have a preference. Certainly, as PM, Julia Gillard was a reader, and that telephone directory would be pretty thoroughly thumbed before this all began. In part the task then was to work out what had changed in the two days since the brief had been put to bed; in part to hold the department heads accountable for the advice their own officials had put in paper; in part a professional courtesy – always an important consideration for this PM. When it worked, the meeting also allowed the major elements of the visit to emerge in some clarity from the detail of each of the particular parts.

On this flight to Washington, Richard Maude and Dennis Richardson (then secretary of foreign affairs and trade) took the lead on this.

In March 2011, downstage right and left were security issues and economic issues – each of these included bilateral, regional and global elements. Centre stage: to showcase the PM's personal commitment to the Australia–US relationship and her personal connection to the president. Making this relationship work, not only at a national but a personal level, is a big part of the Australian prime minister's job.

This would not be Gillard and Obama's first encounter. There had been phone calls on her taking office in June and again in September. They had met at summits where, as the only progressive leaders of big English-speaking countries and among the only progressive leaders of any democracies, a collegial relationship naturally emerged. They were the same age, shared a rationalistic and reserved personality and a modernised social democratic outlook, they were both activists in the face of the global recession – and paradoxically, they shared a scepticism about the glamour of international relations. In an interview during her first overseas trip the previous year, the PM had said, 'If I had a choice I'd probably more be in a school watching kids learn to read in Australia.' In 2014 in an interview with the *New Yorker*, the president would say, 'I didn't run for office so that I could go around blowing things up.'

The upstage issue, always in view, was China. The rise of the great civilisation-state – the world's most populous nation, the global centre of economic change, and the world's biggest authoritarian regime – was the most important new thing in the world. Richardson had a great expression for the upstage issue, which involved quoting himself, from his time as ambassador to the US: 'We have two friends and one ally; we know the difference and we know what it means.'

Only Dennis could genuinely sound down to earth while quoting himself. Quoting himself, on a VIP, to a PM. You can't not be fond of this bloke. He could only be an Australian.

On the flight, the PM would also go through the speeches. She and I would have had a meeting or exchanged written briefings at least a week earlier and the speech drafts would be in the briefing pack but face to face on the flight was usually the first feedback I'd get from her on the drafts. Sometimes forward in her cabin, hooray! Going through changes with the person who'll actually deliver the speech is fine. It really is their speech. Sometimes in the main cabin, boo! This meant enduring comments from everyone with an interest in them. You can't write policy speeches without detailed policy advice; if you want complete creative control, you get to write in a garret, not in a BBJ. When staff and officials apologised for bastardising some nice expression or conceit by pointing out a policy or factual problem, I'd often say, 'Mate, it's not my first novel, it's fine.'

This doesn't mean I didn't grind my teeth.

Either way, I'd write all that up during the hours in transit, and the PM would then get another draft based on her comments while we were on the plane. (Often the first speeches of a visit had to be finished before we landed.)

But the final and most important part of this meeting was that it was a chance for the PM to speak. After all the detail, she had the chance to tell everyone what *her* purpose was for the visit – while they were right in front of her, and couldn't miss it. That Saturday afternoon, while we were still on our side of the Pacific, that's exactly what she did.

The proximate occasion of the visit to Washington was to mark the sixtieth anniversary of the ANZUS treaty between us. This brought with it dealings on all the detailed business of the relationship, security and economic: the biggest new thing on the table was the Trans-Pacific Partnership, a new proposed agreement to encourage free trade. In New York we would also campaign for one of the elected positions on the UN Security Council.

But now Gillard gave the meeting her view of the real purpose of visit. The Australian prime minister wasn't going to advocate for American *engagement* – she wasn't going to call for the United States to play a role, or even continue a role, in our region. She wanted to assume that, to take it as a given, and in turn lock it in. Instead, this visit was going to advocate for American *confidence*. She would do whatever she could with the voice she had to reinforce American self-belief. That's where our national interest lay. Australia and the world needed (and needs) America confidently going for growth in global economic forums and lowering barriers to trade, confidently seeing the mission through in Afghanistan, confidently seeking a modus vivendi with China that means there is peace in Asia and the Asian democracies are secure. Her bottom line: 'They're in a funk. We've got to do our bit to snap them out of it.'

People – everyone – listened and made notes. It was good stuff, and it put a new twist on every part of the visit, from the talking points for the Oval Office to the speech to Congress (out with my draft theme, 'Look West', which for whatever reason the officials had always hated anyway – too interesting? I'm honestly not sure; and in with the PM's theme, 'Be Bold') – Australia's PM would speak to how, not whether, America plays its role in the world.

—

These were exhausting meetings. I was always buggered at the end of them and I only had to follow every third word. The PM's stamina for such discussions amazed me, as did that of the public-service senior professionals like Richardson and Maude. And they would then be followed by hours of drafting and redrafting by the whole team – not just of my speeches, but all the papers for the visit. The plane landed to refuel at Hawaii in the middle of the night and we raced across the apron to a business lounge, where we plugged in phones and printers and laptops and iPads to every outlet and hosed down little eight-ounce cans of Coke Zero and kept writing and printing – redrafting remarks and press releases and itineraries and reviewing new briefs and cables from post – until we carried all our crap back across the apron and took off again, and did it all in the air for hours more.

The best part of that job was always hating parts of that job; catching yourself not being excited any more and then thinking, Man, I'm really doing it. This was everything we'd come for – from the most junior personal assistant to the most cynical professional staffer, the most senior public official. I think the RAAF aircrew even got a kick out of a day like that.

At the end of that thirty-hour day, it was still only Saturday when we landed outside Washington DC. A twenty-car motorcade took us from Andrews Air Force Base to the president's guest house in Pennsylvania Avenue, Blair House. Kim Beazley was there – now Australian ambassador to the US – and grand on a walking stick, sipping a Diet Coke. I said, 'Oh Kim, it's so good to see you here in your element.' He said, 'No, mate, you're in my element, back there.'

After the formal reception, the staff escaped to the Willard Hotel where we toasted the alliance under a portrait of President Ulysses S Grant, and I told the story I'd read back in summer 2006 about the young Lieutenant Grant and his mate Lieutenant Benjamin, menaced by the 'unearthly howling of wolves' while riding one night outside Corpus Christi, Texas:

> 'Grant, how many wolves do you think there are in that pack?'
>
> ... suspecting that he thought I would over-estimate the number, I determined to show my acquaintance with the animal by putting the estimate below what possibly could be correct, and answered: 'Oh, about twenty,' very indifferently. He smiled and rode on. In a minute we were close upon them, and before they saw us. There were just TWO of them ...
>
> I have often thought of this incident since when I have heard the noise of a few disappointed politicians who had deserted their associates. There are always more of them before they are counted.

Of course, underestimating his opponents' numbers is probably why Grant's post–Civil War presidency failed. Well, in addition to the corrupt hangers-on, and the post-traumatic stress disorder, and the drink.

—

The PM had left a lot of howling behind at home. Asylum seekers were dying. Queensland was under water. And her fix for carbon – the only option now emerging from the multi-party committee – was a fixed price.

Between Advent 2010 and Easter 2011 the heavens seemed close to falling. From December to April we lived through boat smashes, floods, bushfires, cyclones, earthquakes, tsunamis, nuclear meltdowns. The human cost was horrific for those directly affected and deeply disturbing for millions watching only through the news media. For a time, the prime minister inspected sites of devastation wherever she went. It's incredible to reflect that every single week between New Year's Day and the budget in May that didn't bring a parliamentary sitting or an overseas visit brought a site inspection of disaster recovery, and parliamentary business and overseas travel was strongly defined by natural disaster as well.

Around dawn on 15 December forty-eight people were killed when their boat, identified as *SIEV-221*, smashed into the Christmas Island coast at Flying Fish Cove. They died in sight of the shore and in view of the people on the island who tried to help. The PM was on leave and returned from her break to give the first of the grim press conferences of that summer. She had been advocating middle-ground policies in this area for years, and for years had spoken of the danger of 'leaky boats'; this was far from the first disaster on a people-smuggler's boat. But the proximity to land, and to people on land trying to help, brought an immediacy that couldn't be shaken off – especially not in an office suite where there are a hundred televisions. Never, after Christmas Island, could we forget the moral and humanitarian imperative to deter boat movements of that kind. It was a sad, horrible day, in a weird week.

The PM spent the next weekend signing Christmas cards and her right hand got stiff and sore; she changed her ring to her left hand while she was doing it, came into the office on Monday afternoon to give an hour-long afternoon press conference about the NBN, and was asked on camera if she had got engaged. Every media outlet in the country, electronic, print and online, covered the story. Special mention to the *Sydney Morning Herald* diarists Matt Buchanan and Leesha McKenny for their speculation that 'perhaps it was a tactic to deflect attention from the [NBN] scheme that will cost taxpayers some $27.5 billion? If so, it was a masterstroke of spin.' No such masterstroke was required.

Through all this, it rained. Flooding that was localised in December (and not limited to Queensland – parts of Victoria had particularly severe floods and most states were affected) had become extraordinary crisis events by 10 and 11 January. In the end three-quarters of Queensland was disaster-declared, the Brisbane CBD had been evacuated, Toowoomba had experienced a bizarre and fatal 'inland tsunami' and dozens of people were dead.

Sometimes an astonishing event changes everyone and everything; sometimes it is as if in their shock, everyone can only keep doing what they always do.

The tabloid media and commercial TV conducted a week-long theatrical review of the prime minister's 'performance' on her visit to Brisbane (a black suit – 'mourning'; a down-beat voice – 'wooden'). Hedley Thomas at *The Australian* got his deer-stalker cap out and went hunting green conspirators among Wivenhoe Dam's engineers – had they let the dam overflow because they thought releasing water wasn't environmentally correct?

The National Party announced that while these disasters proved nothing about the climate, they certainly did prove something important about environmental policy – it was too hard to build dams in Australia. The Liberal Party said we should pay for rebuilding Queensland schools by cutting aid programs to Indonesian Islamic schools.

And the Gillard government did its thing: got together the best advice it could, worked out what was required, and despite real political and economic barriers to progress, got it done. Rebuilding had to be paid for; there was also a tricky question of how to do the actual work without pushing up prices for the kinds of material and labour that would be needed; and the budget process overall was in 'consolidation' mode. We'd promised a surplus, after all. So the prime minister pushed to get the hard decisions made, the treasurer worked hard to make it fair for low- and middle-income people, and on 27 January the PM went to the National Press Club and announced a package of budget savings – delays in infrastructure spending, cuts to industry support, and ending various direct carbon abatement schemes that (when we had a carbon price) wouldn't be required; plus a 'flood levy' of 0.5 per cent on taxable income between \$50 001 and \$100 000 and a levy of 1 per cent to be applied on taxable income above \$100 000 to pay the damage bill. It was the first press club speech I'd written in five years.

The climate kept doing its thing too. Three weeks after the press club speech the category-five cyclone Yasi absolutely smashed Queensland, virtually destroying Mission Beach and Tully and a making a fair mess of Innisfail and Townsville on the way. The majority of Australians kept doing what they have always done, supporting government-funded action to fix national problems; in early February Newspoll showed 55 per cent in favour of the flood levy. But the government – and the PM personally – had lost a hell of a lot of paint.

The Australian economy also took an extraordinary punishment from the floods. The damage to exports were so bad it was like a one-day recession.

But a press club speech about a levy to fix a weather problem was only the overture – a courtyard press conference about a tax to fix a climate problem was the full symphony. That would come four weeks after the flood levy announcement, on Thursday February 24.

At lunchtime that day the PM made her call. In the 2010 campaign she'd foreshadowed action on climate change, ruling out a 'carbon tax' but not emissions trading, with the broad proviso that a 'national consensus' should be reached – in effect, indicating a future scheme would require bipartisan support. The key point of this day's announcement was support for a plan where carbon pollution permits could be bought and sold, but with a relatively long period (three years) during which this would be at a price set by regulation, not by buyers and sellers within the trading scheme. Emissions trading or carbon tax? In a sense, this was both; in another sense, this illustrated the rather arbitrary, even semantic, distinction between the two.

She announced this in her courtyard, alongside the Greens party (as for the multi-party committee the previous year) and this time also bringing in the independent MPs. Look, it said, parliamentary numbers are locked in, this is not a hypothetical any more – she had the will, and it would be done. An hour later in question time the PM would describe the carbon price as 'a scheme that would start with a fixed price for a fixed period, effectively like a tax' – no lawyer language or weasel words, no hiding: she was going to make the case.

I was one of those who thought it seemed like the best of a bad lot of options at the time.

Instead, it became proof that she'd lied.

And that same afternoon the PM announced by press release that she would visit the United States from 5–13 March for discussions on the strategy for transition in Afghanistan, developments in the Asia-Pacific region and the global economic recovery – and to mark the sixtieth anniversary of the ANZUS alliance. She would have a meeting with the president, among other senior officials, campaign in New York for Australia to gain a seat on the UN Security Council, and the Speaker had invited her to address a joint meeting of the

Congress – the first such invitation to an Australian leader since John Howard, nine years before.

—

The war in Afghanistan was bipartisan business again. Earlier that month, the Liberal Party's nibbling around the edges of the commitment, looking for ways to say the government didn't support the troops, had come to a howling end when Mark Riley and Michael McKinnon of the Seven Network revealed probably the worst mistake of Tony Abbott's time as opposition leader.

In September the previous year, the Liberal Party had picked up on rumours that fire support to the Australian troops had been reduced following the Dutch drawdown in Uruzgan Province – and rumours that this was a factor in the engagement in which Jared McKinney was killed. The man died, his widow went into labour with his third child at his funeral, and the opposition defence spokesman David Johnston (later briefly minister for defence) blamed the government, saying we should send more helicopters, artillery, troops and even tanks. Abbott himself repeated references to this argument in the October parliamentary debate, before claiming to accept 'assurances from senior commanders on the spot' that our troops had enough support. Those assurances had in fact been delivered to the opposition leader personally by US colonel James Creighton at a firepower demonstration in Afghanistan itself. Abbott had visited the country alone on his way back to Australia from the Conservative Party conference in the UK in October 2010. There, the commander on the ground had responded directly to the Liberal Party's commentary on the tactical questions, saying, 'But we're all in the knowledge that all the stuff you see here and more was available on the day [that Jared McKinney died].'

Abbott's response? 'Nah, well, it's pretty obvious that, um, well, sometimes shit happens, doesn't it.'

Having disgraced himself by deliberately politicising this combat death, he had now embarrassed himself by accidentally trivialising it; he hid. After months of efforts by his office finally failed to suppress this footage against freedom of information requests, Abbott was confronted with his own words on 8 February, in an interview recorded with Mark Riley in a courtyard in Parliament House and broadcast that night. Word raced around the building during the afternoon that the news was not to be missed. We watched, amazed. At one point, in response to a question from Riley, the opposition leader held a strange twenty-eight-second silence while his head rapidly nodded back and forth. A physical altercation genuinely didn't seem impossible. Abbott's most sensible response came just before that strange silence descended: 'Look, a soldier has died, and you shouldn't be trying to turn this into a subsequent media circus.'

Wise words, even if uttered in hindsight; physician, heal thyself.

If the dirty war over the politics of the war at home now largely went away, the real war Australia was committed to certainly did not. Corporal Richard Atkinson of the 1st Combat Engineer Regiment was killed by an improvised explosive device on 2 February. On 19 February, Sapper Jamie Larcombe was shot in the Mirabad Valley. The name of the Afghan interpreter shot alongside him was not published in Australia. They were dead before the helicopter evacuating them could get them back to Tarin Kot.

The Prime Minister flew direct from Canberra to Sapper Larcombe's funeral on Kangaroo Island in a nine-seater RAAF Challenger Jet – the 'little VIP'. The chief of the defence force and the secretary of the defence department were on the plane; as always, one of the PM's press secretaries also travelled to the funeral. The blokes had brought black ties and the girls had brought black dresses. These difficult days were part of their lives now. The leader of the opposition was also on the plane. Abbott travelled with his press secretary but made no controversial public comment that day.

The PM sat ten feet from the coffin during the service at Flagstaff Hill and followed the procession to Kingscote Cemetery about a kilometre to the west. Sapper Larcombe was buried in front of hundreds of people: in front of his partner, his mum and dad and his three younger sisters. He was twenty-one. He was buried at home, on Kangaroo Island, on Friday 4 March 2011, the day before the PM went to the United States. She would speak about him by name in the US Congress the following week.

—

So there we were in Washington, in the early hours of Monday morning, going through the program for the next day and not really longing for the politics of home – we were in Blair House.

The PM was going to visit the Vietnam Veterans Memorial in the morning and give a speech in front of the Lincoln Memorial to announce funding for an Australian wing for the Vietnam Veterans Education Centre. This would not be front-page news at home, but I saw it as a slightly complicated engagement that needed deft handling. We were about to begin a week dedicated to strengthening the Australia–US alliance with a commemoration of the biggest strategic error and the hour of greatest partisan controversy in the alliance's first fifty years.

But John Howard spent years after 1996 saying that Australia had been alongside the United States in every armed conflict of the century. It now seemed to have become almost impossible to convince almost anyone that the Howard idea – we always fight when they fight – is just one, partisan account of the alliance. Thus at this late hour, it caused a sudden controversy in our travelling party that the PM's speech for the next day – which I'd drafted and she'd approved – was to describe the Vietnam War as 'controversial then and controversial now'. You might think that is the most neutral statement available to the pen; I found out in Blair House that Sunday night that it is anything but. It's a tribute to the power of persistence that such a highly tendentious political claim as Howard's could come to be seen as the neutral view, while a characterisation as flat as 'it was controversial' could make officials nervous.

On the other hand, the discussion reminded me that no one is ever nervous, no matter what the occasion, when you say something that actually is really political about the Vietnam War: that we learned that we should honour the troops regardless of our opinion of our commitment. Now, that's true. But it is a very direct reflection on the peace movement – who were right about the war! – and it is certainly not the only lesson we were taught by Vietnam. If you imply it is, it really sounds like you think we were right to go to that war. Which is fine. If you're Prime Minister Howard.

While I was explaining my view of this, it became clear it was even possible for senior Australian public servants and military officers, people who are not idiots and who sincerely believe they are also not political, to say firmly that the PM shouldn't even reflect on the *Iraq* War with regret – and possible for them to look blank when a speechwriter shouts back at them across the table, 'But the prime minister OPPOSED the Iraq War and the president she is meeting today is only president because HE opposed the Iraq War – what do you think we should say: they were both WRONG?'

Maybe I shouldn't have raised my voice.

But no matter how right you know you are, you still hesitate to get the PM out of bed to tell a meeting you are right. So I caved and made some late changes to shut them up. It wasn't morning in America quite yet.

In her press conference the next morning after the speech, the PM was asked a question premised on her reference to the 'democratic processes' our troops had 'protected': 'Are you suggesting . . . were you actually a supporter of the Vietnam War?' (No, but thanks for noticing that we failed to clear that up.) At least some of the good stuff had survived. The speech still quoted Lincoln on 'binding up the wounds' – which risks overreach for an Australian politician, but if you can introduce the quote with 'Lincoln's own words are carved in stone here' then I think you're on safe ground; it still contained a tribute to the distinctive Australian experience of the war; and the example the PM gave still spoke about my family's experience of 1970.

> I know Australians who visit this city will visit this centre. The 'nasho' who patrolled Phuoc Tuoy. His sister who marched in the moratorium. They will remember what the war meant to Australia and what it meant to them. Many other Australians will pay tribute here. The children, the grandchildren. They will not only remember . . . they will learn.

Once it was delivered the next morning, I emailed my dad a copy and asked him to send one to my aunt. I'm proud of them. You have to say thanks sometime.

Later that day, the PM met the president. Their Oval Office meeting was followed by a classroom visit to Wakefield High School across the Potomac in Virginia (when the president visited Canberra in 2012 the PM took him across the lake to Campbell High School to return the favour). Before they left the White House, they had tossed a Sherrin around the Oval Office, the PM demonstrating how to handball; when they left Wakefield to return to DC, the president asked the prime minister to join him in his limousine for the drive and then stopped the motorcade and literally dropped her off at the steps of Blair House. It really was unheard of; official Washington was agog. There was genuine warmth, but more to the point, empathy and respect between Gillard and Obama; that day and in the two years that followed there was a lot more hard talk than handball.

It's pretty hard not to sound starstruck telling yarns about DC; even saying 'DC' rather than 'Washington' is one sign you're losing the plot. Every Australian prime minister since Curtin must have been accused by someone of being too close to the Americans, or perhaps worse, too easily impressed. In his waspish cabinet memoir, Paul Hasluck groaned inwardly at Harold Holt, who he said 'overvalued almost absurdly being on "first-name terms" with the President' and 'being able to start a letter "Dear Lyndon" and with a few sentences of family gossip'. Maybe that's true of Holt. But the relationship matters to Australia's actual interests, and that means the relationships matter; it's part of any PM's job and part of the job of many Australians. My observation – extending to six party leaders I've seen up close, but all of them Labor leaders, admittedly – is that if their alliance thinking is at all influenced by encounter with presidential glamour, this is easily outmatched by the sour distortions imposed on the thinking of those inside and outside politics who regret their exclusion from the charmed circle. We're all subject to subjectivity. (Since at least the time of Hawke, it is rarely one of the journalists who travels with the prime minister to Washington who writes the grouchy weekend review piece saying the prime minister went over the top.)

The alliance was stronger at the end of Monday 7 March 2011 than it was at the start of that day; it was stronger at the end of June 2013 than it was in June 2010.

—

The PM delivered an important speech to the US Chamber of Commerce on Tuesday morning in which the essentials of her international economy agenda were drawn together for the first time. She made the case for the Doha Round, the Trans-Pacific Partnership Agreement, shared reform agendas in 'education, energy and the environment' – she told the story of Australia's success in 2009 while adding that 'stimulus and recovery are not enough', connecting her own domestic reform agenda, 'human capital, innovation and clean energy' to the challenge of getting the world economy growing after the financial crisis.

Two years before the PM would deliver an Asian Century White Paper, she was already explaining the changes on the west side of the Pacific – 'In sixty years China's share of global merchandise trade has grown from one *one-hundredth*... to one *sixth*' – and making the case that every nation could benefit – not a message the more conservative or more hawkish in the US wanted to hear.

And above all, the PM preached confidence to American businesses – the 'snap them out of it' strategy:

> Just in my own lifetime, the mid-1960s, the late 1970s, the early 1990s, and now this decade, have all seen their phases where plenty of columns were written and books were sold claiming to read 'the writing on the wall' for these United States. There is always someone to say, 'Your days are numbered.' They've never been right yet.

The little girl who won prizes in catechism classes for Bible verses, who still lived inside the PM, enjoyed a biblical phrase.

The other great set piece of the visit still lay ahead. Through all of that Monday I was in my room at Blair House writing, then on Tuesday I was at the Willard Hotel doing the same thing. I ground away at the address to Congress, making revision after revision in response to the PM's thoughts, suggestions from officials and staff, and adding corrections and clarifications to the material we kept introducing. It was working; every change we made was a good one – clarifying stories, confirming policy, and layers of what we called 'cheese', the warm, comforting rhetoric that an American audience expects in almost any public speech – but it was starting to feel like a pretty big deal. At least I was too busy to be nervous; by Tuesday lunchtime, when I dropped version four thousand or whatever it was in the PM's pigeonhole, I hadn't been outside during daylight hours since Saturday morning in Canberra. It was Shrove Tuesday, and my dear itinerant buddy Kirk Kramer, a 'Sooner', as they call sons of Oklahoma, came in from his latest home in Cottage City, Maryland, to rescue me for a couple of hours. We went to confession at St Matthew the Apostle, the church where President Kennedy's funeral mass was said (this day the old priest seemed almost completely deaf, which was absolutely fine by me), then we had a beer and a bowl of oyster stew at Billy Martin's Tavern where (some say) Senator Kennedy proposed marriage to Jacqueline Bouvier, and then went for an actual walk in the actual outside! In Dumbarton Oaks Park I squinted into the sun.

When I got back we were ready for final read-throughs, final rehearsals, final changes, final panics. How will you say 'President, *pro tempore*' when you acknowledge the Senate president at the start? Don't they say '*pro tem*'? How will you say 'boys of Pointe du Hoc' when you cite President Reagan's line on the D-Day landings? Is there YouTube of Reagan saying it? Wait, what will you do if the autocue breaks during the speech? Who can put a copy on the podium before the PM walks in? The 'helmet story' – is it still confusing? Should I rewrite it again? And the editing went on.

At every meeting one or two officials had complained about a line that read, 'The eyes of the world are still upon you. Your city on a hill cannot be hidden. No one lights a lamp to hide it under a bushel.' The national security adviser, Duncan Lewis – a public servant, not a member of the PM's staff – now had yet another go and said again that it just didn't make sense to go from this big image of a city to this little image of a lamp. I looked at him and said, 'Duncan, they come one after another in the Sermon on the Mount.' Ah, that Gillard laugh; I can hear it now. We still took it out; we must have wanted to preserve the poor bastard's feelings, and in truth, one or two of his more literary suggestions had been good ones – 'side by side, step by bloody step' was a particular winner.

The next morning all the boys were wearing navy blue suits and ironed white shirts. The PM's jacket was the colour of a flame tree. Dennis Richardson stood up and said, 'Righto, here we go,' and we were off to the motorcade. In the Congress buildings the whole group, including the PM, her staff and officials and the embassy people including Kim, paused in a 'green room' just down the corridor from the chamber and sipped water, waiting for the senators, congressman and others to be ready for her to enter. (The joint sitting would be in the House chamber; we would enter from a side entrance and take our seats just before the PM did.) I wanted the PM to concentrate on her text in these last minutes, not to make small talk with us, so I looked around the walls, and found a framed illustrated manuscript: it was the address to the Congress during the second famine in February 1880 by the great nationalist leader of nineteenth-century Ireland, Charles Stewart Parnell.

The Chief, the Blackbird of Sweet Avondale.

You've got a job to do for your boss and for Australia and you can't get carried away, but in a moment like that you do feel like your family's come a long way from nineteenth-century Munster. It was the middle of the night at home. I texted my dad, *I'm about to walk out onto the floor of the US House of Representatives. Thanks for everything that got me here.*

There are, necessarily, a lot of people involved in a big job like that. You're as much a publisher and editor as a writer. It's always interesting to see an idea emerge in the conversations and then live or die through to the final speech – and then to see when and how the principal takes over. One way or another, this was very much a Gillard speech, in word and especially in thought. She meant what she said about the alliance when she took the opportunity to describe it in terms that reflected the politically progressive, even social-democratic ideals of Roosevelt and Curtin in the 1940s and of her own leadership and that of President Obama. The great themes of the speech were the great themes of her diplomacy with the United States in three years in office. An 'alliance in war and peace', no safe haven for terrorism in Afghanistan – an 'alliance in hardship and prosperity', stimulus and reform, clean energy, education and jobs – and an 'alliance in a new world', jawboning her way to the best outcome for Australia, reminding all that China's prosperity is a threat to no one and America's security presence in Asia is a threat to no one, in order to make it so.

After the speech, Kim gave me a handshake in the chamber that nearly took my arm off; then the Speaker hosted us for morning tea. There were still tears in his eyes and everyone wanted to know more about the 'helmet story' — how Aussie firefighters found a helmet belonging to American firefighter Kevin Dowdell who died on September 11, and the Australian Rob Frey brought it back as a gift for Kevin's two uniformed sons. One of them, James, was present with Rob in the gallery that day, the helmet under his arm. The PM in her speech had wished Rob and James well in very Australian terms; one of the Speaker's staff asked me to explain the expression 'good on you' over and over.

During morning tea a group of staff and officials were shown out on to the porticos high over the National Mall. It was the sight of a lifetime. Below is where the inauguration happens, we were told, just below us. Someone asked, 'So President Kennedy spoke right there?' and our host explained that no, that was on the east side of the building. It wasn't until 1980 that the inauguration was moved over to this side, partly to allow for crowds on the Mall, but also because as a symbol of American optimism and the future, President Reagan wanted to 'look West'. Some of the team were even generous enough to notice; it turns out my first draft wasn't complete crap. If only the PM had been there to laugh.

Back home, a radio caller said the PM referring to her memory of the moon landing as a symbol of America's abilities reminded her of something Bono said at a U2 concert once. The (laughable) inference that the PM had 'lifted' a section of her speech (or that I had, I suppose) led the television news coverage of the speech that night in Australia and got more print coverage than hindsight can credit. No satirist could invent the ways that our media finds to trivialise our national life; Lindsay Tanner in his jeremiad frankly could have gone harder. But we didn't only get bad reviews – there was even incredibly generous praise from Bob Carr, then still in retirement, comparing the work on the speech to that of Graham Freudenberg; I sent Bob a message saying it was 'praise from Caesar'. Next time I was in New York I'd end up writing for him.

So whatever the mood was like in front of the TV screens in Canberra, that day on the plane from Washington up to New York nothing was going to take the fizz out of the champagne. After dinner I walked half the length of Fifth Avenue to meet my predecessor Tim Dixon, now consulting in social enterprises in the US. It was finally me running late for a drink because of work.

In New York the PM campaigned for Australia's bid for a two-year seat on the UN Security Council, spoke about the problems of the small and medium countries of the world, and continued the argument for bold US engagement and for enlightened Chinese leadership in a century of Asian growth. She was setting a course for a visit to China, Japan and Korea over Easter and ANZAC Day, relationships in which there was a lot of work to do.

At about four a.m. on the day of our departure, an earthquake and tsunami hit Japan.

It was still a season of disaster. And Asia was always there.

# 5.
# Delivery and decision

*Any government which tries to fight an opposition on its own ground of short-term media pandering is doomed to policy and political failure. My approach is quite the contrary. Consensus and discipline, method and delivery . . . difficult decisions to meet the big challenges, my honest best judgement and leadership in the national interest.*

*As an optimist and an activist, I keep my faith that good policy and good politics converge in the long term.*

PRIME MINISTER JULIA GILLARD

Every day in the prime minister's office I walked the corridor that runs past the rooms where Caterina worked on the diary, past the lounge with a round couch where Emma bent over the question time folders – 'the round lounge', we called it – to the policy unit. Sometimes I had work to do, sometimes I had jokes to tell, sometimes I had a coffee buddy to pick up, sometimes I just needed to find out what was going on. This would take me past the office of Ian Davidoff, the PM's ingenious, neurotic policy director, until he left in the middle of 2012. If his door was open I might say g'day. If it was closed and he was in a meeting, I might ring his mobile and then hang up when he looked up; if he was ranting at some poor adviser and things looked really tense ('But *what* is the *counterfactual*?!'), I'd sometimes do a blowfish on his window.

Ian never really accepted this conduct. But if he wasn't there, I'd often stop and admire a newspaper front page he had stuck up on his wall – only a few days before polling day, when the campaign policy shake-up he helped lead had drawn a massive headline screaming something like *Labor's policy push*. Nothing beats looking up from your desk to a big old front-page win to remind you of what you are capable of. In federal politics, governing is the story.

But that doesn't always mean the yarn is policy – other times it means the yarn is events. In 2011, events were cruel.

In January the PM had worn a suit in Brisbane next to Anna Bligh, who was in workmanlike blue jeans. In Parliament in February she wept for young Jordan Rice who died during the floods to get his brother to safety first and for rescue worker Mark Kempton and the aircrew who couldn't save a young mum's child in arms. March had taken her to Christchurch, a week after returning from the US, for the memorial service for the earthquake which ripped up the ground underneath the New Zealand city eleven days after the earthquake, tsunami and nuclear meltdown in Japan; the PM had spoken to New Zealand's John Key within hours of the disaster, saying simply, 'Tell me what you need.' And in Japan, in April, she walked through Minamisanriku; the first foreign leader to visit since the tsunami disaster, it looked like she was inspecting the site of the end of the world.

Still, policy could also get a yarn.

—

Kevin Rudd once inked a change on a draft speech before growling at my predecessor, 'I don't do "significant". I do "first", "biggest", or "best ever".' That's exactly what he had gone for in April 2010 when announcing a 25 per cent increase in tax on cigarettes – which equated to over two dollars a pack, effective immediately – alongside new 'hard-hitting' anti-smoking television campaigns, restrictions on internet advertising and a measure that really was first, biggest and best all at once: plain packaging of cigarettes, with legislation to ban brand imagery on cigarette packs from 1 July 2012. This was big news by early 2011.

When you think of human lives saved, plain packaging of cigarettes might be the most important and enduring good thing the Labor government did between 2007 and 2013. Cigarettes kill tens of thousands of Australians every year; it's quite likely nothing we did will make more difference to more people over time, not least because it seems the least likely of Labor's major initiatives to be reversed or repealed by a future conservative government. In many ways it's also a miniature of all that was bravest and dumbest about our years in office. We had a real knack for doing just enough of the right thing to almost kill us, preferably in a policy area we couldn't definitely and directly control.

As health minister and then attorney-general, Nicola Roxon's glory was that she fought and won this massive fight with an industry that has more lawyers, guns and money than does the state. This was a genuine world-first and a massive threat to the industry's global businesses, and it was desperate to beat it any way it could.

British American Tobacco campaigned against the laws, saying they'd encourage the rise of black-market cigarettes dominated by organised crime. They also threatened to cut prices of branded tobacco to compete with this, and pointed out this would mean more kids taking up smoking and more smoking deaths. In thirty years Big Tobacco had gone from denying that its product killed to threatening to kill people with its product; gutsy stuff. By June 2011, Imperial Tobacco were running TV advertisements saying plain packaging was a symptom of a new 'nanny state', featuring an angry middle-aged woman.

Plain packaging was the right thing to do: the experts all supported it, the evidence was perfectly clear. (We probably still had a preventive health taskforce or something on our side; I forget how many lawyers, guns and money they sent us.) So from now, indeed for most of the first two years of Julia Gillard's prime ministership, we were in a fight with one of the toughest industries in the world. We spent months bogged down on it in Parliament and the High Court, kicked a lot of people at home right in the wallet, signalled a kind of moralised disapproval of millions of Australians (about their recreation and consumption habits, which are so important to personal identity), and sent out Nicola, her successor as health minister Tanya Plibersek and Prime Minister Gillard to explain that it was for your own good.

Importantly, like the flood levy, this remained a proposition with narrow majority support; inevitably, like the flood levy, it came at a real political price. The industry lost; Nicola won and the government saved lives. It was probably worth it. And then we attempted poker machine reform.

Since being elected in 2007, Labor had been working on policies to limit losses by problem gamblers. There was some public concern about the spread of gambling, not only in poker-machine venues, but at sports grounds and on live sports television coverage in particular. But most poker-machine venues aren't corporations, so the Commonwealth's legal power over the industry isn't clear, and our approach resembled Churchill's Cold War advice at the White House in 1954: 'To jaw-jaw is always better than to war-war.'

Now, though, we had a deal with Andrew Wilkie, MP – a big change. We had agreed to make mandatory a precommitment by gamblers of how much they were prepared to lose when they played poker machines mandatory – we agreed to force the gaming industry to force people to make a decision to control their own gambling. The newly elected Tasmanian independent was only one of the balance-of-power MPs, but he was perhaps the one most likely to walk out on us and cause a general election. He first got a taste for quitting jobs over differences of opinion in the army in the 1990s and in the 2000s he quit working in Australian intelligence in the lead-up to the Iraq War (I didn't say he was always wrong). Over time, his preparedness to bring down the government and force an election if precommitment wasn't resolved to his satisfaction was more and more public and explicit, forming an important undertone to the politics of the year. What's more, nothing could further emphasise the non-Labor (albeit, not strictly anti-Labor) elements of this endeavour than his public role. I don't know Wilkie the private man, but Wilkie the public personality is a textbook wowser and moral snob, one of the few genuine prigs in Australian public life and a man at times seemingly determined in principle to ask for more than is achievable while offending those he is asking. In essence he wanted the Parliament to make a law requiring people to use a technology which definitely didn't exist in an area where Commonwealth power didn't definitely exist – and to do so with immediate effect.

The essential elements of the policy and political dynamic of mandatory precommitment for gaming machines hardly need describing: read the earlier paragraphs on plain packaging and it's all there, complete with the origins in long-forgotten Rudd hyperbole ('I hate poker machines and I know something of their impact on families', 11 September 2007) and expert reports (Productivity Commission 2009), legislation from the Commonwealth that tested the limits of its own powers, High Court challenges and bitter advertising campaigns from a powerful cashed-up industry, and the final expectation that yet another female minister, this time the families, community services and Indigenous affairs minister Jenny Macklin, should be asked to carry the can for the government and sell this medicine to every irritable fifty-year-old bloke in Australia.

Bill Shorten, who shared some portfolio responsibility for the area and could see the policy logic and the political difficulty, worked hard to express a community-friendly version of our argument that eliminated the inflections of wowserdom and snobbery present in the arguments of many anti-gambling voices outside politics. On one memorable occasion, Tom Cameron on his staff asked me if I had any gags or funny suggestions for a speech his boss had to give to the clubs movement; I said, 'What, like, "Wow, this poker machine reform stuff is a real schnitzel sandwich"?' and before I knew it Tom was running back up to Bill's office to put the joke in the draft. Days of begging him to take it out failed, and not for the first time, it turned out Bill's judgement about how to show people we supported their aspirations was better than ours. The 'joke' went down a treat as part of a good speech that really helped, for a while.

But only for a while. At the peak of the industry campaign against mandatory precommitment, Labor MPs who attended branch meetings, ethnic new-year functions and football presentation nights in suburban clubs in their communities had to walk through club foyers past enormous posters tailored for each electorate, personally addressed to the MPs and including a picture of their face, saying, *Tony* (or David, or Deb, or whoever) . . . *Why are you voting to hurt our community?* Eventually, it began to seem like a fair question. I remember then NSW ALP secretary Sam Dastyari fogged in to Canberra overnight around this time, sitting on a couch in our office saying something like, 'Our blokes know they have to fight for the carbon tax, but fair go, this one really is too much.' He was right.

Unlike the flood levy and plain packaging, mandatory precommitment was too much, and too hard; in time the government would agree to abandon legislation and instead planned a trial in the ACT. This was the opposite of a backdown; without Wilkie, this would have been Labor's approach from the start: not to rely on the stroke of a pen, but to work with the industry while pushing them at every stage. Like plain packaging and the flood levy, precommitment was basically sound progressive public policy that retained narrow majority support; like plain packaging and the flood levy it made us a government determined to tell you what to do with your spare coins in your spare time.

Through 2011 all this, and the decision to concede that the fixed price for carbon trading 'operated like a tax' – followed by the announcement of the full detail of carbon pricing in June – defined a negative personal image of the prime minister for many Australians for the remainder of her time in office.

As the carbon and budget committee processes ground on with the work of the Gillard project, and the fevers over flood levy, smoking and gambling worked through politics, Laurie Oakes wrote a Saturday column for the News Limited tabloids on 12 March that was in equal parts brutally unfair and brutally insightful about the situation the PM was in.

> Former US vice-president Walter Mondale once observed that political image is like mixing cement. When it's wet you can move it around and shape it, he said. But at some point it hardens, and then there is almost nothing you can do.

In the *Herald-Sun*, this column appeared under the headline *Julia Gillard Is Following Kevin Rudd's Spiral*. In the *Daily Telegraph*, it was *Like Concrete, Lie Could Sink Gillard* – a headline that buggered up the metaphor of Laurie's lead paragraph and also introduced 'lie', a word that didn't appear in the column at all. It's reassuring to know that sub-editors can be unfair to journalists and politicians at the same time. Oakes continued:

> As soon as she broke her 'no carbon tax' pledge, Gillard's satisfaction rating also dived from 50 to 39 per cent – and Labor's vote fell six points to a record low of 30 per cent.
>
> ... [at the election] enough voters gave Gillard the benefit of the doubt to allow the Government to survive. But now we have a blatant breach of trust – a solemn election promise cast aside without apology or any adequate explanation of why. And the message from Newspoll may be that voters will not trust her again.
>
> In which case her fate, like her image, is set in concrete.

Was her image set in concrete already? Well, even for us, it could never be absolutely all bad. The US visit had gone well, as Laurie said – and a week after Easter, the royal wedding of Prince William and Kate Middleton passed without incident and the magazines declared the PM's outfit a success, and we almost wept with relief back home – but yes. You can only frown in so many pictures and ban so many things before people get the message the country is in strife.

One way to deal with growing unpopularity is to claim it as proof that you'll make hard decisions. In a budget preview in April to the Sydney Institute's annual dinner the PM wanted to be pretty plain about the path she was on. In response to commentary on her standing, which combined general panic about our political prospects 'if an election were held this Saturday' and specific assertions that our minority government was sure to collapse short of a three-year term, I offered up another military analogy.

> I'm increasingly sceptical of exaggerated and overdetermined claims about politics and public opinion from any quarter. Remember when the NBN was going to break us? Or the flood levy? Or health reforms? Each of these overhyped claims . . . each overcome by perseverance and patience. As with governing progress, so with public opinion: the measure is in the years . . .
>
> . . . I will not go down a populist path, pursuing short-term politics, lacking serious policy convictions, whipping up negativity, following the opinion cycle. The Australian military scholar David Kilcullen has reminded us that Bernard Fall wrote fifty years ago:
>
> 'A government that is losing to an insurgency is not being outfought it is being outgoverned.'
>
> I find the analogy with modern politics compelling.

It was an explicit reproof to the negativity of her opponent and an implicit contrast with the populism of her predecessor. Let the years judge.

Whether the fate of the prime minister's popularity was sealed, the fate of the Australian economy was not and nor was the fate of the Gillard project. The economy really was going through something important and strange in 2011.

My years working for Labor's Amazonian class-warrior leader didn't turn me from a social democrat who goes to mass on Sunday into a classical Marxist or a classical feminist. But writing speeches about the economy went close to turning me into a materialistic determinist, and reading what people said about my boss firmly made me a practitioner of gendered literary critique. I'll leave the Lacanian psychoanalysis of male anxiety in the text of Australian politics for a later chapter, but for now, let's talk about 'superstructure' and 'base': by 2011, two big things had happened in the forces and relations of production in Australian society that certainly defined and arguably determined the culture and politics of the joint.

First, the millennium drought had broken. This began in 2008 in New South Wales and on through 2010 in Victoria and Queensland. Melbourne's water restrictions were reduced to stage three on 2 April 2010. In September 2010, the PM had announced the formation of the Multi-Party Committee on Climate Change on a rare fine day during the wettest spring ever recorded in New South Wales and the Australian Capital Territory. In early May 2012, the final 'exceptional circumstances' drought support ended. This was the final, formal declaration that an eleven-year drought was over, everywhere in Australia. The Gillard government's carbon-pricing scheme commenced operation at the end of the following month. (Ironically, this meant it wasn't the worst time economically, as at least one sector was on the improve.) But the end of the drought was the real end of broad bipartisan support for hard action on climate change.

Bob Hawke's first-term government benefited hugely from the

economic boost of the breaking of a drought in 1983; in fact he might even have been saved by it, when you consider how close the 1984 election turned out to be. Twenty-five years later, we were buggered by the end of a drought. The dry conditions easing then ending, and urban water restrictions lifting, meant that when the opposition changed its mind on carbon pricing and climate change the community was open to the argument too: when you could turn the taps on again in the kitchen, the bathroom and the lawn, climate change just didn't seem as urgent to people. It couldn't. This is key in understanding the politics of 2011: it started raining again for a few years. That's Australia.

Second, the first and biggest phase of the mining boom started going down in 2011.

At its peak, after an eight-year climb, the prices we got for our exports compared to what we paid for our imports reached *double* their average for the previous twenty years. It was in September 2011 that they began to fall, nearly as fast as they had risen, and they are still falling in 2015. (The PM emphasised this in speeches in the following two years, notably to the small miners in Perth in September 2012 where she spoke of a boom with three distinct phases – prices, then peaking; investment, peaking in the coming year or two; and production, with years and decades still to run.) Indeed the economist Ross Garnaut, in his characteristically self-assured survey in *Dog Days*, writes that the positive impact of the China resources boom on the overall Australian economy was over by late 2011 – a huge underlying shift away from economic good times. He's far better qualified to tell you that than I am. What I can tell you is the positive impact of the China resources boom on the Australian government's standing in the electorate ended in late 2011.

To add a layer of complexity, this moment didn't fundamentally change the macroeconomic task of budget policy in the immediate period. Since the end of the stimulus spending, we were in this funny position of growth being higher than it had been in the crisis of 2009, higher than it was now in the rest of the world – but less than we wanted, and at risk of slipping backwards. Fragility was one word for it, so keeping jobs growing was still the key. But there was also a contradictory nervousness that demand could 'break out' – that people might suddenly start buying things faster than they could be made, pushing prices up.

To use an old-fashioned car analogy, we had to hold the throttle back but not allow the economy to stall.

But as export prices slid, particularly for resource exports, revenue slid and as revenue slid, all the politics changed.

Making good decisions about the economy in this period was hard; explaining what was going on in the economy was hard too. On one occasion in a speech the PM used a line I suggested, that all these contradictory pressures arising from underlying strength meant the economy was experiencing 'powerful growing pains'. I had been reading *The Tin Drum* and had in mind the character Oskar's dramatic and searing bone and muscle pains as, after years in the body of a small boy, he suddenly starts growing to adult size while travelling west across Germany by train in the last days of the Second World War. Awesomely dumb and out of touch. It sounded trivialising; when it was headlined as *PM plays down job losses* in *The Age* and then 'growing pains' (obviously 'powerful' was lost) was shouted at her in question time I really regretted it. I might as well have suggested nicknaming the Liberal Party room after the nightclub in the book, for God's sake.

Car analogies are much better; even when the economy was going through the end of a drought and the end of a boom and a slow recovery from a global crisis. The engine would keep working fine and we were going to get to the destination – but we would be driving thirteen hours with the air conditioning turned off and we were going to eat the sandwiches we brought with us instead of stopping for lunch. That's a really bad-tempered trip.

The changes unfolding through 2011 became ever clearer in

preparing and delivering the budget. In turn, the political 'opportunity cost' of not spending grew: we never seemed able to do just a few simple good things for people, a few measures that weren't 'tough reform', that just helped make life easier. PM Gillard's spending commitments for the 2010 election had already been the smallest ever recorded in real terms. Now the Gillard government's first budget, 2011–12, proved to be the first tough budget in more than ten years; the first since at least the introduction of the GST in 2000 that wasn't a good-news budget and wasn't a budget from which a government could expect to win votes. She and her deputy, Treasurer Wayne Swan, had got the argument back onto the economy when the 2010 campaign was about to be lost by accepting the advice that a surplus could be achieved in 2012–13 and, in turn, insisting that a surplus was the measure of success. It had been critical to winning the confidence first of the country and then of the cross-bench; the impeachable mess of the Coalition's costings failures had reinforced all this. In that period, it worked.

The internal price of the struggle to respond to the falling revenue and reach surplus would be high. The economic ministers, their staff and officials all ground on, through the meetings of late 2010 and the first five months of 2011, on what I thought of as a plan to 'thread the needle': first, above all, don't stop growth; second, get to surplus, get there by one dollar; third, it'll be hard but we could use the scarcity to impose fairness on expenditure, because even after one term of Labor, there were four terms' worth of unfair or untargeted Howard-era spending to get rid of. That was the principle that meant that we needed a flood levy; it was also the principle that meant that people who earned less than $50 000 paid nothing, people who earned $60 000 paid under $1 extra per week, but a person earning $100 000 per year paid five times as much. A good principle, but one that also saw them send ministers away angry and frustrated that spending plans with their name on them would remain just that – plans, not programs. Spending cuts don't just bruise relations with communities and constituencies – colleagues don't enjoy them either. Simon Crean couldn't get his 'creative nation mark II' arts plan funded; Kim Carr saw his cherished 'green car' fund gutted.

Conservative critics point to headline deficit numbers to make a general critique of our performance – you should have just fixed it, is the basic line – but this really can't be sustained once you read into the complexities of the time. Garnaut's hindsight on this period in *Dog Days* is generous to us on the economic substance ('There can be no credible argument that the Budget was too loose from mid-2011 ... The Government's position looked worse because its revenue forecasts were consistently too high ... the government had accepted official advice, as a good government should, and paid a high price'). But this can't erase the tremendous political tensions of the 2011–12 and 2012–13 budget periods.

My windowless room was about forty paces from the cabinet and committee rooms where the hardest of these decisions were made. That was close enough for me.

But the Gillard project was still on the road. The NBN kept rolling out, funding was found for the health reforms close to agreement. The plan for a carbon price was on the table. And there was a new key, close to the PM's own heart: changes to the incentives for people to move off welfare and into work. After months of internal debate over principle and detail, in which she imposed herself in an area where many feared to go, so-called participation changes were there. Job creation and welfare reform; both are needed in order for the long-term unemployed, young people with disabilities, teen parents and young parents to feel those famous benefits of 'work and the dignity of work'. More changes followed in the budget the following year. There were plenty who thought they went too far then and more who now agree – that the jobs just didn't exist, that if they did, the changes to get people to take them were too mean, or even that it was unreasonable to expect these individuals to do some kinds of work or work in some places. Gillard has since written that in better budget circumstances, wider changes allowing people to keep more earned income as they moved from welfare to work would have been considered.

But you won't convince her that a single parent whose youngest child is well into the primary school years wouldn't be better off working, and that her or his child wouldn't be better off with a job in the family. You won't convince me either.

As the PM put it in words she personally drafted for that Sydney Institute speech in April:

> The old way saw a victim . . . the old way offered an excuse. Some today see a problem . . . they offer blame. I see a person . . . a person who can work. I offer only opportunity . . . I ask only responsibility in return.

Or as the treasurer would put it on budget night the next month: it was the year for a budget 'based on our firmest convictions'. But thanks to the resources boom, budget night had been like Christmas morning for a decade, and all that had now changed.

The opposition leader hadn't; his budget reply speech began, 'My three children are still in the education system and Margie, my wife, works in community-based childcare . . .' Subtle. Arthur Schlesinger wrote of President Kennedy's scorn for Nixon's speeches which opened with 'the "Pat and I" greeting', recalling Kennedy saying with contempt, 'He has no taste.' Indeed.

—

The months brought more pain in Afghanistan. In May and June I wrote condolence speeches in the Parliament for the PM to honour the lives and deaths of Sergeant Brett Wood, Lance Corporal Andrew Jones, Lieutenant Marcus Case and Sapper Rowan Robinson. Sitting alone in the windowless room writing about Marcus Case was a dreadful trial. Earlier that year, he had deployed in support of the

Queensland flood emergency. His family said he was an 'idol to his niece and nephews'. Our climate adviser Clare Penrose bounced into my office before question time to ask if I wanted to grab coffee and found me in tears.

In July, Sergeant Todd Langley was killed; the PM went to his funeral. He went to Afghanistan seven times; he had a brother in the army.

The mission was just so hard.

—

By the middle of winter, the PM's public standing, and support for the Labor Party in Australia, had never been lower. On the eve of announcing the full details of the carbon price in what would be formally titled the Clean Energy Future package on 10 July, Newspoll measured the Labor primary vote at 27 per cent, the lowest ever recorded by a government; the Coalition's two-party preferred lead (58 per cent to 42 per cent) was the highest ever recorded by an opposition. And there was no reason to think some natural correction awaited us, or that this couldn't be reproduced on election day.

If hope in ourselves wasn't a reliable source of personal energy in the office, our disgust at our opponents would have to do.

On 22 August, Tony Abbott addressed a rally outside Parliament House – the 'convoy of no confidence', calling for an immediate election to stop the carbon tax. (The opposition leader had even driven in one of the trucks in the convoy en route to Canberra the previous day.) The convoy was organised by right-wing radio commentators and conservative activitists and supported by climate sceptics groups, the anti-Semitic Australian League of Rights and One Nation. After weeks of publicity on radio talkback and online, a laughably small crowd of a few hundred people fronted up, boosted by the large and noisy presence of a number of trucks. The crowd was reassured by radio host Alan Jones that 'thousands' of people and 'hundreds' of trucks had been 'stopped at the border' – 'the most disgraceful thing that has ever been done to democracy', which, given the healthy state of Australian democracy, is possibly true. Then, in front of a placard held by a demonstrator that read *JuLIAR . . . BOB BROWNS* [sic] *BITCH* and another that read *DITCH THE WITCH*, Tony Abbott said, 'As I look out on this crowd of fine Australians, I want to say that I do not see scientific heretics, I do not see environmental vandals, I see people who want honest government.'

The leader of the House, Anthony Albanese, called it a convoy of no consequence, so they went to his office in Sydney's inner west a week later to tell him what they thought of that. He fronted them on the street while staff and police watched on. When one idiot shouted, 'And your mother would be ashamed of you,' Albanese just said, 'No, my late mother is certainly not ashamed of me,' before giving them a speech about 'the most cheap and efficient way to reduce our emissions'! Albo woke up that morning a tribune for the NSW Left and went to bed that night a tribune for the Australian Labor Party.

Through the madness of that winter Gillard stayed the course and worked to keep the party and the movement on the course as well. From the disillusion and despair of twelve months earlier, she had led us to narrow victory and restored our Labor purpose – but that had now led us into real 'there is no alternative' territory.

She told families at home that while the changes would mean 'some businesses will put prices up', she would look after their interests as this change took place: 'nine in ten households will get a combination of tax cuts and payment increases. For five million households this will fully meet your average extra costs.'

She told the National Press Club it was good for the country and made sense, a smart market reform like the ones they all knew had been unpopular in the past but had worked – complete with a nod to Adam Smith: 'The carbon price is our dollar float . . . We've heard a bit of talk about how carbon permits are an "invisible product". They're not – they're just the "invisible hand".'

She told hundreds of NSW conference delegates in Sydney Town Hall to join a Labor battle, a conviction fight for real Labor principle.

> Ben Chifley, in this very hall, talked about 'the things worth fighting for'.
> These are the things worth fighting for. These are the things that make us who we are . . . Chifley was in failing health but there was no self-pity. Just the uncompromising message: 'Fight for the right, and truth and justice will prevail.'

(SCG boss and party reform advocate Rodney Cavalier, in his private capacity as history buff, later reminded my fellow speechwriter Carl and I that the year Chifley had said that the conference was held over at Trades Hall in Sussex Street. Thanks, mate.)

Events were cruel and when policy was the yarn this hardly seemed to help. But the PM showed no self-pity. She told anyone in politics who would listen that the government would ride this out, the false predictions of economic disaster would hurt the opposition, the 'lived experience' of the household budget would rebuild public support, the tide would turn – remember the GST in 2000? – we would get this done.

And I don't know what she told herself, when she woke up in the morning or went to bed at night; but whatever it was it worked. Whatever it was, it was enough to keep her putting one foot in front of the other and to keep her eyes on the road. There were better times ahead.

# 6.
# The shadow of the past

*The responsibilities of government are the responsibilities of hard choice. Curtin knew that when he raised conscripts for military service overseas. Chifley knew that in the industrial winter of 1949. Whitlam knew it when he ended the bitter debate over state aid. Hawke and Keating knew it every day they governed. And we know it now.*

PRIME MINISTER JULIA GILLARD

On 16 September, three months before the ALP national conference, the PM went to National Circuit in Canberra to unveil Peter Corlett's sculpture of former prime ministers John Curtin and Ben Chifley — Labor's great leaders of national victory and postwar reconstruction. Just larger than life, so that from a distance they appear full size, Curtin and Chifley walk together and speak to each other in confidence. The statue reproduces a photograph taken in the 1940s of the two men walking the half-mile from the Hotel Kurrajong in Canberra where many MPs then stayed to the old Parliament House, and stands roughly on the site where the picture was taken. It's a remarkable thing to look at, just as democratic and heroic as a Labor statue should be, in a part of Canberra that from many angles appears unchanged in all the intervening years.

In the remarks I drafted for that day, the PM had some fun with what they might have been discussing – billiards? the colleagues? – and offered a wry shout-out to the minister for communications, Senator Conroy, whose battles with the Murdoch empire over broadband infrastructure and media regulation were growing with the years: 'When Curtin made Arthur Calwell minister for information he said, "He's been fighting with newspapers all this time – now he can learn to live with them".'

But there was serious purpose to her words on this day and she spoke very much as Labor leader rather than prime minister. Curtin and Chifley are genuinely national figures, but she claimed them as Labor partisans too – one man jailed, the other dismissed from his job, for political action during the First World War. These were no disciples of consensus who would be embarrassed by a fighting Labor government, these were two 'men of conviction', sons of thunder like the apostles James and John. She claimed her personal proximity to them – her own position as leader, her reflections on time in their homes and at their graves, and on her own life in the Lodge where both spent so much time and where one finally died. She characterised them as activists, modernisers, agents of change – not workingmen-conservatives who would be appalled by the social or political complexion of a progressive Labor Party in postmodern Australia.

And she claimed them for the messy contested reality of their own history and life in politics; she claimed them for the reality that Labor was and is opposed, and that this tells us something precisely about their strengths, as politicians and as men. In turn, she claimed them for the inspiration she drew from them in the circumstances of her own time:

> With history's hindsight, we see two great Australians, 'without fear or blemish'. But Curtin and Chifley were tested by their times
>
> One biographer wrote of Chifley's failures in opposition,

> 'He had responsibility far too long ever to be a destructive oppositionist'. The engine-driver who became a nation-builder couldn't become a wrecker. Another writer reminds us that Curtin lost an election in 1937 'when he stood for air strength for Australia'. Four years later the bombing of Darwin brought a terrible vindication – and an education in the bitter ironies of politics and war.
>
> Tested by their times . . . but history judges them well. Their courage became its own reward.

Of course this wasn't really a speech about Labor in history – it was a speech about modern Labor. The leader couldn't command stable support in the synods of the caucus, because its human divisions and failures had made it too fallen and impure, and couldn't master the mystical body of the movement, because it remained too perfect and abstract. By day the Labor leader would try to drag this ragged hundred of actual politicians across the desert into Canaan; by night the Labor leader would wrestle the angel of the Labor tribe's dream-vision of its past. Even in victory, she limped away.

And at the centre of the events of the final months of 2011 – the muted, modern pageantry of a royal visit and a Commonwealth Heads of Government Meeting in Perth; the real business of a visit from President Obama and US troops prepositioning in our north; the announcement of an Asian Century White Paper; the appointment of Peter Slipper to the speakership of the House of Representatives; the debates had, and not had, before and at the ALP national conference; the hysterical opposition of Tony Abbott and the Liberal Party to the government's every act; and the emergence of a public campaign for the Labor leadership by Kevin Rudd – at the centre of it all, really, was this question of authority.

Not just the authority of the prime minister over the nation, or of the leader over the party, but the authority of the Labor present over the Labor past.

This question of whether Labor today is worthy of its predecessors is not new, and not one we invented. There is a long Australian tradition of the conservative side praising Labor's past to detract its present: give us the good old workingman's Labor Party, not this rotten middle-class mob of today. Poor old Nick Cater, then writing for *The Australian*, now leading the Liberal Party's think tank, probably sincerely thinks he invented this critique; the truth is he could have fished it out of any Tory ashtray or brandy glass in the eastern suburbs in the past hundred years. The conservative NSW premier Sir George Fuller was shouting it in 1921:

> The men who were in the Labor Party now were not the old pioneers . . . who had the interests of the working men at heart. Today the Labor Party were representing the extreme section of the community, and they were led and influenced by an outside junta.

It has never ceased; and you can still meet people who solemnly tell you why they really are Labor people . . . and who last voted Labor when our leader was Bob Hawke. But we're the ones who've changed. Or how they didn't leave the Labor Party, the Labor Party left them . . . in 1955. In its own way, it's a tribute to the power of Labor identity: there are no 'ex-Liberal voters', like there are no 'non-practising Anglicans'. They just switch.

Then there are the paradoxes of the ratchet effect of social change: that the conservatives wind up agreeing with the progress we fought for twenty years ago, and then when we want to go further today, they say this proves we have changed!

Tony Abbott learned this argument in his youth. His regular invocation of Ben Chifley as the kind of Labor leader he admired made us grind our teeth; never more so than in May 2011 when he quoted from Chifley's famous Light on the Hill speech in his budget reply. It's false history. Abbott's predecessors were conservative snobs who dismissed Chifley's contribution on the financial system royal commission in the 1930s, saying he had been 'brought off the street' and hadn't known a bank from a public toilet; Abbott's contemporaries are ideologues who in 2014 would put Chifley on an Institute of Public Affairs magazine cover as an 'opponent of freedom'. (The same year, as prime minister, Abbott would quote Chifley as opposition leader at the UN!) We know what the barefoot child of Limekilns, who left a minister as austere as Dedman in charge of rationing, would say about a conservative opposition leader who quoted him like this – and then in the same speech went on to attack a decision not to increase family payments for people on $150 000 per year, declaring, 'I know you're not rich.'

But at least in the movement itself we were once confident that this was crap.

What was new by 2011, as I wrote speeches about jobs and growth – and statues – was that the use of Labor's past achievements as a critique of Labor's modern activism was now fully extended to the prestige of the 1980s. That iconoclastic, Oedipal, 'don't be Whitlam' generation of government, the Hawke–Keating generation, had become another Great Era of the Past Labor Can't Live Up To. How any government can betray both Chifley and Keating at the same time I genuinely don't know; it is like being told your latest album isn't worthy of the musical legacy left to you by Paul Robeson and the Clash. Yet it is said, and more importantly, we do now ask ourselves if it's true.

The same branch-meeting bores who buttonholed us in the nineties about Gough buttonholed us in the noughties about Paul. (Often, not just the same type of bore – the actual same bore.) And some of those bores have newspaper columns. The nostalgia for the 1980s as a lost golden age had been growing every year since at least 2001, and by 2011 the intellectual and political authority of the Hawke and Keating generation hung very heavily over a caucus and cabinet that comprised so many people who had grown up genuinely motivated and inspired by the substance and the style of those years, and who naturally enough wondered if they were worthy of their position today. From time to time, the PM struck out in a direction that challenged, or at least modified this – as in the 2010 pre-election press club address describing 'a new kind of microeconomic reform from that of the 1980s and 1990s' – but this was all around us. It was present in our policy frameworks, our political assumptions – and above all in our language, especially when it was directed to opinion leaders and the Canberra press gallery. The carbon price was 'our dollar float'; the national disability insurance scheme was our Medicare; I wrote that the structural separation of Telstra was 'a real white whale which has escaped many a reformer's harpoon in the past' – as if everyone carried around the Keating–Beazley cabinet fights over Telecom in September 1990 as their private political dreaming.

The amazing thing is how many people did.

All the staff suggested lines like these (all right, only I was mad enough to suggest that harpoon business) because the senior figures of the Rudd and Gillard governments genuinely looked over their shoulder many times, wondering what the predecessors thought of them and what they would have done. Most remarkably, even on the economy, where the Rudd government in 2008 pretty specifically learned the lesson of the Hawke–Keating generation's terrible failures in 1991, the more general moral of the story, that imperfect modern Labor was thoroughly worthy of its thoroughly imperfect past, was lost; lost even on many of the leaders of modern Labor itself.

It was the Labor press secretary and writer Don Rodgers who wrote those words about Curtin losing the 1937 election on air strength for Australia, in a heartbroken obituary to his boss in 1945. Rodgers, the man who in 1941 wrote, 'Australia looks to America, free of any pangs' for an opinion piece for his PM – and who stayed to serve Chifley after Curtin died. *Sans peur et sans reproche.* It isn't only the caucus who sometimes look at pictures of their predecessors and wonder about their place.

I wrote the draft of the speech about statues in the windowless room inside the windowless room in a deeply reflective mode. I never genuinely thought we were doomed, but I knew we were fated. This was it for us – whatever we made of it, this was our time. If nothing else, 2011 made me think about what makes successful Labor PMs.

—

It wasn't only the black and white age of the forties or the golden age of the eighties that we saw over our shoulder. From here until the end of the Gillard prime ministership, over our shoulder we would see Kevin Rudd.

When did the second front open? The truth is it never closed. Rudd never accepted the result of the caucus mutiny of June 2010. In private I never really doubted this. Too many people who had been present at the Lodge on the evening of 24 June spoke privately of the atmosphere of surreal temporary departure, not permanent resignation in defeat. A few even knew that in that July, just ten days after losing office, Rudd had rung a former adviser who had stayed with PM Gillard to wish him happy birthday; when this adviser carefully commiserated with Rudd and asked how he was, the reply was a light, 'Oh never mind me, mate, I'll be back.' Rudd is a master of the bald statement of intent masked as wit; he didn't even care that this adviser, loyal to his party and his PM, would pass this on.

But there was a public period where the sheer improbability of a Rudd return meant that private and even public detraction of the PM by Rudd wasn't usually considered part of a real leadership campaign. So when, after the 2010 election and having gained the foreign ministry, Rudd exceeded his authority and exploited the resulting differences of opinion to foment questions over the PM's judgement, this was reported principally through the lens of a foreign policy debate. As the prime minister's successful visit to the United States in March had reached its high point, a rebellion against Libya's dictator Gaddafi escalated to near civil war; Rudd toured the Middle East calling for a no-fly zone to be established against the Gaddafi regime and even allowing speculation about an Australian contribution to its enforcement. The PM was in New York meeting US and UN officials, and moved to correct Rudd, saying, 'I think it's appropriate for the [UN] Security Council to consider a full range of options; I don't believe that range of options should be narrowed.'

This intervention – combined with an anonymous statement, attributed to a 'government adviser' that was reported in the *Sydney Morning Herald* about Rudd being 'out of control' on the issue – created perfectly legitimate grounds for headlines that the PM and foreign minister were in open conflict. (We never worked out if the remark was deliberate or a mistake, from a staff member or a public servant, in Canberra or on the road; and to this day all I am certain of is that it wasn't me and it wasn't Richard Maude.)

Of course, back during the election a series of damaging leaks had been directed against the Labor election campaign, and personally against the prime minister. The source for those leaks is known only to the journalists and the leaker or leakers. What is known is that they stopped when the offer of foreign ministry to Rudd was privately and publicly renewed two weeks out from election day. I prefer a natural to a supernatural explanation of secular events. (*Age* journalist Michelle Grattan, gamely defying both this principle and Occam's razor, wrote that leaks were 'not in [Rudd's] interests because it has worked against his chances of obtaining a good post-election ministry'. But even this is revealing: a veteran reporter was so dismissive of Rudd's future leadership prospects she couldn't understand what he stood to gain from the leaks.)

Even Laurie Oakes, in his 'set in concrete' column, while commenting on the no-fly zone controversy and arguing that the latest Newspoll showed that 'more people want Rudd back as PM than support Gillard', had written, 'Since Rudd has no prospect of making a comeback, that should be the aspect of Newspoll least worrying for the PM.'

So there was a public period in which even those who wouldn't have denied Rudd's involvement in disloyal actions saw them as acts of vandalism, attention-seeking or sour grapes rather than acts of deliberate political intent as part of a real leadership campaign. It wouldn't last. The spring days when the PM was unveiling her greatest predecessors also brought the effective opening of hostilities on the second front.

Measured public opinion of the government was still horrific. On election day 2007, 5.4 million Australians voted Labor; by election day 2010, when we got 4.7 million votes, about seven hundred thousand Australians had changed their minds. By September 2011, extrapolation from a typical poll suggested another million had changed their mind in thirteen months. Public support for Australian Labor was as low as it would ever be.

Rudd had spent most of August on another of his regular long recuperations from ill health. Now came the first genuine public assertions that not only Rudd could or should challenge, but that there soon would be a vote in caucus, and when there was, he would win it: assertions which leaped from opinion page to news page to front page, from News Limited to Fairfax to the ABC. From here, it was on like Donkey Kong for pretty much the next twenty-one months. The gallery had learned its lesson from July 2010 – no Australian journalist would ever again be guilty of failing to predict a challenge against a prime minister. This prime minister would never lead a united party against the Liberal opposition again.

There was a pattern: government sinks, Rudd emboldened, Rudd destabilises, government sinks further. It seems evident that for Kevin Rudd himself, falling polls were not motive, but rather means and opportunity. This was no doubt true for some of his supporters; but others in the caucus, who would have been content to support Gillard, or take leadership as a given, if things were working, were clearly coming to a view that things were not. Some probably contained both views inside their private selves. Others of us only dug in harder; I don't say this is necessarily the better or braver course. In any event, there's no question that it was our falling popularity that enabled Rudd to renew his attack. Every one of us whose vocation was to make the Gillard government a political success has to accept our own role in failing to create a political environment where the government was popular enough for leadership questions to be irrelevant.

And there's no question that our falling popularity was ultimately about carbon – even the questions of character and personality, about trust and lies, were really about carbon – and no doubt that in pricing carbon, we were doing the right thing. If anything, our resolve hardened on the substantive question – should Australia cap emissions and allow them to trade at a fixed price, to float over time. Whenever attention turned from carbon to other policy issues and political matters the PM and the government would recover. The 2011 trough came in August, a month after the detailed carbon announcement. It returned in the middle of 2012 at the time of commencement. At other times, as in late 2012, we would recover to a competitive political position.

Of course we blew the politics of carbon. It was a hard problem and we didn't solve it. Conceding that a fixed price worked like a tax was, in hindsight, 100 per cent wrong; no one denies this. The pragmatic desire to avoid playing word games and the pedantic view that a fixed price really *was* the same as a tax was combined with an underprepared announcement, developed in response to cabinet committee leaks. Our candour, even exaggeration over the nature of the policy change and our paradoxical hesitance in describing the reason for it turned a new carbon plan into our broken promise and then into her lie – and this, combined with our crypticism, even silence over the leadership change, smashed trust in the PM. It delivered the worst political error of the Gillard prime ministership, and one that so damaged her personal reputation that the resulting fall in her popularity and support for the government created a context for leadership destabilisation from which she and her government never ultimately recovered.

The mistakes that drove her popularity and support for the government to unprecedented lows don't become any less mistakes with the passage of the years. Nor do the years make the mistake of saying the carbon price operated 'like a carbon tax' the moral equivalent of the decision of the Greens to vote against an ETS twice in 2009 or the decision of Tony Abbott to oppose carbon action from the day he became Liberal leader in December that year. To confuse these two failings is like confusing a footy team that brings the ball too slowly out of its backline with a footy team that cheats on the salary cap or takes drugs.

Only Gillard the negotiator could have fought on through an issue as uniquely difficult as carbon to deliver legislative action; only Gillard the resilient could have fought on through a challenge as uniquely extended as Rudd's to govern for three years and three days and to fulfil so much promise.

Yet somehow, even as she was making decisions and delivering outcomes, the appearance of authority – over her government and party, over the events of the present and the legends of the past – was eluding her, and eluding us.

# 7.
# We are us

*In a word, the Prime Minister's speech to the party faithful yesterday was lacklustre.*

AUSTRALIAN JOURNALIST TROY BRAMSTON REVIEWS<br>THE PM'S SPEECH TO NATIONAL CONFERENCE 2011

In 2011, the first week of September was a hinge point in the politics and the final week of September was a hinge point in the project. Whether it had worked or not, the 'fixing tour' phase of the Gillard prime ministership was long gone. In the politics, even as the campaigns against the government by the opposition and on the second front intensified, we really were masters of our own destiny; our own performance was the biggest fact about the politics of the joint, not that of any of our opponents, and if we weren't popular, there was no one else to blame. The same was ultimately true of the policy project. Gillard's own approach now defined the government on the many issues that had been unresolved in June 2010: on carbon, population, refugees, mining tax, health reform, broadband, jobs. By no means had all been 'fixed' in the terms hoped for the previous year; some had hardly been resolved and some never would be. But we owned them now and couldn't blame – or thank – anyone else's legacy.

It was time for the PM to break new ground.

That month, a divided Collingwood footy club surrendered the premiership and coach Mick Malthouse left. I saw him at a Boxing Day Test function in 2012 and introduced myself and thanked him for the 2010 premiership. He said, 'I'm sorry I couldn't get you the 2011 one too,' and when I went to say, 'One is rich reward,' wagged his finger right at me and said, 'DON'T say one is enough!'

—

Despite the battering the government was enduring in public opinion and the opening of the second front, I recall this period as a constructive and creative one, marked by some successes and memorable events. Now, thanks to the PM and the minister Mark Butler, the release in October of the Productivity Commission's report *Caring for Older Australians* didn't destroy the government; thanks to the PM and the minister Tony Burke, the release in November of the draft Murray-Darling Basin Plan also didn't destroy the government. It might sound modest but compared to 2010 it felt like progress. At times in 2009 and 2010 it had seemed the government couldn't think of any way to respond to an issue or even release a document without either endorsing insane so-called reforms, hurting every Australian we represented, or, at the other extreme, putting a white flag on a black T-shirt and issuing bumper stickers saying *Labor – we're scared of the people*. Think about how Ken Henry's tax review's late release – especially the mining tax that came out of it – hastened the fall of a prime minister. Now, with the completion of the problems of transition, everyone's growing experience in their roles (including the PM herself) and the arrival of some new senior staff, I finally began to feel that we were able to solve some problems and that capability was growing in the PM's office. The new chief of staff, Ben Hubbard, had now had a few months to tidy up the operation and a lot had changed. The PM celebrated a second birthday in office; preparation for a second budget began.

The Queen visited. Another tricky task for the PM – republican Labor leaders haven't always managed their royal engagements with courtesy and authenticity. I lumbered Carl with the real work on these speeches – he had a better tone for it and is less of a Fenian – but we kicked some ideas around together. We wondered if there was some way to express the respect a typical Australian has for this woman, who has been here so often over the years and might be visiting for the last time. In the end we just couldn't think of a good way to get to this sentiment without sounding morbid, and the PM put it aside. (In a very self-conscious and eccentric performance, the opposition leader told the royal reception a joke about a young journalist interviewing the nonagenerian Archbishop Mannix on his birthday and hoping they would meet the following year.) Instead, Carl gave the PM lovely details on the Queen's father and her own first broadcasts, and the PM congratulated the Queen on what lay before her as she stood at the gate of the year of her diamond jubilee. To put it mildly, during her period in office the PM's clothes were sometimes discussed in public. So here's a remarkable thing: I truly can't remember what the PM wore when she met the Queen. In its own trivialising way, it was a sign that we were all getting used to it.

November brought President Obama to Australia, eight months after the PM's visit to the States, en route from the Asia–Pacific Economic Cooperation conference in Hawaii to Jakarta. Welcoming him to a joint sitting of our parliament, the PM spoke about the Four Freedoms, Roosevelt's characterisation in the Second World War that we were actually fighting for ideas, not just against aggression; again stressing the progressive political origins of our alliance. The president's assertive speech to the parliamentarians and dignitaries who gathered in the house, which put in bold type not only the US focus on Asia but a democratic confidence that China's own polity must eventually change or fail, was followed by the announcement that hundreds, and in time thousands, of US marines would 'preposition' in Darwin during training and operations.

It was a show of confidence by our government and their administration that America was sticking around; this wasn't without critics. Many would say that the Obama visit and the Darwin announcement reflected naiveté, that we'd been used by the Americans to send a message. Others were sure that our meetings with Chinese ministers must have become 'tetchy' in the months that followed. The strategist Hugh White and former prime minister Paul Keating, in differently modulated ways, were among these critics. Each of them at times made a sophisticated argument, that a 'concert of powers' which included China and the US would be the best outcome for Asia; White conceded this mightn't work but was worth a try; Keating said that the Chinese leadership would need to change its behaviours for this to work. But many who heard them — and sometimes they themselves — converted this into an arid strategic triangle, and then wanted to know which axis Australia would 'choose'. Whatever else that is, it's hardly a more sophisticated view than the view held by Gillard, Rudd and Howard that we could trade with China as a US ally. In any case, by the end of the Gillard prime ministership, we'd have done enough in China to suggest we hadn't got the Obama visit completely wrong.

The days of the Obama visit were ones in which we often laughed and smiled and said, 'There's a chapter for the book in this.' There wasn't, really; but there were bar stories a plenty. These were days when I found I had a White House counterpart who struggled with the people who comment on his speech drafts just like I did. (US embassy officials have opinions about the speechwriters' jokes, just like Australians do.) Days when swapping stories about the Guam primary in 2008 and the Canberra preselection in 2010 seemed exactly what the Hotel Canberra was built for. Days when you could put up on Facebook, *Who wants to shake the hand of the man who shook the hand of John L Sullivan?* and all your friends knew what you were telling them. We flew up to Darwin to see Obama and Gillard and hundreds of troops and Kim Beazley and Corporal Mark Donaldson

VC and Jessica Mauboy all under one hangar roof and to hear the president say, 'Aussie Aussie Aussie,' and the troops shout 'OI! OI! OI!' to laughter and applause. And on the plane back down from Darwin, with all the inspiration of flying over central Australia twice in two days and all the freedom that fatigue and a Friday-afternoon flight brings, I wrote the first draft of the conclusion of the national conference speech that we would need in a month's time.

My draft began with a statement of Australian social democratic ambition:

> Delegates. Australia is a special country and we can do something special here. We can set a goal for which few peoples in the world can realistically hope. Australia can be both rich and fair. We can be the world's fairest rich country. We can be the world's richest fair country. Sharing the wealth and the benefits of hard work with all. Showing the world that a prosperous people can live in an egalitarian society still. And silencing the many voices who say it cannot be done.

It moved on to draw this ambition from an exceptionalist version of Australian history:

> There are still those who say we have a simple choice between growing jobs and being fair . . . friends, because we are Australians, because we are Labor people, we know that they are simply wrong. We have proved the world wrong many times before today. Australian achievements have amazed the world in times of war and peace. While we have surprised many . . . we have not surprised ourselves.

And a materialist version of Australian history, which united black and white in responding to this particular homeland:

We know Australia is a hard place peopled by strong women and strong men. Indigenous Australians, the first people on this land, knew its hardness and left on its rocks fine traces of their love for it. Europeans too left the traces of hard work and hard days as they mapped and then named our land. Lake Disappointment. Cape Tribulation. Mt Despair. But the names they gave this place captured more than the hardness. They captured the newness too. Mt Surprise.

Then with an eye to Nassim Taleb's book about big surprises and to the poems of 'Ern Malley', it continued:

Friends, on this old continent, they saw many things anew. For ours is the continent of the black swan. From the dawn of civilised life, the black swan stood as the proverbial example of something all are certain does not exist . . . but while the philosophers of antiquity could say 'no swans are black'. . . they knew they could not prove there was no such thing. And before Socrates taught, there were men and women here – men and women who had long seen black swans on Australian waters. So when the Europeans arrived, the black swan was one of the greatest of Australia's surprises. They knew when they saw it . . . Australia would be different.

Today when popular writers take as their topic the great surprise, they still choose as their sign of contradiction the black swan. And in doing so, they pay a tribute we can claim as our own. To our nature's capacity to confound the world. To our people's limitless ability to surprise. To our national determination to walk our own path. A path we walk as trusted allies, good neighbours and reliable friends . . . but in the ultimate, a path we walk as our own people who follow our own way.

I wanted to finish on identity and people – shifting from Australia to *Australians* as the final subject:

> Australians can be different – we must be different from the rest. It is that very difference which makes us who we are. We are the people who share and stick together. We are the people who hold on to mateship and the fair go. Who want to grow and who want to spread the growth. We create jobs and while we do, we demand that every job be a job worth having. We know ours is a people who work hard and we deeply believe all deserve a share in the benefits of their hard work.
>
> Those first Australians who first knew our black swans knew this place as a place entirely its own. And they knew that here, you can only prosper if you share. That is Australia's way. Our uniquely pragmatic and practical, progressive path. We follow it simply because we are us.

It was a first draft; it wasn't perfect, and I reach out to redraft it even now. But too little of it survived.

———

The ALP national conference, held every few years, makes important political decisions, about policy platform and executive committees. These are too easily dismissed as weak – a platform prohibition on a given policy measure is still a powerful fact in a Labor government, and conference elections are only as tame as the pro-leadership majority is secure. Conference is also a showcase and a snapshot of the poltics within the party in the time when it is held.

National conference 2009, the only one during Kevin Rudd's prime ministership, had literally no votes, as the leader remarkably demanded and even more remarkably received actual unanimity on every policy resolution and platform line. Not just no dissent and no debate, but not even a headcount on an issue; it's amazing someone wasn't kicked out for dumb insolence. Perhaps no political party can completely look like a democracy governed by its rank and file members, but it can definitely be a republic in which the leadership is subject to reason and rules. It was inevitable and indeed desirable that 2011 contain a bit more of that.

Conference also has elements of campaign launch and nominating convention. A favourite media adjective is 'choreographed'; the leader's speech is a major public and media event. In 2011 the leader's speech actually opened the conference, and the real business of that conference – the opening to India that was part of the decision to change policy on uranium; the decision to overturn Rudd's ban on a conscience vote on same-sex marriage; and other modest party-reform measures – were completely overshadowed by my failings in the PM's speech on that first day.

The only good reason to go over all this again is to share the lessons learned. Righto; here we go.

The PM gave a speech that said all the things you are supposed to say. She described the government's achievements and referred to people she'd met and places she'd been. She drew out connections with Labor in history. The theme of conference was 'jobs, growth and fairness', so there was a section on each of these. Through these, we weaved the idea that 'Labor says yes to Australia's future', and then concluded with a riff on the link between these Labor values and enduring Australian values.

In the room, I thought it got a fair reception, no more or less. I was probably optimistic; others found the reaction flat. It wasn't enough. We hadn't made a major new announcement (nor should we have) and in the absence of that, the speech frankly just wasn't sufficiently interesting.

Through the late morning, in the hours following the speech, it became clear that the only two really interesting things in the speech were bad things. One was that the PM had acknowledged the work of many of Labor's prime ministers in history but had not mentioned

Kevin Rudd by name – evidently a conspicuous omission. The other was, a line late in the speech that said, 'This is the Labor way. This is the Australian way. We follow it simply because we are us.'

Where on earth did that line come from? I wrote it on the plane back from Darwin, and it was there in every draft I ever did; none of us ever thought it sounded funny, which is weird and dumb, because clearly it did. Maybe if I examine my creative sources, 'we are us' came from the same place where things like English football's 'No one likes us, we don't care' or 'This is Anfield' come from; the place where you find AFL footy's 'us against them' or rugby league's 'Queenslander!'; or Irish republicanism's 'our day will come' and 'ourselves alone'.

What did it even mean? Honestly, I never thought deeply about this line at the time because, of course, it wasn't intended to define the speech; part of the reason it did was because the lines that I hoped would define the speech didn't make the cut. But yes, I have occasionally asked myself about it in the years since. So, I think what it means is what it says; that the reason we follow a path of sharing the growth, a social democratic one, not just a path of individual advancement, a liberal capitalist one, is because of who we are and who we want to be in this country – because we're Australian! Because we're us! – not just because it makes the economy grow better in the long run or because a rationalistic cost curve tells us what measures generate well-being cheapest or best. The fair go is our identity, not just our idea.

I freely accept this is not what people heard. Good grief.

Kevin Rudd told anyone who would listen it was the 'Toys'R'Us' speech and, referring to 'Labor says yes to Australia's future', greeted a group of journalists in a nearby restaurant with a raised middle finger and the cheery slogan, 'Fuck the future!' But he was hardly the only critic, and he wasn't even wrong. The story grew (and got worse) as the days wore on. By the following week back in Canberra, when the PM was actually asked in a press conference if she was getting a new speechwriter, I would have been grateful if we could dial the criticism back to 'lacklustre'.

The speech to national conference was by far the worst moment for the prime minister that I had real responsibility for. I didn't roll up into a foetal position and cry my eyes out on a boardroom floor like a beaten Liberal opposition leader but I certainly cracked the frowns for a while and I was pretty determined to get another chance to do a big job. I didn't really get the monkey off my back until NSW state conference 2012, when the PM smashed it out of the town hall with the 'I will not lie down and die' speech.

Given eighteen months, even I would laugh about it. It became a stock interjection at any given moment, whether in a tense meeting or during a wedding speech – 'we are us?' – and my mates were always good about it, bagging me just enough to keep me on my toes but never quite going too far. So was the PM. She never mentioned it ever again, except to laugh when someone made fun of it.

But there were no laughs in it at the time. What went wrong?

Graham Freudenberg's best advice to speechwriters is to make an argument, not just a presentation. I comprehensively failed this one. The slogan for the conference – 'jobs, growth, fairness' – was pretty general already. But to try to fit in with it completely, I kept moving the sections of the speech around and that destroyed the argument. From the start, the speech had sections on each of these three points. We reviewed versions where the sequence of the argument was, 'We need fairness – which means we need jobs – which means we need growth,' and we reviewed versions that went, 'We deliver growth – which delivers jobs – which delivers fairness.' But to actually construct an argument that went from jobs to growth, then back to fairness just couldn't work. It read like three unrelated essays, not an argument of the whole. (Heaven knows why I thought the order had to be the same as the order on the straplines.)

Add to that the other main conceit, 'Labor says yes to Australia's future.' Not bad, but not great. I feared it might be too pointed a reference to our media lines that Tony Abbott was 'Mr No' – though when people missed that and decided it was a riff on Obama's 'Yes, we can', I just thought our line was too vague; either way, it really had nothing to do with jobs, growth or fairness. It just wasn't enough.

Don Watson's best advice to speechwriters is to get in first with a draft before the political guys have time to catch up. I did that, but then didn't fight for the draft. Even when everyone is working co-operatively, if you get overwhelmed by all the changes being suggested, the document just becomes four hundred sentences in a row, not a speech. And people make their case for changes pretty firmly in private; you have to hold your ground. But I tried to be collegial within the office, build good relationships with a newish chief of staff, Ben Hubbard, an incoming communications director, John McTernan, keep the party office guys happy, listen to the policy advisers, take on board the thoughts of the conference comms team . . . too many compromises. I definitely wanted to work within the overall communications strategy for the week, which was more important than my creative satisfaction. That was fine, but I also wanted people to know that I'd done that; I definitely didn't want to kick up a stink on a big job. Definitely the wrong call.

So by far, my single greatest regret in three years is not taking the 'black swan' idea to the PM. It's hard to believe it could have made the reception to the speech worse and even if it had been cut, it would have set the bar higher for the drafting process as a whole. Instead, when it got monstered in an early staff meeting before the boss had seen it, I backed off, suggested a less ambitious version – and abandoned it altogether when it was smashed again. I should have gone past them, or at least I should have tried something else just as bold next.

My second biggest regret is not having a tantrum in the final rehearsal the night before the speech when communications advisers, listening for the first time, told the PM they thought the 'we can be the world's richest fair country and the world's fairest rich country' lines should come out – because these would run all over the country and hurt us. I can't quote the precise words used but it was something to do with cost of living, and the fact this line might be read as a suggestion that we'd never had it so good and people should stop whingeing. This didn't make sense and I should have said so. (Apart from anything else, didn't we *need* something that would run all over the country?) Instead I put my head down, grabbed my pen and got ready to cross out the lines, before frantically rewriting so that the final section on the autocue wouldn't have a gaping non sequitur or complete grammar or usage fail, a big risk when gaspingly late changes are made.

In both instances, I put my own reputation and self-image as a proper staffer, not a prima-donna creative, ahead of what I was sure was the best call.

One reassurance for me was the knowledge that people who've really done the job, as opposed to people who wish they had, also just know that sometimes these things happen. That doesn't make it okay; it just means that's what working at this level is sometimes like. Hawke's infamous 1987 'no child' campaign launch speech wasn't his staff's finest moment. Nor was the preparation for the 1990 campaign speech when Freudenberg and Hawke's other speechwriter Stephen Mills had a frightful blue in front of the PM in the lead-up. (They won their elections, of course.) But these speeches are big engagements: they are grand finals, where you're paid to perform, and the reality of life is that sometimes you play badly. Bachelors' children are better behaved and music critics never sing a bum note.

Another reassurance was that John McTernan took me aside to tell me I reported to him and he took responsibility. He didn't have to. He also batted for me, completely unbidden, fifteen months later, when Dennis Richardson asked me about it on a flight in front of half a dozen staff and senior officials. I was there being the good soldier again, saying, Oh yes, it was my biggest regret, and talking about Mick Malthouse losing grand finals, and not mentioning anyone else's name, and John cut in with, 'What Michael's not telling you is that we cut his best lines in the final rehearsal, and if we hadn't, it would have been the "world's richest fair country" speech, not the "we are us" speech.' Which was too kind in substance, but a very good thing to do. I grew up in Canberra, and for me a plane full of secretaries is a pretty important forum. It took a fair bit of guts and decency for John to do that.

Yet another element we'd never really fully taken into account was the press gallery now reporting a speech like this live online, and tweeting each other during the event. This hyper-responsiveness and desperate need for colour right up front influences their coverage; we use the expression 'feeding the beast' but it's more like feeding hundreds of tiny birds one after another twenty-four hours a day. They don't actually need meat, they need seed. You'd almost be better off dropping a pen or breaking a heel because if you don't get something tiny wrong they'll talk about something big.

I just didn't grasp the scale of the task. And too many people were performing their specific role at national conference for the first time, me above all. All I could tell myself was that I'd learned my lesson. When the next speech as big as this one came – the campaign launch – I wouldn't make the same mistakes.

There were happy moments that week; comedies of error, comedies of manner. We signed McTernan up to an erectile dysfunction hotline on the new phone he was so proud of; we went out with Rudd's old press sec Lockie Harris, now safely *hors de combat*, and laughed so much about what PMs are like – they are more alike than you (or they) would think; we sent emails from Sean Kelly's new iPad while it was unlocked, and didn't tell him until the VIP flight home so he had to wait til it landed to fix the mess    but they will never erase the regret of having served Gillard so badly.

—

We limped away from conference, our only consolation that we wouldn't have to front question time the next week. The parliamentary year had already ended on a remarkable note with the appointment of newly independent Peter Slipper, up to that point a Liberal MP, as Speaker. His appointment further secured the government's majority, ensuring that even if one of the independents Tony Windsor, Rob Oakeshott, Andrew Wilkie or the Greens' Adam Bandt were to vote with the opposition, the government would retain a majority in the house. The government would now serve its full term.

Specifically and immediately, it meant the government could abandon the lost cause of immediate implementation of mandatory precommitment for poker machine gambling, instead going to a trial of the plan in one jurisdiction, the Australian Capital Territory. (Bizarrely, Wilkie had openly and often said that were the government to abandon this commitment, which was opposed by the Liberal Party and the Greens, he would be prepared to switch his support . . . to the Liberal Party.)

More generally, the appointment of Slipper was an additional vote for the government's agenda. In the complex game theory of the lower house between 2010 and 2013, this was a key benefit. Before Slipper took the chair, every independent member voting with the government held a potential final vote. It gave each of them an effective individual veto over legislation, and a potential individual veto over the government as a whole. It also made each of them the individual target of great external pressure – they could never argue that their vote didn't matter. The PM and her leader of the House, Anthony Albanese, lived this reality every sitting day. This is why some bills that all the independents voted for still might not have passed without Slipper's support: because with Slipper in the tent, the dynamic changed, and it was possible for each of them to vote for a bill but dilute their individual responsibility. Bringing Slipper over meant Labor legislation would pass in 2012 that couldn't have passed in 2011. And Gillard intended that it would be fair dinkum Labor legislation when it came.

Finally, on the 'second front', Slipper had long been touted as a key House supporter of Rudd. When Windsor of New England and

Oakeshott of Lyne would say publicly, as by this time they occasionally did, that their agreements to support the government would be vitiated by any switch to Kevin Rudd as PM, supporters of Rudd could argue – usually privately – that Rudd could attract the support of the Queensland MPs Slipper and Bob Katter; all would be well. Whether that would have been possible will never be known, and wasn't tested when Rudd returned to the Labor leadership in 2013. It seemed a ropey old argument at the time; but in any case, once Slipper was in the chair, any incentive for him to switch back to Rudd was lost; his appointment was a strong symbol he wasn't going to switch.

After conference, the PM reshuffled her ministry. I saw the glass half-full: Bill Shorten and Tanya Plibersek entered the cabinet, Greg Combet added industry and innovation to his responsibilities for climate change, Nicola Roxon became attorney-general.

But only half-full. The PM wouldn't promote Jason Clare to cabinet – she said to some that she just didn't think he was ready – and that meant the NSW Right's ageing son Robert McClelland remained in cabinet, in a made-up sort of junior emergency-services ministry carved out of the attorney-general's responsibilities. Peter Garrett, who might have chosen this moment to exit school education for a less demanding role, one where he'd be further from the growing political combat over education policy, wanted to stay, and did. He would remain very loyal to Julia Gillard. Kim Carr was ousted from cabinet, but not the ministry; Martin Ferguson remained in place; Chris Bowen was still left stranded in immigration.

We had finished the parliamentary year strengthened by the PM's international leadership and by new numbers in the house – and then handed it all back when the conference was one of our worst weeks. It was to cost us dearly.

But we stood for something on climate change, on the carbon price – and for fairness, on the flood levy. And the party had even survived the year without changing leaders. The staff had something to celebrate by the time we got to the Lodge for Christmas 2011. The previous year, a lot of new staff hadn't been quite sure what to expect of visiting the PM's home: would it be some kind of cucumber-sandwich garden-party scene? Now everyone knew their boss, so we brought some scotch as a contribution and cleared the afternoon. And the evening. We were definitely getting better at this.

# INTERLUDE:
# the movement

*The Prime Minister . . . faces a torrent of critics within the Labor family. This reflects a belief that the Gillard government is derailed and has failed to build on the Hawke–Keating legacy. It also reflects a private position Rudd had recently begun to develop – that Gillard's party is too enthralled to the trade unions, old-fashioned labourism, class warfare, hostility to business, internal patronage and excessive regulation . . .*

*Labor's tragedy is that a party created in the 1890s to represent the industrial wing has achieved its historical purpose with rising community prosperity, affluence once unimagined, and the shrinking of trade coverage in the private sector to about 14 per cent of employees. Given this reality, Labor must change.*

PAUL KELLY, *THE AUSTRALIAN*, 30 MARCH 2013

I want to tell you a story, about why some people like having unions in the Labor Party.

On 31 May 2012, the day after the PM told the Minerals Council of Australia's dinner, 'You don't own the minerals . . . this is Australia, and it has a Labor government,' we flew from Canberra to Sydney for dinner with the Transport Workers Union (TWU) and the Maritime Union of Australia (MUA). The transport workers' delegates had met in Sydney during the week, and their annual dinner was in Sussex

Street. A tremendously happy coincidence of the parliamentary calendar meant that this week, as well as telling the minerals council who was in government, we'd shown the union movement who controlled the Parliament, and now we were going to celebrate with them; because this was the day two absolute Labor totems, Safe Rates and Save Our Shipping, had passed the house, with passage through the Senate assured.

It was Thursday afternoon and the sittings were done for the week when we raced out to RAAF Fairbairn. Anthony Albanese joined us on the 'little VIP' from Canberra to Sydney. He and Gillard had been working toward these changes for five years: she as industrial relations minister and now prime minister, he as minister for transport and, almost as importantly, as leader of the House.

Safe Rates was the culmination of an issue the TWU first raised in the 1990s: the deadly impact of long hours and low pay for contract truck drivers, as they took on extraordinary workloads without breaks to make ends meet. A committee report in 2000 sparked a community campaign, which by 2005 had signed up people like Cardinal George Pell and talkback hosts Ray Hadley and Alan Jones – but couldn't get any traction with the Liberal government in power. The election of Labor in 2007 brought an opportunity, but the party was cautious and had a whole industrial-relations system to create in that first term. It would be polite, and not quite misleading, to say progress had been 'gradual' in the five years since, but in 2008 the National Transport Commission explicitly demonstrated the link between driver safety and rates of pay. The following year then Deputy PM Gillard had committed the government to deliver; fully two years of consultation and another six months of legislative debate followed.

The MUA's Save Our Shipping campaign had been working to guarantee Australian wages on our coastal shipping routes for even longer. It too had passed the House that day. There'd be some emotion in the room tonight; we'd be among friends, and we were champing at the bit.

I caused some hilarity among the cops on the plane as I struggled with a complicated lap-sash seatbelt on the side-facing bench seat. While the PM sat up front and went over her speaking notes for the dinner, our staff sat with Albo and his staff and cracked a few cans to toast a fighting week. We landed at Sydney and the PM's car raced off, while the staff car's driver buggered around with the boot and missed the coveted window – the chance the staff car has to tuck in behind C1 as it whizzes past synchronised green lights out of the airport precinct. Precious drinking time was lost, but we made up for it in the end. (Did you know Sydney has a small bar called Small Bar? This is either peak irony or zero irony; I can't work out which.)

A Labor prime minister speaks at a lot of events where the money raised goes to people who fund conservative campaigns. We would send our leader not just to the Business Council of Australia or the Australian Chamber of Commerce and Industry, but the Sydney Institute and the big mining firms and the small mining explorers and plenty of other rooms where the audience didn't just oppose us, they disrespected her. I undertand making the case across the community, but I always thought letting the conservatives actually sell tickets to hear a Labor leader speak was as dumb as shipping pig iron to imperial Japan in 1938, and I loved not attending those events. This was a different crowd (actually, it was the crowd who fought to stop that pig iron being shipped to Japan before the war).

Jim McGiveron was the national president of the TWU. He warmed up the crowd in his piping Liverpudlian accent. He paid an emotional tribute to the PM, who had joined the various tables and posed for photos with delegates for half an hour before taking her seat: 'You've just had photos with hundreds of us, put your arm around us ... we have a prime minister today who's here *with* us and who's one *of* us. I want to introduce the Labor Party's leader, Australia's prime minister, *our sister*, Julia Gillard.' They roared their support.

WA Labor senator Glenn Sterle was there. Sterle was an owner-operator who drove in northern Australia for fifteen years. In the 1980s he trucked jarrah timber to Canberra, where it was used to make the parliamentary benches in the chambers of the new Parliament House. Twenty-five years later, he sits on them. This night Glenn was awarded life membership of his union. He stopped halfway through his speech to point to the prime minister sitting two metres away from him and said, 'And PM, I don't want to piss in your pocket, but it wasn't the 2007 election that got us Safe Rates – it was the 2010 election. And we all know what's going on and we don't forget, and you will always have the support of the TWU.'

Next, Albo was called up; they had a presentation to thank him for what he'd done to push the legislation through. Albo can be so sentimental sometimes I wonder if he's half-Irish. He stood there and told us about his mum, and about their council flat, about selling papers a few blocks away from this hotel, about a lifetime in the Labor Party Left, mostly losing to blokes on the right like the TWU national secretary Tony Sheldon, and about fighting Tories, and he put his arm around Tony and said, 'My mum taught me what to believe, but it's you blokes in the New South Wales Right who taught me to fight!' And we all teared up again.

And that was before Tony Sheldon spoke. Proving the link between low rates of pay and truck drivers dying, and then fixing it, is one of his life's passions; to see Prime Minister Gillard stand in front of him and his mates and say, 'Today the Bill became an Act and the campaign became law,' was a moment in his life. In that moment of personal achievement, he spoke about two other people – Suzanne de Beer and Lisa Sawyer. Their husbands died together on the side of a road – one a man who pulled on to a roadside to help a traveller whose car had broken down; the other an exhausted trucker who fell asleep, ran off the road and hit him. Earlier this year, Lisa and Suzanne had met their local member Tony Crook, the 'independent National Party' MP for Kalgoorlie, to ask him to support Safe Rates. Lisa told him that while she wasn't very religious by nature, she had taken comfort in the scriptures since her husband's death. One verse in particular, which spoke about 'righteousness', had become very important to her, and she had asked her pastor to tell her more about its various translations and original meaning; she'd learned that the word 'righteousness' originates from the Hebrew idea 'to stay on the right road'. Her last words in the meeting had been, 'Mr Crook, if my man had stayed on the right road, both our husbands would be alive today.'

Sheldon stopped, looked up and said, 'And then Tony Crook went into the House and voted NO.' Then he looked at the PM and said, 'Labor's worst day is always better than the Tories' best day, and we don't forget.' It was an extraordinary night. I've don't think I've ever been at a more emotional public event. It was a good night to be Labor, and a good night to work for the PM.

The Abbott government believes Safe Rates is red tape and will attempt its amendment or repeal.

—

Plenty of people roll their eyes when they hear all that. It's just blokey, beery, sentimental bullshit. The world's changed, the economy's changed, politics has changed, get over it and move on.

These people are in the Labor Party and out of it; people to the left of the Labor Party and to the right of it. Some of them in the Labor Party think issues like Safe Rates matter, but the unions cause too many other problems for us – that we can do good things like that without the problems and costs of having direct union representation in Labor decision-making structures. Some in the party don't mind policies like that, but don't care about them very much and see them as a weird political distraction, a minority interest that hurts us in the media and makes us seem backward-looking and out of touch.

Some to the right, outside Labor, think policies like Safe Rates are the kind of regulation which puts economies on an inevitable trajectory to decline. Some further to the left of the Labor Party definitely do not care about, and do not like, blokes who drive trucks.

I want to tell you another story, about why some people don't like having unions in the Labor Party.

On 17 February 2013, as the prospect of another Rudd challenge grew in strength, the PM delivered an Industry and Innovation Statement: a 'one billion dollar plan to deliver productivity and jobs', it was the culmination of years of work. Some wanted it sold as a plan for future jobs, with the emphasis on future. We should have listened. Instead we tricked it up in the PMO as a 'plan for Australian jobs' (with a blunt emphasis on the Australian – like, the website was called www.aussiejobs.innovation.gov.au) and the tagline was, 'Modern Australia can have a great blue-collar future.' The day after the launch, the PM travelled to Queensland to the annual conference of the Australian Workers Union. Unlike the TWU delegates dinner, the AWU has cameras in the room; the high profile of the union and its national leadership ensures the speeches are front-page news. The union's then national secretary Paul Howes praised our policies on industrial relations, praised our plans for manufacturing jobs, and praised the PM personally, finishing with a heavy reference to his union's support for Gillard's leadership against Rudd:

> Thank you for being here, PM, thank you for [the] honour – *and we've got your back.*

So on Sunday we'd taken a pretty substantial piece of policy work designed to help the economy through a tough transition as export prices fell and the dollar stayed high, and made it look old-fashioned on the economy and even faintly xenophobic (Aussie jobs, oi oi oi); and on Monday we'd made it look like the reason we'd done it was to get support from a blue-collar union in a parliamentary leadership contest. Not a bad thirty-six hours' work – and that was even before the PM gave a fairly short, fairly standard speech, summarising the

Aussie jobs message and policy of the previous day, paying tribute to the union, reminding them of the work we'd done together in industrial relations and reminding them that we had an election to fight that year. She finished by saying:

> I come here to this union's gathering as a Labor leader. I'm not the leader of a party called the progressive party. I'm not the leader of a party called the moderate party. I'm not the leader of a party even called the social democratic party.
>
> I'm a leader of the party called the Labor Party deliberately because that is what we come from. That is what we believe in and that is who we are.

Ewin Hannan for *The Australian* reported the speech as a 'standard stump address', which nevertheless got a standing ovation. But people who weren't there saw it differently: what I had drafted for the PM as a really standard speech ending, something I'd been hearing from Labor podiums all my adult life, turned out quite nicely to summarise and symbolise everything that people thought was crook about the previous thirty-six hours and indeed the previous fifteen years. Powerful prose.

We had committed a scandal to the left and foolishness to the right. Conservative critics took the opportunity to link their criticism of Labor's economic policy to Labor's internal leadership contest. When Paul Kelly pressed Chris Bowen about the implications for government policy the following weekend on a Sunday-morning talk show, Chris made the very sound point that the distinction between Laborism, social democracy and progressivism is ultimately irrelevant to the practical details of governing, because the very same policy measures promote growth in a progressive way, spread opportunity in a social democratic way, and lift up working people in a Labor way. Unarguably true. Kelly was followed by Peter van Onselen saying, 'Let's call a spade a spade' (really – in fairness, spoken English is not sub-edited) and asserting that the only reason Gillard said anything at the conference was to win support of an internal audience supporting her in an internal contest.

Critics on the left seemed genuinely and literally to misread the statement that we are not *called* the progressive party, et cetera as a statement that we *are not* a progressive party, et cetera. Tim Soutphommasane in *The Age*, for instance, wrote, 'Gillard declared that she didn't lead a party that was social democratic, progressive or moderate – it was simply a Labor party.' Dennis Altman of La Trobe University on *The Conversation* wrote, 'The prime minister claimed the party was neither progressive nor social democratic,' while Geoff Robinson of Deakin University in *Overland* magazine got it even more wrong, writing, 'Prime Minister Julia Gillard boasted that she led a Labor government, not a social democratic one or a progressive one.'

Uh-oh.

I don't really accept responsibility for academics who can't or don't read, but there's a pretty sound principle that if smart people – including your own mates! – don't understand your speech then that's your problem, regardless of fault. So when even a serious, politically independent journalist like Geoff Kitney and a serious, politically engaged Labor speechwriter like Denis Glover rent their garments at what I had honestly thought was a bromide, I couldn't only roll my eyes. (Doesn't mean I didn't. It just wasn't the only thing I did.)

If I'm left saying don't over-read seventy-five words at the end of a stump speech on a Monday night, I suppose I need to concede I oughtn't over-read half a dozen opinion pieces bashed out in the next ten days. Nevertheless this little brouhaha was revealing in its way – illuminating as it does some of the furious convictions and confusions among those who call for Labor's self-understanding to change, and especially the passions of those who want the union link to change or die. So it's worth considering what it means for the way Labor, and labour, is seen.

First, in my opinion, and for what it's worth, Labor must remain a labour party, with a constitutive identity and formal organisational connection to trade unions.

This doesn't mean I think we can leave the existing relationship between union leaders and factional organisation unexamined. I'm not here to score cheap points against the hundreds of my mates and thousands of factional activists (left, right and centre) who organise within the party and within the community: I've been a member of Labor's right faction since the day I joined Labor (in fact, I joined a right-wing campus club before I had party membership, so biographically the Labor Right precedes Labor in my life). But you can have union members represented in Labor decision-making without having union bloc votes forming part of faction bloc votes in Labor conferences – this is largely how it works in the UK, for instance – and we must consider this.

The Labor Party would also be stronger if we added more connections to a wider set of formal groups representing phases of Australian life. But it's a fact that if we offered formal party 'affiliation' to progressive community organisations like environmental NGOs or welfare organisations or aid campaigns, we'd still almost certainly only have unions affiliated, because no one else wants us; that should tell us something. It's also a fact that the ACTU and many major unions have stronger connections to those progressive community organisations than the federal parliamentary Labor Party does. This means that the unions are a gate between Labor and progressive Australia, not a fence – you often literally go through a mate in the unions to find a connection in the welfare sector or at a peak NGO – and that should tell us something too.

The economy hasn't changed as much as some reformers want to believe, either. The famous growth of self-employment, the emergence of a new class of independent contractors, the detachment of these former Labor voters from progressive politics and the subsequent need for Labor to become a party of liberal reform, is mostly myth. There's a lot going on in the growing flexibility of the work contract in Australia – some of it bad insecurity; some of it good flexibility; some of it hard to assess, a complicated mix of good for people who already have a mortgage, skills and savings, but bad for people who have none of those things. (We won't know until the next recession if even the 'winners' from workplace change, the stereotypical high-wage, high-mortgaged, trade-skilled self-employed aspirationals of outer Sydney, were better off in the long run from this change.) No matter how many speeches and columns and books are written making that claim – and it's more than ten years since the first one I helped to write, which argued, 'The new middle class is here to stay, with its army of contractors, consultants, franchisees and entrepreneurs' – they can't change the fact that owner-managers were 18 per cent of all employed people in 1982 and 17.8 per cent of all employed people thirty years later in 2011. Most contractors are not their own boss. That's the Productivity Commission's finding, not an anecdote of mine. The thing about that economic 'new model army' is there never really was one. Fact.

It's also a fact that Labor is advised to sever the union link by *The Australian* and this should be serious pause for thought. They know what they are doing and we should know what they are doing.

We would also be stronger if we added more individual people to our movement and our party – more members of all kinds – and we can't expect new people and groups to take a share in our membership without taking a share in power. That's real. Community preselections, where any Labor supporter in an electorate can help choose a Labor candidate, must spread and must include a wider variety of people, vitally including working people.

We need to evolve, but nothing is gained by an attack on ourselves.

Second: Labor is the only hope for progress in Australia. Forget about the Greens party.

On 20 February 2013, their leader, Senator Milne, ended the parliamentary agreement with Labor – because, having attempted a compromise on the mining tax, we had walked away from our agreement with them and 'into the arms of the big miners'. Some days I thought the Greens would make my eyes roll out of my head and across the floor like big fat sticky marbles. A tax that hadn't existed on the day they made their agreement with us was now in place. It didn't raise as much money as we'd forecast and intended. So they quit. It's like Leonardo da Vinci's housekeeper resigning in disgust because he's only designed the helicopter, not built it – or like Andrew Wilkie threatening to bring down the government and make Tony Abbott PM if the government couldn't overcome *Tony Abbott's* resistance to Wilkie's poker-machine legislation.

Good riddance, you morons. You are barely progressive and you're certainly not Labor's conscience. The agreement had its moments, but had been sinking for a long time; the PM had her own take on the difference between the two parties in 2012, at NSW conference, in that 'I will not lie down and die' speech, one where I drafted words based on things she'd been saying in recent unscripted comments.

> The politics of progress – the cause for change – the work of Labor – never passes through a wide gate or an easy way. But a hundred and twenty years after our founding in this country, political Labor is still a unique force in the politics of Australia. Only one party in the history of our democracy has ever stood and fought for working people – for progress . . . and for the responsibility of governing Australia.
>
> The great vested conservative interests always find their parliamentary voice – the party names change but the song stays the same. Other parties come and go – often promising more, always delivering less.
>
> But we endure – not a brand, a cause. Not captured by the privileged few, but sworn to serve the many. Not a party for the moment, a party for the ages. And, twelve decades on from Barcaldine and Balmain, not done yet.

Not a brand: a cause. Not called progressive, moderate or social democratic: called Labor.

Third, and this is really important: Gillard's statement about the link with the unions and the fact that we are called a labour party is a statement of party identity, not of function. It isn't a statement about the party's relationship with progressive Australia (or its attachment to social democratic means). Laborism alone isn't enough and labour alone isn't enough, we know that. It never has been, we've always wanted to reach out; we did it in 1909 when we recruited a liberal lawyer and future Queensland premier TJ Ryan to run for the seat of Barcoo, and we do it again now.

I think about progress in politics in this country as a column moving forward, with a broad rear narrowing to the front. At the rear, the whole progressive constituency taking in liberals, middle-class families, migrants and their children, public-sector workers and the old working class. Then a progressive movement in front of them — then the unions in front of them — then the Labor cadres — and the federal Labor Party in the van: the tip of the spear. All that is contested, of course — economic and social change create new pressures on this, no one in those constituencies has to vote for us, and plenty don't. We have to work to keep this column together, and that can be hard. It really can't be done if there isn't within it all some kind of relationship of understanding and respect — at least within our own show. We have a place in our movement for liberals and QCs and environmentalists and entrepreneurs, but we have no place for snobs.

Leading a movement in which the party and the unions are connected also really can't be done without a sophisticated understanding of that connection. So it is worth responding to more thoughtful observers — even those who didn't read the AWU speech closely enough to quote it correctly. What had the speech meant for this complex task?

Here's what I think: because ours is a Labor Party, the centre of our identity is a vast group of people, not any narrow set of ideas. That's the real beauty of Chifley's matchless phrase 'the light on the hill' — that it

Julia Gillard advises my bosses Mark Latham (above) and Kim Beazley (below) during her time as manager of opposition business 2004–2006. *Photo credits: Auspic*

The prime minister in cabinet. Gillard came to the prime ministership determined to restore policy process and collective responsiblity. *Photo credit: Auspic*

Swanny and the boss on a budget day. The relationship between my PM and her treasurer was considered better than the historical mean. *Photo credit: Auspic*

'Be bold.' The PM addresses the United States Congress, March 2011. An admiring speechwriter can be seen on the floor of the House. *Photo credit: Auspic*

'Rob, James, good on you.' Rob Frey and James Dowdell in the United States Congress – friends, firefighters, allies. *Photo credit: Auspic*

A great Aussie bird. Above and below, the PM is greeted by workers in Tasmania during the election campaign in 2010. She saved their penalty rates. *Photo credits: Auspic*

My funny boss. Above and below, the PM campaigns as the best prime ministerial holder of a beer since Hawke. *Photo credits: Auspic*

The beginning of the 'picture mountain'. Two safe pairs of hands but one very unpopular coat. Simon Crean, Stephen Smith and the PM in 2010. *Photo credit: Auspic*

Minamisanriku: the PM in Japan, April 2011. It looked like the site of the end of the world. *Photo credit: Getty Images*

About to leave the Lobby restaurant, Australia Day, 2012. The Australian Federal Police were able to protect the PM's security but not her dignity as she fell and lost a shoe. *Photo credit: Auspic*

Exit signs are the enemy of any good picture. Here the PM is under the biggest exit sign I've ever seen, in Western Sydney, March 2013. *Photograph by John Iass-Parker*

On the way to the US in March 2011 we refuelled in Hawaii. Everyone had work to do. *Photo credit: Auspic*

On the way back, we were more relaxed. I am wearing my school rugby jumper and disputing accounts of my insobriety. *Photo credit: Auspic*

Kirribilli House has a tiny office where a lot of work can be done. Here the PM is surrounded by media, policy and events staff. John McTernan (left), the PM's director of communications, is googling himself. *Photo credit: Auspic*

Ryan Batchelor, the PM's policy director, advises her in her Canberra office.

*Photograph by John Tass-Parker*

'You don't own the minerals.' The Minerals Council of Australia got the message and so did First Dog. I pinned this cartoon on the wall for darker days. *Image credit: First Dog on the Moon*

The shadow of the past. The PM looks over the shoulders of her great predecessors Curtin and Chifley, September 2011. *Photo credit: AAP Image/Alan Porritt*

The foreign minister makes notes at Labor National Conference 2011. He was not happy with the 'we are us' speech. Nor was he alone. *Photo credit: Jacky Ghossein/Fairfax*

Above: Cheers, big ears. We have one ally, but we do have two friends. Let's do business. China, March 2013. *Photo credit: Auspic*

Below: No matter what was happening in the world, we struggled for an audience at home. Western Sydney, March 2013. *Photograph by John Tass-Parker*

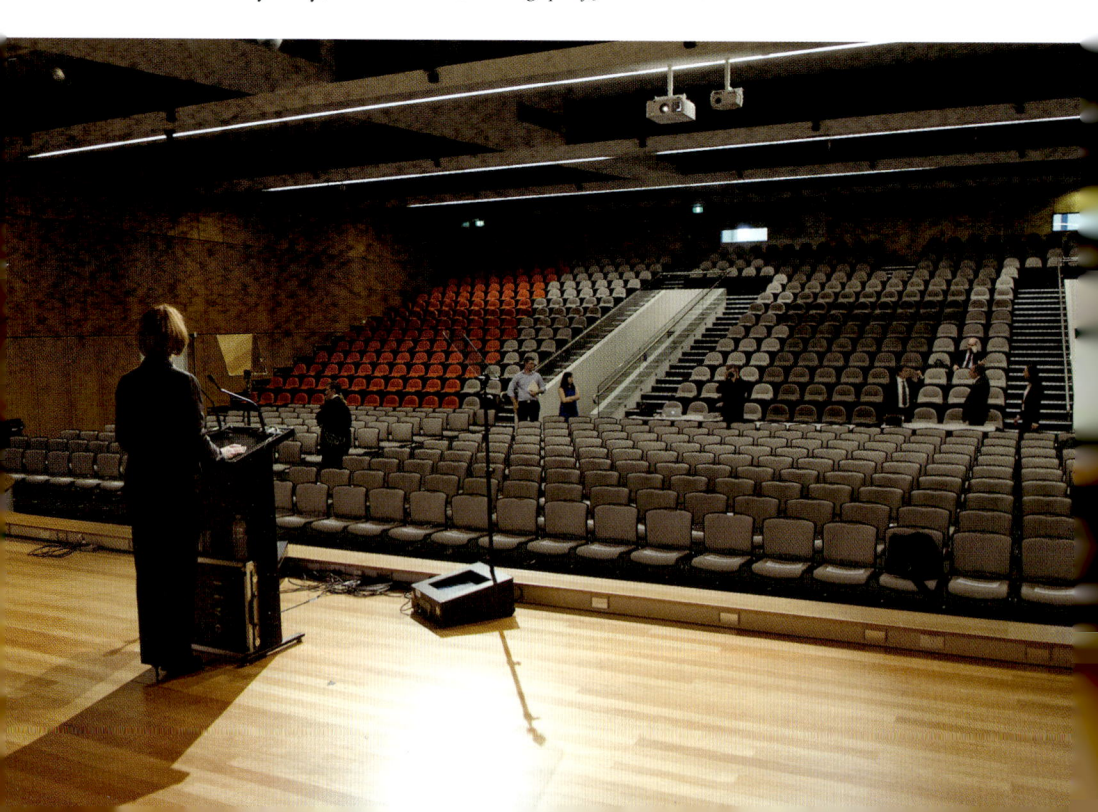

Gillard signing up to her own deepest passion, handily renamed after someone else. Not the first time the teachers' union annoyed me. *Photograph by John Tass-Parker*

Two powerful and impressive women meet. International Monetary Fund managing director Christine Lagarde and the PM. *Photo credit: Andrew Meares/Fairfax*

Cabin fever. In the final days, this pig became my closest adviser. 'Mate, talk about cost of living,' he would plead with me. *Photo credit: Debra Biggs*

Leadership spill, 26 June 2013. She would be back soon. We were so proud of our boss.
*Photo credit: Laura Chalmers*

Calling on the spill. While rumours circulated, the PM acted. *Photograph by John Tass-Parker*

Last words. What the PM saw as she gave her final press conference. She doesn't miss the gallery very much. *Photograph by John Tass-Parker*

The PM so often looked the part. Above, representing Australia at the royal wedding. Below, thanking our troops. *Photo credits: Auspic*

is connected to a statement of a practical objective, 'better standards of living, greater happiness to the mass of the people'. That's also the real heart of what Keating said on the occasion of the centenary of the federal parliamentary Labor Party, when he celebrated the variety and energy of Labor's movement of ideas:

> We were and are a pluralist party; we've given a home to all sorts of people – Fabians, Marxists, single-taxers; all sorts of characters.

It's what Neville Wran said – Wran the moderniser, the cosmopolitan, the progressive, the moderate – in his dramatic final speech to the NSW conference as premier in June 1986.

> Preserve at all costs the union links. You can have a party of social democracy without the unions. It is even possible that such a party would win elections.
> But it would not be a Labor Party. And above all, delegates, it would not be, it could never have been, and never could be, the great Australian Labor Party.

No, this doesn't mean Laborism is enough; no, it doesn't mean we don't need new ideas; but it does mean we never put the cart ahead of the horse. The ideas are there to understand and to serve the interests of the people. As the historian Bede Nairn put it in 1989, describing the practical, populist, democratic sentiment of the founding generation of Labor in Australia:

> Labor people weighed the confused promise of an alien earthly paradise against its high price, including the constriction of the human spirit, and decided to continue their efforts for betterment in the society to which they belonged

Just as critically, this sentiment Nairn describes is never simply one of electoral pragmatism or even of practical moderation. It is, rather, a spirit of deep empirical conviction, of profound attention to the social and economic facts of contemporary Australian life – and of clear-headed service to the contemporary social and economic interests of the people who we represent. Of course unions don't represent everyone, but they represent more people than anyone else walking around Parliament House trying to tell us what we should do (and even more especially, what we should think). The union link is precisely a connection to 'the real world' and a mechanism of policy pragmatism and modernisation. The challenge is to make that truer, not to make that go away.

Fourth, because we are a labour party, a party organised in a certain way and representing certain people, this allows us to be a distinctively Australian party. To be a party that reflects on the interests of the people it represents in the future of the nation it seeks to lead. There isn't a Labor 'ideology' about how to respond to two ageing generations or to the peak of the mining boom or to the rise of Asia or to the new digital economy – and that's the point. For Australian Labor the starting line isn't a deduction from liberal, social democratic or progressive principle, it's an observation from the future of Australia, from what's happening to the people we represent and what can best help them through that. And the finish line isn't ideational consistency with a political philosophy – the finish line is a histogram of the distribution of wellbeing. Labor is the party of *cui bono*, the party of 'who benefits', and that makes us the party of 'which *Australian* benefits'. The culture of our movement and our connection to industrial organisation is part of what makes us an Australian political institution.

Arthur Calwell's glorious assertion, repeated so often during his leadership, that 'we are Labor because we are Australian and we are Australian because we are Labor' was surely the ripest example of confidence in this; speaking in and of the Australia of Eddie Ward and Russel Ward, Calwell believed it, and probably so did the movement as a whole. The historian John Hirst had a serious and sophisticated expression and critique of this Labor dreaming in his Allan Martin Lecture 'Labor's Part in Australian History: A Lament'.

> The Labor Party has cared too much for itself and not enough for the central institutions of the polity . . . Those who have lived within the Labor tribe have loved it. They think it is the essence of Australia. But I doubt whether it was the ideal vehicle for fully realising the social democratic potential of this place.

We have done the state some service; and they know't. But perhaps we have loved Labor not wisely but too well. Hirst recalled that Freudenberg put it this way:

> More than any other political party in the world, the Australian Labor Party reflects and represents the character of the nation which produced it.

And that Keating said it even more boldly.

> We are the people who make Australian history. We are the ones who nominate the heroes, we anoint the heroes of Australia, our Party sets the ethos of Australia.

In early 2013 Tony Abbott went through a little phase of saying the prime minister needed to be 'a national leader' rather than just 'a tribal chief' — a clever formulation implying you can't be a fighting Labor leader and be a prime minister who governs for all. Offered in self-defence in the face of another Gillard evisceration of him in the House, it could sound like he was asking for quarter. I'd hear this while sitting in my office during question time, grinding away on some useless speech about the economy for next week or arguing with Carl about how to fix our diary processes, and it would make me think of John Guard's lyrics for 'Men of Harlech' – 'as our trusted chief surrounding/march we Harlech men'. I'd find myself humming, and I found it hard not to feel that the tribe is enough. Of course, in more sober surrounds like the National Press Club these sorts of comments sometimes worked for the opposition leader, sounding elevated rather than patronising, and harmonising with the masculine modes of 'grown-up' politics that he sometimes liked to affect.

And we knew it sounded different to ears outside the 'tribe'. We'd always been conscious that the story Labor tells about itself to itself isn't a campaign theme and we needed to think about how we looked and sounded to the people we reach out to in order to support and govern – exactly the kind of people who don't think about 'tribe'. We never only used our history as a form of ancestor worship within the movement to inspire us – we also used it to express a kind of popular patriotism, and to rebut the recurring conservative claim that we didn't love Australia enough. Hilaire Belloc said, 'Europe is the church, and the Church is Europe'; between them, Arthur, Graham and Paul essentially said, 'Australia made Labor and Labor made Australia.' This often worked.

When Hirst spoke in 2006, the self-regard for the ancestors of the tribe and the tribal discipline had been growing together through twelve decades. Grant that even then he spoke explicitly of Labor's history and past ('I don't know how to talk about today's Party. I am still in mourning for the loss of Qantas and the Commonwealth Bank') and yet it is still unnerving and sad to read his statement of the classical view of Australian Labor's cult of solidarity, because it was made so recently and seems so ridiculous – that our caucus was *too* disciplined, damaging not only ourselves but 'the social democratic cause and the quality of the parliament'.

If only that were still true.

—

I can't prove to you that all of this isn't just sentiment and sediment, or even special pleading on behalf of powerful mates. All I can do is tell you one more story, about why I like having unions in the Labor Party.

Not about a dinner this time but about a union summit – the community summit assembled in Old Parliament House in March 2013 to discuss the change in the workforce from permanent and ongoing jobs to more casual, temporary and insecure forms of employment.

This summit brought together welfare-rights advocates, representatives of think tanks, environmental reformers, independent economists, Catholic social activists – new and established voices for progressive ideas in Australia. Peak bodies and service providers – for immigrants, refugees, the unemployed, the unskilled – who serve millions of Australians. Union leaders in some of the most toughly contested blue-collar battlegrounds of the economy, union leaders in some of the most poorly paid pink-collar parts of our workforce, who represent millions more. Academics, public servants, retired parliamentarians.

This summit represented exactly the kind of broad coalition for change that real social progress demands: touching on the true diversity of modern Australian life, seeing the needs of the disadvantaged and the aspirations of those who are lifting themselves and their families up, and hearing the ideas of those who want to make a difference in the lives of others. That broad coalition for progress and change in this country ranges as widely today as it ever has. The community summit illustrated the breadth and diversity of the progressive side of Australian politics – and yes, Labor needs to reach out to that.

It's also a fact that the summit was brought together by the ACTU. That is why these people were there debating the ideas, working through the evidence, considering the solutions – never as an abstraction, always connected to the contemporary conditions of the lives of the Australian people. That is why secure work – not an agenda pushed forward by vested interests or political commentators, but one arising from the working lives of millions of Australians – could be aired and debated that day. That is why there were the resources and the support simply to organise an event of that kind.

The unions booked the room. They almost always do. We have to keep that in mind.

—

Yes, a party without a link to the unions might draw on different suburbs and schools for its leadership and might be less likely to generate a prime minister who inexplicably mispronounces hyperbole as 'hyper-bowl' on national TV. Some of those who couldn't come at Gillard's 'the party called the Labor Party' speech are just snobs and ideologues, captured by a false consensus and scandalised by the fact of labour (and Labor) in politics; they don't fit, and that's fine. We were a stumbling block to those sorts of people in 1891 and in 1943 and we were in 1983 and we still are in 2014. We'll always be a bone in the throat of the sort of people who sneered that Chris Watson's government was 'steering from the steerage' and who said Ben Chifley 'wouldn't know a bank from a public convenience' or who gave parliamentary speeches in the 1980s about the 'Hawke–Keating socialist government' – the sort of people whose secret hearts still really ache for a millionaire leader with a corrected accent. It is so embarrassing to see them tell us (and themselves) that what they like about Turnbull is his stance on climate change. I don't worry too much about them.

But a party without a link to the unions would also be less likely to do Safe Rates, to make sure cleaners get paid more, or pass new laws to help stop the exploitation of outworkers, to make safer building and construction workplaces, get Australian wages on ships working the Australian coast, have higher wages and better training for aged care workers, build higher superannuation, achieve equal pay for caring workers, create Fair Work Australia, have unfair-dismissal protection, keep penalty rates.

I know which matters more to Australia, and it's a trade-off I'm prepared to make.

# PART THREE

# RAINING STONES

# 8.

# The sleep of reason

*Fantasy abandoned by reason produces impossible monsters: united with her, she is the mother of the arts and the origin of their marvels.*

EPIGRAPH TO GOYA'S *CAPRICHO NO. 43*

When 2012 began, Julia Gillard, Wayne Swan, the cabinet, their officials and staff, were obsessed with the economy. No one else was; the world was about to go mad. While the PM and her government battled through complex economic circumstances and determined political resistance to deliver reforms and investments of which 'the measure is in the years', extraordinary events were about to bring us dramatic pictures that essentially signified nothing except their own symbolic power. Governing and politics would diverge, as rarely in the past, and the Gillard prime ministership would be politically tested by pictures that told us little about the way Australia was governed in this period but much about how Gillard, and the government she led, were perceived.

—

When Bill Clinton's 1992 campaign manager James Carville wrote 'It's the economy, stupid' in his office, he was talking to his own campaign staff. In that campaign, which followed the recession of 1991, the insiders had to remember that the people's focus was the real challenge of jobs and growth. The staff (and the candidate) had to be sure not to get distracted by the daily politics shoved in their faces or by the unwritten memoir of their own ideas pressing into their heads at night. The object of their convictions had to be the things the people were interested in.

There Gillard was, governing after a lifetime of growth – and it's a lot easier to tell your own staff something than to communicate it to the country. It's the economy? Such an abstract debate, so boring. Stifled yawn; and the only thing more boring than an economic debate is a fiscal debate, one just about the levels of government spending and taxing. So there we were, halfway through the electoral term, still making a fiscal argument, saying, 'It's the surplus, stupid,' while Tony Abbott chanted 'debt and deficit'. Many critics implored us to shift away from arguing about the surplus to argue about the bigger economic picture of jobs and the future.

After all, our policies themselves were clearly broader than repairing deficit and repaying debt. Through the whole Gillard government a strong employment agenda was delivered, above all in the form of the investment in clean energy funded by the carbon price and in the form of the NBN. Undoubtedly getting this done supported the good jobs outcomes achieved in 2011, 2012 and 2013 – the hundreds of thousands of new jobs created – and undoubtedly the destruction of these programs by the Liberal government in 2014 is one of the causes, not just one of the correlates, of rising unemployment since. Labor was talking about (and acting on) the wider economic elements – but we weren't saying they were the big picture. Should we have changed the line? Were we swallowing a conservative economic frame?

I think no: because in 2012, fiscal policy actually was the main economic story. Abbott's talking about 'debt and deficit' was a distortion of the main issue, not a distraction from the main issue – he was offering a bad answer, but he wasn't talking about the wrong question.

Fiscal *was* the question. We didn't swallow the frame, we fought the good fight.

You can only assess this seriously by thinking through the sequence of events. Following the second stimulus package, in February 2009, the official forecast was that the federal budget would return to surplus in 2015–16. As a recovery grew, the independent advice in the first half of 2010 was that a surplus could be achieved earlier than originally planned; and so in May 2010, the budget forecast a return to surplus in 2012–13 – 'in three years, three years ahead of schedule'. As the 2010 election campaign approached and in the campaign itself, with the political urgency to demonstrate that the stimulus packages of the global financial crisis had been a deliberate cyclical measure, not a permanent loss of discipline, we turned a forecast into a promise. The months that followed witnessed the miracle of the campaign, when we got the conversation back on the economy and won; the years that followed witnessed the long struggle with declining revenue forecasts from Treasury ('writedowns').

You can also only assess this seriously if you choose to start with a judgement about the economics of the period, not the politics. Which one you start with is a crucial divide between the decision-makers in government, whose object of interest is the material world, and many of the disappointed independent and progressive critics, whose object of interest is political discourse.

———

When critics start with the discourse, they and the electorate itself become an audience instead of a citizenry. Interested voters are reduced to couch-bound politics fans imploring their coaches to 'play the beautiful game' rather than 'win ugly'. Disengaged voters reduced to politics viewers are reduced to preferring a leader who won't annoy them so much they have to change channel – while engaged activists reduced to politics fans are reduced to preferring a leader who will say something worth cheering for.

Even on an issue as emotional and serious as asylum-seeker policy there is great energy expended on arguing about the language used, and some people seem to want a different kind of politics on asylum seekers as much as they want different actual treatment of people who arrive by boat. I don't really get a clear sense that for the politics 'fan' a better political style would have any connection to the governing endeavour to fashion a better society. It would just mean less distressing politics TV. This creates a situation where even the best people with the greatest commitment to politics are closer to theatre critics than activists; complaining against a caution of style rather than a centrism in substance. Everyone is the political equivalent of a cricket tragic and no one is the political equivalent of a club cricketer.

This is what we are witnessing when people say politics is increasingly 'boring' and politicians are increasingly 'dull'. You know, maybe it's not actually a failing of democratic politics that if you watch it on television for hours and hours a week it's boring.

People who watch the same politics news over and over instead of relying on the wider accumulation of statements and events remind me of author Flann O'Brien's character the holy fool De Selby, who considered human existence 'a succession of static experiences each infinitely brief'. It is a suggestive way to think about life in Parliament House. But O'Brien's narrator in *The Third Policeman* speculates De Selby thought of this while going through old cinematograph films, which he found 'repetitive' and 'tedious', having 'examined them patiently picture by picture and imagined that they would be screened in the same way, failing at that time to grasp the principle of the cinematograph'.

There is a life to be lived active in politics, and there is a life to be lived in voting every three years, but I'm not sure there is a life to be lived watching panel shows on a couch all day or even every weekend, and I'm not sure it's the job of the Labor Party to make that life on the couch more fun. What did the English football manager Alan Durban say when he was at Stoke? 'If you want entertainment, go and watch a bunch of clowns.' Join the struggle or take your kids to the park but don't tell me we're boring you.

This difference — between caring mostly about governing and caring mostly about talking — isn't the same as a difference between preferring big sudden leaps forward in policy or step-by-step progress through the years. And it isn't the same as a difference between left and right.

The 'Labor swallowed the frame' argument doesn't miss the economics of the period by accident — it's essentially indifferent to the economics of the period, starting instead with the words. But to understand this period, you must forget the frame and look at the big picture. Stop thinking about whether or not to think about an elephant — it's not an elephant, it's the economy, stupid. Less George Lakoff. More James Carville.

In fact, the fiscal-policy argument sits at the centre of Australia's economic challenges and in turn at the centre of the economic argument between Labor and the Liberals in the current decade. Indeed it is now central to our competing visions of the role of the state. Labor believes economic growth that includes everyone is the key to a unified society, a clean environment and to healthy public finances. That's why in the Gillard government, our fiscal policy started with growth. We want growth now, because jobs are morally urgent; we want public fiscal balance over the long term, because that's practically important. We know there are massive fiscal challenges — not because of debt, but because of ageing — not over a year, but over a decade and more. They are in the long term, and we must grow now if we are to be rich and strong enough to meet them over time. Growth now, plus revenue adequacy and expenditure restraint over time, will pay for the fiscal balance.

By contrast, the Liberals say healthy public finances are the key to economic strength. They want cuts now, because they don't trust growth and the future to resolve the fiscal balance; and because they are genuinely morally offended by public debt, while they don't see joblessness as anything other than a number. (Paradoxically, in this respect their view is both less pragmatic and more state-centric than ours.) Job creation doesn't seem so urgent to them. In my opinion, the simplest explanation for this is because the interests they represent will be the last to suffer in a shrinking economy. It's like a twist on that song by the Who: the conservatives can go nuts with cuts, kill off growth and take a hammer to low-wage private-sector jobs, and still drive home over the bridge whistling, '*Our* kids are all ri-i-ght.'

You can see this fundamental argument between the parties over the relationships between and relative importance of fiscal policy and economic growth illustrated in our competing interpretations of Europe's financial crisis. Greece is the Rorschach blot of the modern political debate. Labor and other progressives look at Greece and see a legacy of years of sluggish growth and the professional class dodging tax; the Liberals and other conservatives look at Greece and see a legacy of government overspending and garbage collectors getting paid too much. (Neither of us is brave enough to see the legacy of a political class complacently conspiring across party lines against the people they represent.)

Of course, Greece is in a deep enough hole for a lot of different explanations based on different political prejudgements to have some basis in fact. The point is that in 2012, the basic Labor idea about growth and fiscal policy was right for Australia: it was a time to repair only as fast as jobs and growth allowed, not a time to grow only as fast as fiscal repair permitted. With fragile growth, a short-term deficit and very low public debt, it was the right time to grow, then pay back – in 2012, the way we preferred to run the economy was the way the economy needed to be run.

But we hadn't just promised to return to surplus as soon as jobs and growth allowed. We'd said the facts indicated that return to surplus as soon as jobs and growth allowed would deliver a surplus by 2013. And then the facts kept changing.

All things being equal, getting back to surplus while keeping jobs growing wasn't hard in the end – it just got harder the faster you had to do it. Think of growth and fiscal repair as two parallel lines, like your arms stretched out in front of you. The left arm – growth – we wanted to keep straight. The right arm – fiscal repair – was the variable; it had to move over to meet it. The closer to your chest that you make the right arm touch the left, the sharper the angle you have to move on. You can move your right arm easily to touch your left at the fingers. Getting them to cross at your elbows is a stretch. Now imagine the countervailing forces of global weakness pulling your left arm away from you, and falling revenue pulling your right arm away, like a pair of malign holidaying schoolkids interfering in your exercise routine. Getting the surplus done 'on time' becomes almost impossible. The stretch was very real. By the start of 2012, the challenges to growth and revenue meant that the times suited our preferred economic strategy, but not our stated tactics. What in 2010 had been a promise to bring our middle fingers together at arm's length increasingly felt like a commitment to make our armpits meet in front of our chest.

As Ross Garnaut put it, 'The government had accepted official advice, as a good government should.' But sometimes the advisers need to listen to the government. Canute knew he couldn't stop the actual tide coming in, no matter what his advisers said. Now Gillard and Swan couldn't stop the metaphorical tide of revenue going out, no matter what Treasury said. The 'thread the needle' plan remained, but by January 2012 it was starting to feel like we needed to thread a camel through it.

Come the new year and the PM was ready to meet the test. Another sign of growing capability and confidence was the arrangements for the PM to rest and recover over that summer. You can't turn your phone off. But you can't not take a break. What do you actually do?

Natural disasters notwithstanding, it had struck me that at the end of 2010 neither she nor her staff had a realistic sense of how you go on leave as prime minister. That sounds odd, but it's in the nature of the prime ministership that everything is different, even taking a holiday.

That summer we largely got it right. The day after drinks and cricket at the Lodge with her staff, on 17 December, she left for a week in Victoria's north-east. Three of the five days there brought a mid-morning teleconference with key ministers and staff about major issues – hardly idle, but strategic discussions on 2012 were a step down from the exhaustions of 2011. Two days of business in Melbourne – cabinet met for the last time in the year on 22 December – and more strategic wrap-ups. Then real leave, three days off in Adelaide: Christmas with family followed by South Australia's Proclamation Day, a cherished routine.

The old year ended and the new one began at Kirribilli House. A few more days off – for a PM, a day off is a day where you pop over to the SCG to announce a new grandstand and do a press conference, or where you pop back two days later to support a fundraising day and attend functions – and then the round of discussions began again. No rushing around, no early starts or late nights, but a quiet mix of planned strategic conversations and relaxing casual interactions – dinners with former prime ministers, barbecues with independent MPs, afternoon teas with key ministers, even tennis with friends. This was Gillard as she wanted to be: purposeful and tranquil, preparing and recovering.

In the third week of January, the machine started up again and the PM hit the road: Hobart, Melbourne, Canberra (for the sad funeral of a young and well-liked press gallery journalist, Peter Veness), Melbourne, back to Canberra. Bizarrely, this did constitute a relatively quiet first week. The first major speech of the year would be on 1 February – on the economic big picture – and so we met at the Lodge first thing in the morning on 25 January.

The PM walked in to her sitting room and the courtly Carl Green stood up and said brightly, 'Happy new year, Prime Minister!' The communications director John McTernan, who had been halfway through sitting down when she entered, hovered in place and weakly waved; the policy director Ian Davidoff, already sitting but behind the PM, cringed like he was having an acute attack of glaucoma and didn't stand up. I had a huge folder of notes and outlines and pens and Post-its and blue editing pencils on my lap so I just raised my eyebrows in a pretty familiar sort of greeting.

'Thank you, Carl,' the PM said, before swivelling around the rest of us. 'God, you three blokes are rude. I get no respect.' That laugh. It was good to be back at work. And the next day, the PM tripped over on a footpath.

—

Australia Day has really grown in Australian life in the past twenty-five years — I reckon native title made it a day many more progressives felt at ease with, and the Triple J Hottest 100 made it a day that matched the lifestyles of more of the young — and it's been a day largely insulated from politicians directly playing politics. Maybe Tony Abbott wasn't breaching that insulation when he was asked that morning about the Aboriginal Tent Embassy, the protest camp near Old Parliament House, and said it was 'time to move on from that'. If he wasn't deliberately politicking (and this must be logically possible) then he was misheard because of the legacy of years of deliberate politicking on the issue by Liberal leaders and ministers, particularly by the revolting Wilson Tuckey during his ludicrous period as minister for territories.

Either way, Australia Day 2012 ended with Indigenous protesters banging on the glass walls of the Lobby Restaurant where Abbott and Gillard were, having heard about Abbott's comments from local Canberra union leaders who heard about them from the PM's staff. With the PM (and the opposition leader) evacuated by the Australian

Federal Police, and with the PM falling and losing a shoe between the restaurant and the car door.

And that was only the first crazy distracting picture of the year.

If there is an 'untold story' of how the protesters from the Aboriginal Tent Embassy ended up there, then our communications director John McTernan and our media assistant Tony Hodges can share it. All I know for certain is that our Tony did his job in good faith, and by resigning because of his role in informing local union leaders about the comments and Abbott's whereabouts, he accepted a responsibility that no one else would or did.

In this, Tony earned great admiration to add to the widespread affection in which he was and is held by Labor people. Put it this way – whoever in the Howard government leaked a Top Secret ONA report to Andrew Bolt in June 2003 during the Iraq War debate, smearing the whistleblower Andrew Wilkie (later MP) and likely committing a criminal offence in the process, took no such responsibility and paid no such price. In the US, that person would be in jail sharing the soap with Scooter Libby, not be paid to tweet demands that Tony Hodges resign or to call Edward Snowden a traitor.

—

The only untold story of Australia Day I can share is of a family barbecue in the suburbs. Now that I run a think tank, I'm thinking of developing an app that gives progressives talking points for debating their conservative relatives over the summer holidays. Nothing beats a good 'chat show' session on the back deck. We all get on well at my mother-in-law's place, but people can't help talking politics.

My brother-in-law, Sean – great man; a manager in manufacturing; fair to call him a Gillard-sceptic – had a new job that year. He'd left the printing business where he'd spent twenty years and was now commuting to the Visy pulp and paper mill in Tumut, in the forested mountains about a hundred kilometres to Canberra's west. Over lunch he marvelled at the new investment they were putting through there – all clean-energy stuff. (Visy is a recycling company too – just ask Chris Judd.)

His father-in-law, Bill – good guy to hang around with; too polite to go full Gillard-hater on me over lunch, but there's a fair bit of 2GB going on in his interior monologue – had a new complaint about the world. Bill and his wife Mavis live in one of the small villages half an hour outside Canberra. He wasn't getting broadband internet soon enough. Paying extra for downloads would send him broke. It'd drive him mad. Couldn't look at grandkid photos. Couldn't do online banking. Didn't anyone understand?

I considered pointing out some wider implications of this conversation, but I didn't have to.

My father-in-law, Neville – rugby league referee, retired public-school principal, an old man who drives through country towns like he lives in them, and in a lot of them he has – is getting pretty old. He doesn't say much and you're not always sure he's listening. But he dropped one right on Bill and Sean: 'Well! You boys had better hope old Julia Gillard gets back, hadn't you.'

They laughed but they weren't laughing. I could have hugged him. What a champ. And then the mad shoe news started coming through.

I am sad that the dramatic events and images of conflict on Australia Day are so unrepresentative of Prime Minister Gillard's cautious and consensual approach to Indigenous affairs in office. That January – a few days before the Footpath Fiasco – the expert panel appointed to create a model for constitutional recognition brought in what was in practice an overambitious report. That is why constitutional recognition was deferred – the right thing to do at the time, given the difficulty in winning support for recognition in light of the foreseeable stance of the conservative parties on the panel's specific proposals. Much of the Indigenous leadership and most people of goodwill in the wider community want a 'yes' vote of 90 per cent or more. Anything less would be a terrible shame;

I certainly don't disagree. But if you accept that this kind of effectively unanimous public support is necessary, what is necessary in turn is that the change proposed be unimpeachably modest, including that it have the total support of the opposition. The PM and minister for Indigenous affairs Jenny Macklin worked with great caution and sensitivity through the year to consult with Indigenous leaders about the next steps, carefully managing the unavoidable transition to a new phase of a frustrating process, and by September a referendum had been put off. (The squabbling public remarks of Rob Oakeshott and GetUp following this decision about whose fault that all was didn't leave me thinking that problems of political culture end at the edge of the major parties.)

In Indigenous affairs under Prime Minister Gillard, there was none of the emotion or drama (or missteps) of Hawke, Keating, Howard or Rudd. The PM was inclined to describe Australia as reconciling, rather than to appeal to Australians to reconcile. The gradualist, empiricist, practical agenda of the Closing the Gap campaign for better health, education, employment and other outcomes that started when we were in opposition, and which both prime ministers Rudd and Gillard had committed their governments to continue, perfectly suited her policy approach and her political sensibility. This was not a period of Makarrata or Mabo, Wik or the apology; it was a period when we started testing every Year Three kid in the country, including Indigenous kids, in reading, writing and mathematics. Progress continued, rhetoric faded.

Gillard being the one to trip on the footpath just doesn't tell us anything about the way she governed.

---

More crazy pictures followed.

February brought us YouTube footage of Rudd swearing and rolling his eyes in outtakes from recording a video message while prime minister – released out of the blue onto the internet on a Saturday night. The pictures told us almost nothing about his prime ministership and nothing we didn't already know about Kevin's temper – and in fact it's not even really Rudd having a tantrum, it's more Rudd pretending to have a tantrum, as people who've seen an actual Rudd tantrum can tell you. Sure, it's funny, and every time I hear that line, 'Tell them to cancel this meeting at six o'clock, will you?' I even wonder if he had a six o'clock – imagine having to tell him there wasn't a six o'clock to cancel.

But the release of this furious video was seemingly one of the rocks thrown at Rudd in this period that seemed to prompt him to a challenge for which he clearly had far less than majority support among Labor MPs. And as much as I was obsessed with the economy, I can't blame you for being obsessed with the leadership in a period like early 2012.

It really is hard to explain Rudd's decision to challenge in February of that year. One theory is that Rudd acted in anger, following the YouTube video and Simon Crean's public 'calling out' of his private campaign to be leader again; but this seems to exceed even journalist David Marr's 'anger is his ruling passion' thesis of Rudd's personality. Another is that he used the challenge to drown out breaking reports that he had been secretly negotiating with gaming interests for a poker-machine reform truce in the event of his returning to office; this isn't proven, and seems so cynical in substance, and so complete a triumph of immediate media management over real political strategy that surely not even a person impersonating the worst caricature of Rudd could do it. Could he have thought that if he didn't get in at the start of 2012, Gillard's ability to deliver during the year would lock him out of new support in Labor? (We won the equal-pay case Gillard had begun for community service workers on 1 February – there would be more where that came from for working people – and of course by 1 July there would be a price on carbon.) Obviously miscalculation is another possibility – but such a substantial miscalculation?

Then again, we had called the carbon price a carbon tax. Never rule out error as an explanation.

Piling paradox upon paradox, a leadership challenge that was prompted by a video that explained nothing brought forth tremendously engaging statements from MPs that told us a great deal about the anger and emotion within the government. The leadership crisis had in some respects been continual for two years now, and the moment brought dramatic, defensive and angry statements of the state of mind about the 'second front'. It was a contest that, for a few weeks in February and March 2012, became the main theatre, with a formal leadership ballot in the Labor caucus the result.

Wayne Swan, in a written statement on 22 February, broke the long silence, spitting out the bitter, widely shared disappointment in Rudd's conduct as prime minister that had been buried in the 'a good government was losing its way' euphemisms of 2010 – and the fury of Gillard supporters at Rudd's conduct in the period since.

> The party has given Kevin Rudd all the opportunities in the world and he wasted them with his dysfunctional decision-making and his deeply demeaning attitude towards other people, including our caucus colleagues. He sought to tear down the 2010 campaign, deliberately risking an Abbott prime ministership, and now he undermines the government at every turn. He was the party's biggest beneficiary then its biggest critic; but never a loyal or selfless example of its values and objectives.

Rudd was travelling in the US as foreign minister; he let fly in a middle-of-the-night press conference before flying back to Australia.

> It's very easy to establish a frame whereby all of the government's problems are the result of one person called K Rudd. Can I just respond to this: It wasn't K Rudd who made a

pre-election commitment on carbon tax. It wasn't K Rudd who made a particular commitment to a Mr Wilkie on the question of poker machines . . . The government's problems, as they've accumulated over time, have been of its own making.

When the leadership decision was taken in June of 2010 on my own leadership, I think I'd been below the 50 per cent mark once – I'd got down to 49 per cent. In the last twelve months, my recollection is I don't think the current government has got in terms of Prime Minister Gillard's support ratings, anything approaching that number of 49 per cent . . .

. . . the thesis that the government's problems exist because of one K Rudd is simply unsustainable, and I think it's time everyone reflected on that. I'm gonna zip.

I listened to it thinking what a complicated mix of truth and falsehood that was. Parts of his remarks spoke only for himself, in an emotional statement of personal grievance at his removal, adopting an odd pose as a victim in a challenge largely of his own making, even openly expressing two-party preferred poll numbers as his purpose. Other parts captured the widespread frustration and anger in Labor at the government's poor support and maladroit politics, emotions shared by many who had not supported him in 2010 and even some who still didn't support him now – reflecting the serious judgements now being levelled against the government and prime minister I served.

On Friday, the prime minister responded in a fighting press conference in Adelaide. My only advice to the travelling media staff was for God's sake, don't hold back, this is not the time to be a good soldier and rely on false reserve – something told me I was pushing on an open door. The PM spoke with great personal conviction, characteristically offering the project, even more than her own person, as the centre of that passion; but with plenty of 'I' in the frame.

Who delivered a historic health reform agreement making changes in emergency departments for people seeking health care around the country? I did. Who has delivered education reforms and is continuing to build on them? I am doing that and will continue to do that. Who delivered the modernisation our telecommunications sector needed with the changes to Telstra through structural separation? I delivered that.

I'm happy to be judged about my credibility on carbon pricing – I've got it done. Didn't talk about it, got it done. Kevin Rudd, when the going got tough couldn't get carbon pricing done.

Over the next eighteen months, among her staff and closest supporters, 'got it done' became a talismanic statement of what Gillard stood for as a leader and as a person. We might have butchered the sell, but she got it done.

And there was one more amazing statement left in that amazing five days.

On the Saturday morning before the ballot, the PM flew to Cessnock to address a NSW Country Labor conference and seek support up there. The big battalions were holding for her – the major unions, the NSW Right – and she went to this event on short notice to create a powerful symbol of that ahead of the caucus vote. I sat at my younger son's cricket match in the Canberra suburb of Yarralumla with my feet in the wet grass and smashed out some speaking notes on a laptop. (This is exactly the kind of suburb Alan Reid was talking about in the 1960s when he said Canberra 'looks like Toorak and votes like Cessnock'.) When it was finished I emailed it to the travelling party and then went to the car to listen to the radio news. So I was in a dirt car park, parked under basketball rings, when I heard Anthony Albanese's press conference announcing he would support Kevin Rudd in the ballot to come.

> I love the Labor Party . . . Mum raised me with three great faiths: the Catholic Church, the South Sydney football club and Labor. She said to be true to all three . . . I have despaired in recent days as I have watched Labor's legacy in government be devalued.

And then he cried. Sitting in the car and listening, I groaned and rested my head on the steering wheel and I nearly did the same.

> Under Kevin Rudd, we had the apology. We brought the troops home from Iraq. We ratified the Kyoto Protocol. We advanced the National Broadband Network . . .
>
> Under Prime Minister Gillard, she has led a government that has achieved outstanding things, particularly under the circumstances of minority government. Two hundred and sixty-nine pieces of legislation. Finally we have a price on carbon; we have structural separation of Telstra; the Minerals Resource Rent Tax and just in the last fortnight, reform of private health insurance . . .
>
> I like fighting Tories. That's what I do. That's what I do. And I have lifelong friends who disagree with me on this. It has been very difficult.

And he nearly cried again, and so did I. Is this what we all worked for all those years?

―

The next week the PM won the ballot by a huge margin, one exceeded only by Whitlam against Bill Hayden in 1977. Talk about a pyrrhic victory. Then, after days of 'will she, won't she' speculation, she announced her support for Bob Carr's return to politics as a senator for New South Wales – Senator Mark Arbib was retiring from politics – and her intention to appoint him minister for foreign affairs. Media commentators seemed universally astonished there was any hesitation among federal Labor decision-makers at inviting Bob into their counsels. How could we be so stupid, they asked. The confusion arising in those days robbed her of momentum and we didn't get the ecstatic analysis and opinion coverage we deserved. It probably wouldn't have happened anyway, and probably wouldn't have mattered if it had.

You just can't keep snatching victory from the jaws of defeat from the jaws of victory; you just can't keep getting it done and butchering the sell; you have to have some proper wins. And even as a matter of politics, the second front is not the most important thing. Governing the economy matters so much more.

Amid all that, there were some good moments that week. One of these was when the PM launched journalist George Megalogenis's *The Australian Moment.* Nothing is more enjoyable than drafting a speech like this (my predecessor Tim Dixon emailed me, *Enjoy – writing a Mega book launch is the Grange Hermitage of writing for a PM*). The PM and I both like George and had known him for ages, and Gillard shows you she likes you by making fun of you in front of other people; so we had some fun with the author.

> We've had leadership, not luck. Take the deputy prime minister . . . If this is 'the Australian moment', and it may well be, Wayne got us here as much as anyone. Swanny should probably have more mentions in your book than Margaret Thatcher. But I might be biased . . .

She had some fun with chairman of the US Federal Reserve Alan Greenspan and Treasury secretary Ken Henry too:

> . . . we're not run by some wise old owl playing the clarinet in the bath, or some solo genius zipping back and forth from

Bungendore in a sports car while the political class wastes its time on doorstops. I think we've got a smart, hard-working people, tough businesses, and, yes, a class of economic officials that the world envies. But we've got politicians who make decisions and get the job done.

The 'lacerating tongue and disarming jokes' that David Marr had once identified didn't hide the affection and respect she held for Megalogenis, a genuine independent and a master explainer:

> When he climbs these little mountains of empiricism he always plants a flag of explanation on the top.

The year 2012 started with a mountain of images. The ones of the PM falling, as her close personal protection moved her from the restaurant to the car on Australia Day prompt raw emotion. The ones of the former PM swearing in frustration at a bad script draw prurient amusement. It's some kind of job to plant a flag of explanation on the top.

Sometimes, I imagine the mountain you could make of dramatic images of the important stuff, the things really going on. The pictures that didn't exist.

A mysterious YouTube upload of Wayne Swan being told in September 2011 that he would be *Euromoney* magazine's finance minister of the year – or two months later, learning that Fitch Ratings was upgrading Australia to AAA, making us one of barely a dozen of the most creditworthy economies on earth.

If only we'd had a camera running.

Or on the other hand, a photo of the PM being told by economic advisers in January 2012 that Chinese growth had slowed to its lowest level during her government, or one from February 2012 when she learnt that the Treasury writedowns of revenue the previous year hadn't been enough, and there were more to come. It'd illustrate something dramatic about the strategic strengths of our economy in these three years, and about the tactical challenges of making it look strong.

But of course, no such photo exists.

There'd be a photo of the PM walking in to her first meeting with Chinese president Xi Jinping in Bo'ao in April 2013, to put the final touches on the amazing achievement of direct currency trading on the mainland and an annual strategic dialogue, and bumping into Christine Lagarde of the International Montetary Fund walking out of her meeting. That day, the two women exchanged a spontaneous high five and a laugh at the door. It'd tell you something real about Gillard's ambition and accomplishments for Australia in the Asian century, as well as something about the personal connection between women who lead in the world.

The snappers weren't there.

The picture-mountain that we actually did get, the one that illustrated Australian politics and the Gillard government in early 2012, tells us nothing about the way Australia was actually governed in this period. But it's precisely in this that it symbolises everything – because the most dramatic moments and memorable images of the period 2010–13 were almost all essentially irrelevant to the governing reality of the Gillard project. Fantasy abandoned by reason produced impossible monsters.

Maybe it is only in this way – remembered as a rambling yarn, and understood as a raging paradox – that the importance of the Australia Day picture of 2012 can emerge.

Julia Gillard wasn't a 'lucky general', but in a world gone mad, she got it done.

# 9.
# Basest things

*What will not ambition and revenge*
*descend to? Who aspires, must down as low*
*As high he soared; obnoxious, first or last,*
*To basest things.*

JOHN MILTON, *PARADISE LOST*

Another Labor winter: 2012; when everything and everyone doubled down.

The poll trough just before the carbon price commenced was even deeper than the one just after it was announced. The opposition's tactics became even more extreme, in the Parliament and out; they would descend to anything. The revenue writedowns got even worse, turning our fiscal breastplate into a straitjacket as the surplus got even harder to achieve. The PM and her treasurer dug in deeper and fought harder a gutsy budget in May was followed by months of fighting rhetoric in June, July and August. These were days when we broke out vintage Gillard, days of Labor purpose, days of resolve, in the face of the most bitter and base opposition we had ever known.

Everyone knew Peter Slipper's appointment as Speaker had risks. The day he took the chair, an adviser asked me what I thought; we all knew he had been accused of misbehaviour with regard to entitlements in the past, by his local paper in particular; I said that was probably irrelevant now; if he behaved himself in the job, he'd be all right.

Everyone knew Mal Brough was a threat. He was a Howard minister who'd lost his seat in 2007. A leading figure in Queensland's Liberals, a self-consciously tough, activist former army officer, still able to get on the *Australian*'s front page. By 2011, Brough had been hunting a way back into Parliament for years. Slipper's seat of Fisher, a safe conservative seat in Queensland's south-east, was a natural target.

No one knew James Ashby. He was just a young bloke desperate for a job in politics. In July of 2011 Ashby met Peter Slipper — probably at a dinner at Slipper's house attended by Slipper's wife, Inge, and others including Bronwyn Bishop — and by October, he was swapping text messages with Slipper about online political campaigns against Brough. In one of those exchanges, Slipper called Brough a 'cunt', Ashby replying, 'You make me laugh sir.' The revolting details that followed would become legend the following year. Later in the same conversation, Ashby suggested that Slipper should seek the speakership. Five days later Slipper had offered Ashby a job in his office, including work in Canberra. Ashby didn't accept. Once Slipper actually was Speaker, he made another more generous job offer. Ashby was in. On 24 November 2011, when Harry Jenkins resigned the speakership and Slipper was elected — unopposed, with the support of the government and the outward consent of a silent, stunned, sullen opposition — Mal Brough's personal interest in taking Fisher from Peter Slipper became the Coalition's collective interest.

Attempted personal attacks on Slipper began within days. In 2012, as new harassment claims against Slipper reached a public peak, *The Australian* would report that 'seething kingmakers in the Liberal Party' had immediately organised a 'dump' of documents considered damaging to Slipper dating back to 2003. When finally published, important details had to be denied by Tony Nutt, John Howard's private secretary of the period; and the relevance to 2012 had to be denied by George Brandis, then shadow attorney-general. The 2003 documents, while unflattering to Slipper, didn't prove wrongdoing on his part; but even if inaccurate and incomplete, they did prove contemporaneous knowledge of the unflattering on the part of the most senior people in the Liberal apparatus. Slipper couldn't be brought down by old claims, much less by claims previously put to and dismissed by Liberal Party decision-makers.

He could only be brought down by new claims, and by claims which the Canberra press gallery would find credible. April brought those.

—

Almost a decade before, in February 2003, I had to bowl the last over for Labor MPs and staff (the 'gentlemen and players' team) in our traditional cricket match against the Canberra press gallery. (The following year's game featured Mark Latham's famous cameo as 'Manboob Habib', our spinner from the subcontinent.) In 2003 we played at Reid Oval, almost in the shade of the War Memorial's dome, in glorious 'summer of 1914' weather. Their team was nine wickets down and needed a handful of runs to win the game. Our captain, Stephen Conroy, threw me the ball and some inspirational words. On the third ball of the over I hit the right-handed batsman's pads while he hovered at the crease. Now, I am 'military medium' the way Dad's Army was a military unit. I'd bowl on coir matting if they let me. This ball didn't smash into the pads, it plonked into them; it wasn't going over the bails in a hundred years, and God knows I couldn't swing it to leg if it had a bias in it. So I ran down the pitch, wheeled around, roared, 'Got him, yeah!' . . . and realised the umpire was the captain of the press gallery team.

Steve Lewis said, 'Not out.' And that's Australian politics.

Steve Lewis had worked for *The Australian*, and we got on fine;

I treasure memories of drinking beer and cracking gags with the late Matt Price (also from *The Australian*) in his backyard pool. I'm not alone in this. Journalist Bernard Lagan wrote a very forgiving piece in the now defunct *Global Mail* – where he might have been expected to rip and tear some News Limited flesh – recording that 'Lewis is no hard-drinking, hell-raising, out-all-night hack. He's a family guy, an industrious, diligent reporter' – one who sings in choirs and raises money for charity. I believe it. What I also believe is that his reporting of the Rudd and then the Gillard governments was at best fundamentally unserious and irresponsible. By the time he broke the Slipper scandal he had a track record in working with troubled informants making sensational allegations against high office holders. His coverage of the fictional 'Utegate' claims in 2009 was so disastrously wrong it brought down the opposition leader who had worked with him on the yarn; all the more reason to be genuinely amazed, and troubled, by his conduct in 2012 working directly with the opposition (again) on sensational claims investigated in secret (again) – and with none of that secret work reported or disclosed.

Government is scrutinised. Labor is opposed. These are not the same things and the journalists who do one shouldn't confuse their role with that of the politicians who do the other.

Ashby started work in Slipper's office in January 2012. By March, Ashby was taking documents from Slipper's office and giving them to Mal Brough; Brough was giving them to Lewis. By 2 April, Ashby and Lewis were on the phone to each other; by 4 April they were in a coffee shop together. Lewis later texted Ashby *we will get him!* By 21 April, Steve got his front page.

> SPEAKER ROCKED BY SEX SCANDAL
> Staffer's lawsuit over Slipper's alleged 'unwelcome advances'

The next day, while the PM was in Singapore preparing to visit Kranji War Memorial, Slipper announced he would step aside while the issues were considered. When Parliament resumed, on budget day, Slipper confirmed his 'stood-aside' status from the chair.

Who knows what happened to the relationship between Slipper and Ashby between October and April to explain Ashby's claim that Slipper sexually harassed him at work. Given how often Ashby texted Slipper saying, *I don't offend that easy*, it might have been something serious. Nevertheless, Ashby maintains that things Slipper said and did even on his first day at work in January were too much. The heart has its reasons and consent matters. Ashby sued Slipper and the Commonwealth.

By January 2015, two judges had found Ashby's civil claim against Slipper for harassment to be an abuse of process, one finding 'Ashby's predominant purpose for bringing these proceedings was to pursue a political attack'; two have found it not so. But of course, it really doesn't matter. Whether or not they did want to 'get him', he was got. And he was got on budget day. While Slipper was pulling the pin, Swanny was rolling the dice.

—

The revenue writedowns of 2011 had been bad, putting the surplus at risk. They took money off the bottom line, forced painful savings decisions on the government, forced us into the very difficult flood levy argument, and, perhaps most damaging, robbed us of the headroom to solve small problems and offer modest benefits to individuals and families. After 2011, everything had a price. Then the revenue writedowns of 2012 had been worse. They resulted in all of the above again, in a budget where there was less room to move than ever before. The government had now gone since the second stimulus package of February 2009 without announcing a new net spend. Remember that thirteen-hour car trip? We were driving past a lot of good places to eat without stopping.

And the writedowns made funding the PM's plans for schools and the national disability insurance scheme harder. These are substantial but affordable programs for the Commonwealth budget over time, a claim that isn't seriously disputed, and both have economic (not just social) benefits. But starting them costs; and if we didn't start them before the next election – and we were stoic, but we weren't stupid, we'd been behind every day for almost eighteen months – then they probably wouldn't happen. We didn't discuss this much, but we knew: this was a race to get the storm windows made before Hurricane Tony arrived. The politics of promising better schools and disability care 'soon' was punishing too. Driving past all those ice-cream shops promising that when we get there it would really be worth it.

Worst of all, once that second set of writedowns arrived, no one could say there wouldn't be a third. Among government staff, confidence in official forecasts snapped like a twig. From here on, economic advisers would be watching the revenue numbers like kids in the back seat peering nervously at a fuel gauge with its light flashing. A procession of budget advisers dropped past my office that winter to lie on my reclining Eames repro and use me as a sounding board. 'How small a surplus do you reckon is a credible surplus?' I laugh just thinking about those conversations, or at least smile, partly because I wonder if any of these people knew that the others were also asking me. I wanted to be Hawkeye in *M\*A\*S\*H* but some days they made me feel like Father Mulcahy.

The era of good-news budgets was just about done. But the hard decisions of the last two years were paying off in the real economy. The week before the budget, the Reserve Bank cut interest rates again – to lower than they were when John Howard promised in 2004 that interest rates would always be lower under the Coalition than under Labor. No single measure could better stimulate jobs and growth across the board; no single measure could better ease pressures on living standards. So on budget night, 8 May 2012, Wayne took the official advice that we'd get there on time, this year, and made one more promise to thread the needle:

> The four years of surpluses I announce tonight are a powerful endorsement of the strength of our economy, resilience of our people, and success of our policies ... The deficit years of the global recession are behind us. The surplus years are here.

Then he really rolled the dice. Since 2010, the government had been proposing a cut in the company tax rate. This was one of the intended benefits of taxing mineral resource rents. In the economists' favoured phrase, by broadening the base, it allowed us to lower the rate – and it helped firms who were squeezed by the high dollar that mining was driving. But the Liberal Party had voted against the company tax cut, along with the Greens – now *that* is a ramshackle Senate coalition – and after a difficult consultation with business, even they couldn't agree to a plan to get it done; they just didn't want it enough. So Wayne said, fine, we'll give that money to middle Australia.

In his speech he announced that the business tax cut was off. Instead, over 1.5 million families would get a boost in family payments; more than a million Australians on Parenting Payment and other allowances got a new lump-sum payment; and little companies would still get a boost, a loss carry-back scheme, to give a capped benefit of up to $300 000 to 110 000 firms.

The 'spreading the benefits of the boom' package was a good Labor plan to lift living standards in the country – as well as a gutsy political gamble, by unravelling elements of the mining tax package we'd 'fixed' – that largely paid off. It was so tightly held that on the Saturday before the budget, when I sat on my back deck and did my customary favour to Wayne's office of reading his draft budget speech to offer any suggestions, there was a square-bracketed section with some bland reference like 'more detail to come'. I knew something was up; I love seeing a draft like that, knowing that for once there'll be something worth watching on TV.

The PM spent Saturday after budget week in Adelaide with her family. But we were in plenty of strife and needed every moment of campaign time there was; we made her fly to Queensland at dawn on Sunday to spend Mother's Day with a Labor MP at a barbecue in a marginal seat.

—

We were not just in plenty of strife. We were in more strife than Burke and Wills, and the PM just would not give up. It makes the hair stand up on the back of my neck to think about it. Three weeks after the budget, on 30 May, she had to give a speech to the Minerals Council of Australia, the industry body for mining companies, in the Great Hall of Parliament House. I thought it was time to chuck out the 'you're so awesome, I'll work methodically with you, hope you don't mind the tax too much' script of 2010 and just tell them we were going to do it because it was right. The PM loved it, agreed, and then recut the speech so the toughest lines were right at the end. By some incredible miracle, no one killed the plan before she left the office grinning with the speech under her arm.

> Now, I know you're not all in love with the language of 'spreading the benefits of the boom'. I know everyone here works hard, competes in a tough global environment; you take big risks and you earn the big rewards. You build something. Australians don't begrudge hard work and we admire your success.
>
> But I know this too: they work pretty hard in car factories and at panel beaters' and in police stations and hospitals too. And here's the rub: you don't own the minerals. I don't own the minerals. Governments only sell you the right to mine the resource. A resource we hold in trust for a sovereign people. They own it and they deserve their share . . .

It got tougher:

> ... The facts endure. Our economy is the envy of the world. Our mining industry is the envy of the world. There's nowhere in the world you'd be better off investing. And there's nowhere in the world where mining has a stronger future.
> And this is Australia, and it has a Labor government.

She was still grinning when she got back. They didn't like the speech, or the spanking front pages, and if they'd seen the First Dog on the Moon cartoon about it, they wouldn't have liked that either – but they actually couldn't argue the point. Poor old Mitch Hooke, the MCA's long-term spokesman, was on the radio the next day saying, 'Oh, of course, we've always accepted we don't own the minerals.'

On Saturday 14 July Karrakatta Cemetery received the remains of Sergeant Blaine Diddams, killed in action in Afghanistan. This was the first soldier's funeral the PM had attended in nearly a year. Private Matthew Lambert had had a private service in September 2011; circumstance had demanded that the PM send representatives to the funerals of three men killed in an engagement on 29 October that year – Captain Bryce Duffy, Corporal Ashley Birt, Lance Corporal Luke Gavin. The PM flew directly from Karrakatta in Perth to Sydney. There, two weeks after the carbon price had come into effect, she fronted NSW Labor conference.

One day I'll work on a NSW conference speech for a leader who's not under pressure to hold their place and perform well in front of a key audience; and this time I had a little monkey called 'we are us' to get off my back too. We both knew we just had to get it right. The morning of conference I went to mass at St Pat's on Church Hill and sat behind a bloke in an Electrical Trades Union hoody, and then walked the length of George Street a few paces behind him. When we got to the town hall he went to the right's caucus meeting and I went to the green room.

She told the audience what she'd done for working people and their unions in the Parliament during this bitter winter – it was a long list that started with Safe Rates and ended with superannuation. (Delicacy forbade that we give Peter Slipper's vote too much credit.) She slammed home the big news, that her work of years had now delivered equal pay for community services workers – reflecting years of her own work, as well as another win for Bill Shorten's advocacy within the government – and announced funding to meet the extra cost for the mostly not-for-profit employers whose staff were going to get a pay rise as a result.

And she had a word for the critics on the right whose response to our Laborite rhetoric was starting to bite.

> If they've started accusing us of 'class war' at least they've stopped accusing us of not knowing whose side we're on.

Then despite a last-minute adviser panic about making a big statement – I personally held the line, don't say I hadn't learned from national conference – the PM batted on and told them straight:

> Tony Abbott got it right, when he told his party room: 'She won't lie down and die.'
> 
> Too right, I won't.

The applause was so long the *Daily Telegraph* blogged about it. The staff stood at the back of town hall exchanging glances of pleasure and relief. I walked into town afterwards with Albo and he showed me the street corner where he sold papers when he was a kid.

—

The PM looked so sad when she got back early from Russia on 9 September. Her father had died while she was away at APEC. We were all glad Defence Minister Stephen Smith greeted her on the airport tarmac and gave her a kiss and a hug; she wasn't alone. (She said afterwards it was 'cute'; her disarming word for touching and appreciated and nice. Funny old Smithy.) While she was at home in Adelaide with her mother and family for the funeral, she sent a few messages to the office thanking us for keeping things going and telling us about what her dad had been like and his gratitude for our work for her. They were very open and emotional words in what were raw days for the PM.

She was away from Parliament for three sitting days. Soon after her father died, with Parliament still in session, she flew to Narrabri, NSW. Private Nathanael Galagher was to be buried there. He and Lance Corporal Mervyn McDonald had been in a helicopter carrying them into combat in Afghanistan when it hit the deck and killed them both. McDonald was buried in Fremantle the following week.

The Queensland Labor conference was the PM's first fully public and political appearance after her father's death. To a reception almost as emotional as that in the town hall in July – tears for her father, cheers for the teachers in the room – she fired more rhetorical shots: 'Newman's budget razor is Abbott's curtain raiser.' Hard to dispute in hindsight.

It was finally spring. In published polling, the worst seemed to have passed – only a few more months could tell. People were feeling the benefits of our budget – payments had been flowing for a couple of pay packets in a row and carbon pricing hadn't sent anyone broke. The PM was finding an argument – I'm on your side, I'll fight for you, I'll stop the Liberal cuts. It could turn negative perceptions of her as a stubborn and ambitious politician into positive perceptions that she would use that determination to everyone's benefit. The opposition's diminished credibility following the failure of the sky to fall in on 1 July was also a vital moment in the politics. The bitter and base elements were not breaking her.

But if we were finally fighting back by the start of spring 2012, the first day had been the treasurer's autumn budget on 8 May.

# 10.

# I will not

*I will not be lectured about sexism and misogyny by this man. I will not. And the government will not be lectured about sexism and misogyny by this man. Not now, not ever.*

PRIME MINISTER JULIA GILLARD

In winter, everyone had doubled down, but at least we had been fighting about whether Australia should have a Labor government or not. In spring, we found ourselves fighting about whether Australia could have a woman prime minister.

When the PM flew into Melbourne from New York on AFL grand final day, Saturday 28 September, Melbourne woman Jill Meagher, who had last been seen walking home from a pub the weekend before, was still missing. Her family was still hoping, and tens of thousands of people were sharing her image online and looking for her in the street. Around 10 p.m. that night Adrian Ernest Bayley showed police where he had buried Meagher's body after he raped and killed her almost a week earlier.

The next morning, Sunday, it became public that the day after Jill Meagher died, Alan Jones had given a speech to the Sydney University Liberal Club in which he said of the prime minister's late father:

The old man died of shame... To think that he had a daughter who told lies every time she stood for parliament.

At the same function, Jones signed a jacket made of chaff bags to be auctioned as a Liberal fundraiser: a reference to his repeated statements the year before that the PM should be put in a chaff bag and thrown in the sea. Better a chaff bag than a millstone, I suppose. Woolworths executive Simon Berger, who had attended the dinner, had the chaff-bag jacket made and donated it for the auction, resigned his job. (He was subsequently hired by a Liberal Party–aligned think tank and then employed as a senior adviser in the Abbott government following the election of 2013.)

This dreadful crime and this appalling rhetoric hung over us in the office. A few of us also knew something was coming and wondered if this was the moment the PM would lower the boom. Eight weeks earlier, on 4 August, David Farley, the head of one of Australia's largest agriculture firms, Australian Agricultural Company, had given a thirty-minute speech at a conference in Adelaide about an abattoir his firm was planning in Darwin:

> This plant is designed to process old cows. So the old cows that become non-productive, instead of making a decision to either let her die in the paddock or put her in the truck... this gives us a chance to take non-productive animals off and put them through the processing system. So it's designed for non-productive old cows – Julia Gillard's got to watch out.

Oh, how they laughed. The week after that speech, the PM had briefed a number of us at the Lodge that she'd had enough. She was dismissive and disgusted, but also dispassionate in her explanation that she'd always believed that calling out sexism directed against herself personally was counterproductive. Fight for women and you can make a difference; make it a fight for yourself and you can only lose. Her politics as prime minister had reflected this: from the first day, when asked about her view of her achievement as first woman to be prime minister, she had said, 'First woman, first redhead, and I'll allow you to contemplate which was more unlikely in this modern age . . .' and laughed, underplaying the point. Part of the logic of this strategy was that whatever political credit she got for the distinction of being a leading woman would flow anyway, but whatever backlash there was would be minimised. But that strategy had run its course. She was now getting the worst of both worlds – all the backlash and none of the credit – and silence risked looking like weakness and even consent. This meant there was now some staff work to do – to pull together some evidence of Abbott's complicity in it all, think about some more events which highlighted what we'd achieved for women in office – so that when she decided to respond, we would be ready.

I wonder if she thought about taking aim at Jones that weekend in September, but was genuinely too upset and angry to trust herself. But we had no doubt, the next bloke who made an arse of himself was going to wear it.

By the beginning of October, Peter Slipper finally couldn't or wouldn't pay his legal bills and in consequence went unrepresented in the civil case brought against him by James Ashby for a period. The government had settled its case with Ashby a week earlier, which meant there was no professional legal team to counter the Ashby team. They saw their chance. On Monday 8 October, they introduced into evidence text messages from before Ashby even worked for Slipper; there was no one to object. These showed that Slipper and Ashby had flirted – exchanged 'ribald texts' was one coy media characterisation – with grotesque crudity. Worst of all, a text message that had been partially reported by Steve Lewis was one of many now put to the court in full. Almost a year before, when Slipper was calling Mal Brough a 'cunt', Ashby had continued that chat by explaining why Slipper made him laugh: *By telling it how it is. But no pollie tells how it is to the public. Everyone is so bloody scared of the civil libs and the vocal minority.*

Slipper's reply was, *Funny how we say that a person is a cunt when many guys like cunts! ;)*

To which Ashby said, *Not I.*

Slipper replied, *They look like a mussell* [sic] *removed from its shell. Look at a bottle of mussel meat! Salty Cunts in brine!*

How the release of these details could help Ashby's case was unclear. Ashby's claim was that months after this exchange when Slipper asked him for a neck rub or asked him to shower with the door open or asked him if he'd ever climaxed while having anal sex, these requests were unwelcome. This isn't a construction immediately congruent with the earlier exchange his representatives now revealed. In any case, the release of the text messages went far beyond Ashby's case. Media outlets had been primed to be ready for the news, which would prove politically devastating to Slipper.

That was Monday. On Tuesday 9 October, a gunman in northwest Pakistan caught up with Malala Yousafzai – then just a local girl advocating for girls' education; today a Nobel laureate – and shot her in the head on the bus carrying her to school. That afternoon in Canberra, the Libs went nuts. Having played the politics of gender for two years, having surfed the wave of every lousy inference from 'make an honest woman of herself' to 'when she said no, I thought she meant no' to meowing at Penny Wong in the Senate committees – through to 'nanny state', for that matter – they now decided that mock-outrage was the right play over the Slipper revelations. A straight-faced deputy Liberal leader Julie Bishop said:

> How the women in this house can be expected to show respect to the Speaker when we are now aware of the views that he holds of women is beyond comprehension . . . These remarks of the member for Fisher that were read into the court transcript, that are uncontested, that are now on the public

record, are offensive. Many of them are obscenely offensive and what female Labor members would describe as sexist and misogynist if anyone else had uttered them.

A ludicrous Abbott raged:

> I must allude – and I only allude – to the gross references to female genitalia . . . This is a government which is only too ready to detect sexism – to detect misogyny, no less – until they find it in one of their own supporters.

And then he said:

> What this prime minister has done is shame this parliament. Should she now rise in this place to try to defend the Speaker, to say that she retains confidence in the Speaker, she will shame this parliament again. And every day the prime minister stands in this parliament to defend this Speaker will be another day of shame for this parliament, and another day of shame for a government which should have already died of shame.

'I see what you did there,' as the kids would say. And so the prime minister gave him what he deserved – the misogyny speech.

> The leader of the opposition says that people who hold sexist views and who are misogynists are not appropriate for high office. Well, I hope the leader of the opposition has got a piece of paper and he is writing out his resignation. Because if he wants to know what misogyny looks like in modern Australia, he doesn't need a motion in the House of Representatives, he needs a mirror . . .

And on the evisceration went. I started watching in the windowless room about halfway through, when I looked up at the muted TV and realised the boss was really getting stuck in; my favourite moment was when she told Abbott to stop looking at his watch.

Then she went back to her office and finally made Slipper resign.

The Canberra press gallery – for the first time in recorded history, or at least the only time I can think of – was distracted from theatre by substance and missed the significance of the moment entirely. The next morning I was reading Peter Hartcher in the *Sydney Morning Herald* ('We expected better of Gillard') and Michelle Grattan in *The Age* ('More desperate than convincing') at the same time as I was replying to a one-word email from my White House counterpart: *WOW.*

While we'd slept and those 'we don't get it' columns had been being filed, the president's staff had been sending the video around their office and stopping in each other's cubicles to watch.

On Wednesday, Kelly O'Dwyer, Liberal MP, used Malala's name to defend the opposition leader against the prime minister:

> I pay tribute to Malala and those women and men who support her, for fighting for her rights and the rights of other women to get an education. Let us never forget that every moment spent on invented sexism and misogyny is a moment lost to fight real sexism and misogyny.

Yep, she really did.

The day after that, I caught the PM at her desk for a minute before she left for the airport, to fly to Bali, Afghanistan and India. I showed her the email I'd got from the White House and told her, 'Good one, boss.'

She said thanks; and then she took my head clean off with scorn for using the phrase 'White House counterpart' 'Oh, that's a thing now, is it?' – before calling in her chief of staff Ben Hubbard to ask him if he had a 'White House counterpart' and when he last got an email from his 'White House counterpart'. She never missed a chance. (Oh, of course I deserved it.)

Around Australia, women and girls were watching the speech over and over, and talking to each other about it as well.

In India, the female security guards wanted pictures with her.

—

Meanwhile, in Australian politics, there was genuine and pathological woman-hating going on online. Almost everyone reporting on the misogyny speech was also having to follow the story of the supposed 'questions to be answered' about Julia Gillard's legal advice to Australian Workers Union officials in the early 1990s. Bruce Wilson, her boyfriend at the time, had set up the AWU Workplace Reform Association; she had given him legal advice in the process. Later the association and money it raised was used for fraudulent purposes. The principal accusation against the PM, which she has always denied, was that she knew about all this and benefited from it at the time.

The reporters following the story also knew that the former newspaper cartoonist and now blogger Larry Pickering was (indeed, remains) among the most rabid promoters of the accusations against the PM. The PM and Abbott were acutely conscious of it, as were the Liberal politicians and advisers who were up to their necks in asking those questions, and the Labor people fighting the defence; it had been the unmistakable but unspoken context for the misogyny speech itself.

And there is no definition of misogyny that doesn't apply to Pickering's work. His cartoon trope of Prime Minister Gillard carrying or wearing a foot-long leather dildo is one of the most revealing things about this period in politics. (It tells us something about the mask of cheery libertinism worn by many men in the 1970s as well, in truth.) Here is a guy who literally can't imagine and literally can't draw a prime minister who isn't in charge of a penis. His imagination keeps correcting the evidence of his own eyes. It's pathological psychology.

———

How on earth did this AWU business grow to be a major national story in the media and in the Parliament? Honestly, I don't know.

Australia's changing media environment was part of it, and strongly illustrated by the dynamic of the reporting of this period. For *The Australian* to cover this was taken for granted by the PM, MPs and staff, and other journalists and political observers. The newspaper's coverage was always discounted – the inevitably misleading elements, both of detail and of scale, were factored in to insider reactions to the *Oz* coverage of the story, and was one reason the story frequently failed to gain traction in parliamentary debate or the independent media.

By contrast, whenever *The Age* covered the AWU 'story' prominently, it became a far more serious political issue. Perhaps precisely because of *The Age*'s long commercial decline and its well-known provincial liberalism; because it couldn't be easily considered to be motivated by the mad partisanship of News Limited or the rank woman-hating of the online conspiracy-theorists, its interventions in the story were a big deal. Mark Baker of *The Age* persisted in getting this yarn on his paper's front page, and this took a kind of courage. For a senior Fairfax journalist to put himself in company with the crew who pressed the case against the PM – 'monsters from the id' like Larry Pickering, the former radio host Mike Smith, the ever-present *Australian* investigator Hedley Thomas, and the kind of witnesses who want to fly back to Australia from decades residing in South East Asia on condition of immunity from prosecution certainly isn't to walk the easy path.

What was it really all about? Was it a serious story at all? To put it mildly, if you want to get to the bottom of the AWU story, there's a fair bit you can read online. For what it's worth, I don't think you need to read all that. The best final judgement on the whole miasma was ultimately offered by *The Age* and by Mark Baker himself; first in a widely publicised editorial the following year, on 22 June 2013, calling on PM Gillard to resign – because:

> . . . under Ms Gillard's leadership, the Labor Party's message about its future policies and vision for Australia is not getting through to the electorate. Our fear is that if there is no change in Labor leadership before the September 14 election, voters will be denied a proper contest of ideas and policies – and that would be a travesty for the democratic process.

If you can, put aside the explicitly media-management and opinion-poll defined view of the future of parliamentary government and look at what it does not say, or even refer to – at the issue it does *not* suggest is relevant to the prime minister's future. This is the only independent media outlet to have pursued the case – and even it didn't think the case was part of the argument for the PM to resign.

Then on 19 October 2013 Baker (incidentally, is 'editor-at-large' a serious title or a joke? I'm not sure I'd consider 'speechwriter-at-large' a compliment) published an opinion piece in *The Age* summarising the Rudd and Gillard period.

It was constructed as a corrective to the argument that Labor's problems were all the fault of one K. Rudd. Headlined *Kevin the sinner, Julia the saint. It's not the full story*, the column covered the period of the Rudd and Gillard governments, quoted Craig Emerson, Nicola Roxon, Anne Summers, Maxine McKew, canvassed the idea that Rudd was a narcissist, concluded that Rudd had, in the 2013 election, saved Labor from 'a disaster of *Costa Concordia* proportions'. . . and there was not one word on the AWU miasma.

Mark Baker's own evident, eventual view, the view of the person most responsible for lifting the AWU allegations out of the News

Limited–2GB privy and into the media mainstream: it wasn't worthy of mention.

Even before the subsequent trade union royal commission had come to its stuttering, pointless denouement in 2014, with nothing to find or recommend, it was obvious the case was closed.

# 11.
# The world at our feet

*Australia's a big country. An' Freedom's humping bluey . . .*

HENRY LAWSON, 'FREEDOM'S ON THE WALLABY'

While Julia Gillard was prime minister, Australia became a big country.

The last months of 2012 brought big decisions – above all, the White Paper on Australia in the Asian Century – which sat at the very juncture of the global opportunites that go with being big, the domestic policies of the Gillard project, and the prime minister's personal determination to 'get it done'.

This was the year Australia passed Spain to become the world's twelfth-largest economy; the year we entered the top 5 per cent of all the nations on earth. Today, the only countries in the world with bigger economies than ours are a handful of civilisation-states (China, India, Russia, the US), a handful of former imperial powers (France, Germany, Japan, Italy, the UK), and the two biggest states of the new world, Canada and Brazil. Economically, 95 per cent of the countries in the world are smaller than Australia. We're bigger than twenty-four EU nations; bigger than every economy in the

Association of Southeast Asian Nations.

This is an impossibly hard thing to get Australians to believe. There's some chance that you can convince Australians that we are the richest people in the world (you ease them into it by saying there's nowhere else you'd rather live, then point out how big our houses are compared to those overseas, then say people in the middle in Australia are better off than people in the middle anywhere else; you can get there). But that's a 'per person' measure. The idea that considered on national economic significance we are on the top shelf is just too much to cope with.

This is true even of many cosmopolitan Australians. One of my best, most cultured and sophisticated mates in business, a bloke who owns and manages a factory, exports intellectual property, works in Australia and Europe and goes to Dante readings with the scholarly poet Chris Wallace-Crabbe, seriously believes – in fact I saw him tell a US consul-general over lunch – that Australia is 'an insect compared to the American boot'. A drop of riesling-fuelled hyperbole aside, he's completely fair dinkum in saying this. And he's far from the only one.

People truly believe that Australia is a middle power in the way that a person earning $140 000 per year is middle-class – despite earning more than 95 per cent of taxpayers. Our real economic size is counterintuitive to contemporary Australian society, and in some respects it is an even deeper affront of our historic self-deprecation. A lot of people didn't believe it in 2012 and a lot of people don't believe it now. But there it is – we've come a long way, baby.

The prime minister knew. Leading a big country created both possibilities and obligations that I saw drive her on every day. This was the story of the last months of 2012 – more than personal survival or partisan service, more than Labor reform – the definite emergence of a strand of 'great nation' progressive thinking in the Gillard government's plans for Australia's future. Gillard had always had a migrant's pride in her adopted country and a sceptical ear for exaggerated national self-critique. Her sense that Australia really is a good place, populated by good people, where we are achieving something remarkable, had long lived in her politics. What grew through her period of office was the sense that this meant something to the world, and that the world meant something to this.

The interlocking commitments of the Asian Century White Paper, Australia's candidacy for the UN Security Council and continuing the mission of training and transition in Afghanistan were the outward manifestations of this understanding.

These were intimately connected to the big progressive domestic programs of the period – carbon pricing, the NBN, school improvement and the national disability insurance scheme. Strength and success in the world were necessary to the medium-term growth that would fund these changes, and these changes were necessary to the long-term growth that would underpin success in the world. In late 2012, Gillard saw a virtuous cycle of growth and modernisation with fairness underway.

—

In New York again, arriving in the last week of September 2012, the PM planned to make some of this argument to the first joint meeting of the Asia Society and the Economic Club of New York. Before departure, and then on the plane in the air, we had worked on a speech with the unstated theme that the times would suit us – that the things Australians want to do to be fair, above all to spread education and skills, will make us the things we need to be to stay strong, above all clever and innovative. She told the audience:

> . . . the big unanswered question facing countries like ours isn't the growth rate of China's economy later next year. It is what the basket of consumer goods and services will be for middle-class Asian consumers later this century. Can we conceive of the new products and services which fill that

basket – will we make and sell those things – and keep our economies strong?

In turn, the most challenging risk to Australia – and to countries like Australia – isn't China growing more slowly than we predict in 2013. Just as the real task of national preparedness isn't fiddling with the dials of the macro economy this quarter to take care of the third quarter next year. The most challenging risk is if we can't make and sell the things that Chinese and Indian and Indonesian and Thai consumers are buying in 2033.

And the real task of national preparedness is this. Building the skills and the knowledge of our people – accumulating and deploying the human capital – lifting productivity, generating innovation, making ideas.

Except she didn't, because she became violently sick in the night after she, and the Aussie newspapers, had gone to bed. The PM had eaten something on the plane that had basically poisoned her – we weren't quite sure what – and by mid-morning, it was clear she could barely get out of bed, much less the room; she couldn't stand up for an hour, and certainly couldn't give the speech. We dragged Bob Carr out of a meeting across town at the UN and raced him over to the speech venue. It was a seriously big lunch occasion, with over a thousand guests present in a truly vast and ornate downtown ballroom. (The recessive puritan gene in American society showed through – it's impossible to imagine a similar occasion in Australia with iced tea and soda on the table and no wine.)

Proving that he missed his calling as the greatest radio actor of his generation, Bob read through the speech once on a chair at the side of the landing on the stairs below the room – heedlessly red-penning lines we had already distributed to the Australian media twenty-four hours earlier ('You're very good, Michael, but I just need to tone some of this down a touch') while adding his own flourishes about the architecture of the hotel where the lunch was! – then went up there and proved that some days brio beats just about anything. In its way, this was an impressive statement about the level of Australian leadership across the government.

For a speechwriter quite convinced his boss was indispensable to the nation, it was also a bit unnerving to think that the speechmaker could be substituted quite so easily.

The PM was up and moving by the evening, and the week spent in and around the UN had the feel of a political campaign. The peak came on Thursday when the PM spoke to the UN General Assembly – it's such a cool mid-century building, part *North by Northwest*, part *The Rescuers*. The night before, the PM and I had talked about how interesting it could be to come back and give a speech to this audience after the UN Security Council election was out of the way and she could speak more freely. But we delivered a safe set of remarks that got the job done. My highlight of the morning was sitting with Tim Mathieson just before our speech, next to a Gulf state leader's several wives; their husband was due to speak shortly before our PM. He emerged from the green room and waved to them all, and they all waved back gaily as he walked to the podium to give the speech. (The thought did occur to us.)

Our tremendously droll and impressive ambassador Gary Quinlan steered us through a week that went so well it prompted *The Australian*'s Greg Sheridan to write a bitter complaint – 'forget the spin, the gig is in the bag' – that not only was a Labor government going to win the UN Security Council spot for Australia but the ABC would probably give Gillard the credit! Tony Walker in the *Australian Financial Review* didn't think much of the speech, wondering 'if the Prime Minister in her remarks to the General Assembly might have been better served if she had taken her shopping list to Bloomingdales'. Oh well, at least he didn't say it read like an old man's bar tab.

If you couldn't pretend that the PM wasn't working effectively in New York, what you could do was pretend she shouldn't be working in New York. So with the PM shaking hands and asking people to vote for Australia, Tony Abbott played politics at home. He directly attacked the security council bid (and insulted the leaders of Africa's nations) at the most sensitive moment, saying the PM:

> ... should be in Jakarta not in New York because that is where Australia's national interest is most at stake right now. Rather than talking to African countries trying to drum up the numbers to get us a temporary seat on the UN Security Council, she should be in Jakarta talking to President Yudhoyono.

The prime minister was meeting with President Yudhoyono, in New York, that day.

There's such pure, sweet human joy in seeing a man step on a rake in public – especially one he's so deliberately placed on the ground in front of himself. (There's also a glorious pleasure for staff in seeing someone else's boss make such a big statement that is so inexplicably not fact-checked.) But you can lose sight of the real substance, that this was a significant disproof of Abbott's foreign-policy instinct for bilateral relationships and against international organisations. Conservative foreign policy in Australia places great weight on precisely this false choice between working well in bodies like the UN and getting on well with individual countries like Indonesia – and then stacks on top of it a whole set of other falsely correlated false choices as well: between regional and global engagement, between people-smuggling and poverty alleviation, between the alliance and the UN, between Washington and New York ... or, to quote Tony Abbott on so many occasions, between 'Jakarta and Geneva'. So it was a lot more than an irony when the president of Indonesia turned out to be at the UN at the very moment Tony Abbott was telling us to put the region ahead of the world. It didn't just reveal Abbott as a line machine, not a decision-maker, it revealed a key foreign-policy theme to be a line motivated by a prejudice posing as an idea.

And in turn, it was a revealing moment in the opposition leader's campaign for a 'grown-up government'. The expression 'grown-up' is an odd piece of baby talk in itself. The theme is strange too: how many people talk or think constantly about being 'grown up' after their adolescence is complete? The pollster Mark Textor is sometimes credited with this line. I always thought its resonance with Abbott reflected the influence of our mutual friend Christopher Pearson, a journalist with *The Australian*, whose most dearly held fiction was that a 'club sensible' – his actual expression – agreed on all the things that mattered. You know, grown-ups, people like ourselves: old man politicians, journalists, judges and divines like Peter Walsh and Gary Johns and Barry Cohen and Tony Abbott and Greg Sheridan and Peter Hartcher and Dyson Heydon and George Pell and Arthur Sinodinos. We all *really* know what's going on.

But the problem for Club Sensible is this – things have changed. The established symbols of realism adopted by many in Australian politics clash with many of the new realities of the contemporary economy, environment, society and international system.

Because Club Sensible can't or won't adapt to these changes, theirs becomes a realism of commentary and style, rather than a realism of practice; a sensibility, not sense. It privileges bad temper over clear thought, has a very obvious element of nostalgia for a recent past (for the era of most of the membership's actual professional practice) – and, above all, positions commentators as fundamentally more serious than decision-makers, especially politicians. Club Sensible's grown-up foreign-policy voices, journalists like Sheridan and Hartcher, strongly amplify this into a strand of 'symbolic realism' in Australian foreign-policy debate.

Importantly, 'grown-up government', government by Club Sensible, doesn't have to be conservative. It just has to look serious and old. The idea is to grumble on (the deeper and gravellier the grumble, the better) about hard decisions. It doesn't matter what particular decision you want the government to actually make. I wonder for instance if a conservative commentator like Greg Sheridan realises how much like the liberal-progressive Hugh White he now sounds – or if Hugh notices how much he now sounds like Greg Sheridan. In a *Monthly* column after the UN bid was complete, Hugh struck all the same notes. Optimism is 'unremitting' or 'jejune'. (I suppose we did start that one, referring to 'intellectually arid strategic triangles'. Sorry, Hugh.) Choices are 'real' and 'hard'; Australia's leaders both lack the 'understanding' to agree with Hugh and the 'courage' to tell people they agree with him; few people in government 'privately' disagree with Hugh but 'Washington' and 'Canberra' are 'in denial'. You can tell what he's thinking: 'These kids. Don't they know how hard life is? Were they even alive in the eighties?'

—

In two days at the end of August, five Australians had been killed in war – Lance Corporal Stjepan Milosevic, Sapper James Martin and Private Robert Poate in an 'insider attack' by one of the Afghan soldiers they were working with, and two of their comrades (Lance Corporal Mervyn McDonald and Private Nathanael Galagher) in a helicopter crash the next day. They came home to Australia in spring.

Not many of the symbolic realists spent much time in Afghanistan. The long war in that country proves many of the 'hard choices' promoted by Abbott to be false dichotomies. By 2012 it was a place where Australian alliance commitments and our UN engagement and our Asian interests were as tightly meshed as could be imagined. It was a place where the UN Security Council would be making decisions in 2013 and 2014 that Australians were killing – and dying – for. Five days before the vote on the security council, the PM was in country again, on the tenth anniversary of the Bali bombing, reminding our troops that every one of the terrorist attacks which had killed Australians since 2001 involved a terrorist who had once trained in Afghanistan. The war in Afghanistan was important to Australia; and she said thank you to the troops, who were important to her.

Then she flew to Delhi. If the Asian Century is going to be a democratic century it will have to be an Indian Century. They are the great democrats of the world's south and east. Our conception of Asia will need to grow to grasp this, encompassing places far west of Jakarta; there's much more for Indian decision-makers to do. (It was a visit of fewer, shorter speeches, so I was spared the travel, and wrote them back home.) The PM's success of substance at the national conference in 2011, allowing uranium exports to India, along with her preference for deft rather than dramatic gestures toward India's rival, China, had opened the door for Australia in Delhi and these were important days.

Naturally the PM tripped over on the grass while wreath-laying at the Gandhi memorial; at last foreign policy made the front page. I had thought after years of the pressures of this job I was achieving some detachment. That was punctured as I read the papers in the 'round lounge' in the PMO. I remember how hot my face was as I looked at the tabloid front pages; it was a peak of emotion unlike any since the near-tears of relief when the royal wedding outfit went well eighteen months earlier. What happened wasn't funny then and it's really not funny now – it makes me kick the drawers under the desk as I write about it, and she really hurt herself – but as every television in the office showed the PM falling, over and over again, three or four times in every news update, which came three or four times an hour all day, I decided that yes, Ginger Rogers really must have been the better dancer. The PM returned home with a badly bruised wrist and a lot of phone calls to make in the final push for the security council, while Bob Carr was in New York playing every card he had; some we hadn't given him.

Canberra, New York, Melbourne, Bali, Tarin Kot, Delhi, Canberra – it's a rum kind of realism that doesn't notice the world is changing, and is grumpy when Australia wins. But we did win, and on 19 October 2012 the PM was driven down to the Department of

Foreign Affairs and Trade to give a speech in the building the Liberals had named after RG Casey when they won office in 1996. (Casey was one of Menzies' foreign ministers and failed rivals, a sort of Peter Costello of the 1950s; his ministerial colleague Paul Hasluck recalled cabinet ministers saying, 'Dick has got more goods in the shop window than on the shelf.') Hundreds of DFAT's Canberra staff rushed to the atrium and stood on the mezzanines inside the building to hear the PM speak; it was quite a sight. The PM told them:

> I would like to thank, in order, firstly Kevin Rudd for having the foresight as prime minister to put our name forward and to commence the bid process, and then to pursue it so energetically as minister for foreign affairs.

No one other than Kevin Rudd would have started the bid; no one would have committed the funding either; he was uniquely responsible as PM and then critical as minister through 2011. Australia's time on the security council is one of Rudd's genuine achievements. Plenty of people who think they are wiser and better than Kevin Rudd said it was a folly – it turns out they were wrong.

Two days after we won the bid, Corporal Scott Smith was killed by an improvised explosive device in Afghanistan. Corporal Smith was operating in northern Helmand when he died, alongside Afghan troops, under a United Nations mandate.

—

No one other than Julia Gillard would have commissioned or delivered an Asian Century White Paper quite like the one she released in Sydney on the last weekend in October. In her words:

> A plan for our nation's future, which weaves together the policy approach we have been pursuing in government with

new policy directions to create the next chapter in our nation's story.

The white paper itself was a deliberate effort to bring together the major policy elements of the Gillard project and define them by the nature of the times in which we live. The PM's speech to launch the white paper would attempt to bring together the major rhetorical themes of her two-and-a-half-year-old prime ministership.

She and I knew it was a very big and diffuse speech, covering a lot of policy ground – from a modulated view of the 1980s as an achievement of the past more than a model for the present, to the understanding of what was changing in Asia, to the insight that this meant that our social democratic preferences now reinforced our regional and global interests. It also needed to have some style and rhetorical weight. It had to be good, really, is all. So we began talking unusually early, almost three weeks out, and there was a fairly developed draft maybe even ten days before delivery. But I will never again say, 'This time we're going to be really systematic and get the work finished nice and early so there's no last-minute panics.' Man, did I jinx it.

A series of incremental decisions to add events to her diary meant the PM endured a ludicrous schedule in the week before this very big governing moment. My end-of-2011 confidence that our office was improving its capability and judgement was stretched; in fact, this probably broke it. One afternoon she drove for over an hour from the Sydney CBD to Campbelltown in the middle of the day to open a research institute then back in the afternoon to Pyrmont to host a fundraiser; the next day she spent a very emotional afternoon in a private visit to wounded Australian soldiers at Holsworthy Barracks, not far from Campbelltown again. On another she visited her own seat, in effect the safest in Australia, to do about eight public events; good thing to do once a year, bad thing to do that week. She then went to South Australia and was driven from Adelaide to the mouth of the

Murray and back for an event on Friday, before addressing the party state convention on Saturday. (Oh, that day was also Tim's birthday.)

The whole mad process ran so late, the proposed changes coming in from staff and officals were so significant, and the questions we had to ask the PM were so complicated, that by the actual morning of the speech I was dropping in whole page-long sections at eight o'clock before an eleven-thirty event. At that time, I should have been printing the reading copy. Instead, I was trapped in a kitchen in Bondi, and I thought I might have to stay there, in our adviser Damian Kassabgi's flat where I had slept over, and talk to the PM on the phone, because there might not even be time for the necessary cab ride over the bridge to meet her at Kirribilli House. I was alone there with only one power cord that worked for my stuff, and I had to keep swapping my laptop and my phone to keep them both alive while using them both constantly. But I had to risk it and get over the harbour, because the cherry on top of the diary that week was a charity event at Kirribilli House on the Sunday an hour before the launch; so we couldn't even just meet at the CBD speech venue a bit early and finish the work in a green room there. The PM was fair dinkum popping out of the charity reception, walking through the kitchen into the little staff office on the north side of the house, reading new drafts over my shoulder and checking things with the policy advisers, then popping back out to do small talk over cake, before having to come back and do it again.

Yet she had locked herself away in the handful of minutes she had left to her each day – even in Adelaide, where it took her away from precious family time – and sifted the multiple drafts and conflicting staff advice of that week to produce a statement that was Gillard from its first line ('History asks great nations great questions. Australia is no exception . . .') to its last ('Can we be a winner in the Asian Century? Absolutely we can get it done.')

The concept of an Asian Century itself was a key element that shouldn't be underestimated. The PM grasped this and pressed for some of the key implications: it meant economic change, rather than strategic policy, was the centre of gravity; but it took in the wider social and cultural context of change in our region — and unlike the idea of a 'China white paper' proposed by some in business community, the Asian Century ensured India and the Association of Southeast Asian Nations, not just China, were firmly in our thoughts. Some who thought of themselves as friends of the US alliance wanted an 'Asia-Pacific Century' instead. But the paradox that Gillard grasped was that the US alliance was strengthened by being ruled out of the discussion; it was a precept, not a concept, not a problem to be solved but among the starting points for our engagement. (The PM also dismissed the persistent concerns of a handful of political professionals who thought putting 'Asia' on the front page of a major announcement was inexplicable political self-harm in the suburbs.)

Above all, in the white paper speech she spoke of her Labor patriotism — the 'great nation progressive' strain in full flow. She acknowledged Australian achievements ('This is a hard place and we're not angels or saints: the big things are never easy and we don't get everything right. But we stand today, a proud people in a free land. Fifty-first in global population — twelfth in global wealth . . .') and she saw these achievements in essentially progressive, essentially Labor terms ('one of the most equal economies and mobile societies in the world'). This was a real 'I see the future' moment and the PM took it. As a piece of governing, it was important; as a piece of politics, it worked.

—

This all took great determination — to press through the toxic politics of the period, and her own personal grief, and deliver a big statement about something that mattered so much. Her most deranged opponents and her most cynical critics struggled to call her weak, and this showed through most in this period. What Gillard prosaically calls 'the resilience question' — what people, especially women, mean when they say to her, 'How did you get up every day?!' – is still the most commonly asked question of her in post-political life.

Bob Carr speaks for many in his diary when he puts forward the negative view; that it was 'selfishness', and that had he been shown disastrous polling during his own time as premier, he would have 'handed over' the leadership. While this is pretty rugged commentary from a seven-year opposition leader who was certainly not in front every day of those years, at least it focuses on the real question: not so much how, but why?

Among those who didn't know Gillard well or didn't watch her closely, Carr's is not an unusual conclusion. They see her persistence as an exercise in personal ambition, or at best stubborn partisanship; and because so much of the opposition to the PM was bitterly anti–Julia Gillard and bitterly anti-Labor, this isn't a crazy conclusion to draw. It's not as if the opposition bothered to prosecute a serious policy argument against her government. If the conservative case was that Gillard was a bitch and Labor a criminal conspiracy, there's some logic in concluding her motivation in hanging on must have been simply vindication for herself and for her party. But this is to judge Gillard by the standards of her opponents and critics.

More serious and informed observers saw the link between the PM's resilience and her 'got it done' ethic. The day the carbon price bills passed the Parliament on 12 October 2011, journalist Annabel Crabb wrote for ABC *The Drum* online:

> Inside Rudd's office, they used to speak of 'kicking the can down the road' – delaying decisions for a future date by which time conditions, it was hoped, would improve. Of all the criticisms that can validly be made of Julia Gillard's Government, this is not one . . .
>
> Julia Gillard is picking up the can that has been kicked down the road by John Howard, Kevin Rudd and, in his own way, Malcolm Turnbull . . . There's a compelling, almost

cinematic quality to her determination; it's like watching a slalom downhill skier deliberately hitting every peg.

Even the hoary old issue of repairs to The Lodge, urgent recommendations for which have come across the desks of various prime ministers regularly over the last decade, has been picked up by this can-collector of a prime minister, for whom it seems no job is too fraught.

On this reading the PM's courage was almost an act of atonement: 'getting it done' on big progressive reforms, doing things that were hard, was vital work to make satisfaction for the lost Labor opportunities of 2008 and 2009 and the collapse of the Rudd government in 2010. Crabb was writing a few months after the PM had told the press club:

> . . . nothing hard ever gets easier by putting it off to later. And because of that, in the moment I truly believed I was going to be prime minister I told myself: don't ever put off a hard call, because it will only get harder ever day. Be a prime minister, a leader, who sees the future our country can have and has the strength to put in place the plan to get us there.
> That's the leader I'm determined to be for you.

Just as some observers sensed this, some critics tried to carve it out, discounting the PM's determination to achieve things like carbon pricing, disability insurance and better schools as 'legacy hunting'. The urgency in the government in 2012 and 2013 to launch and fund DisabilityCare and the National Plan for School Improvement further provoked this argument – that Labor wanted credit for these changes before we lost office.

I don't accept that at all. The people I worked around and for just wanted these changes to happen before we lost office. If we could give them life, the chance that they would survive a Coalition government would be slim enough; if we deferred, the chance that they would be born under a Coalition government was zero. Whatever you think of the kind of government that winds back free primary healthcare and free emergency treatment in hospitals, you can't think it's the kind of government that establishes national disability insurance or reforms the funding of every school.

But the drive to 'get it done' on 'big Labor reforms' is still a higher recasting of the 'partisan stubbornness' interpretation of the PM. The Asian Century White Paper showed there was something else going on as well: a governing project of growth and modernisation with fairness. Two years into a three-year term, the Gillard project had definite shape. More and more suburbs were connected to the NBN. There was money for DisabilityCare – the insurance scheme was being created and had a launch date of 1 July 2013. The government's National Plan for School Improvement had been released in September, delivering on the so-called Gonski model; the moderate NSW Liberal government, then led by Barry O'Farrell, was working privately to find a way to agree. Education and disability, the big guns of social policy under Gillard, had finally started firing. And yes, by November 2012, twenty years after the Rio Summit and fifteen years after the Kyoto Protocol, the most energy-intensive economy in the world had put a price on carbon.

—

November brought dramatic evidence to inquiries in two states about the extent of child sexual abuse in Australian institutions, including in the Catholic Church. The PM's quiet empathy and her determined rationalism found their moment. On 12 November she announced a royal commission into institutional responses to child sexual abuse. I'm what the Americans call a 'religiously active Catholic', political jargon for a Catholic who goes to mass, and I had an occasional role advising her on relations with the Christian churches; so I was privileged to be part of a number of meetings that Monday where she discussed the options and decided to go ahead. The commission will run for years – I would not be surprised if it runs longer than the Gillard government did – and it will change Australia. This is not an easy discussion to include in an essentially political narrative – especially when the politics was so foully enmeshed in struggles over power and sexuality. But it was a terribly important decision the prime minister made, with lifelong consequences for many people, which ought not be trivialised or forgotten.

—

The Gillard government now had a definite chance. In September and October, the fortnightly Newspoll showed what we politely call 'volatility'. Our primary would go up and down by three points every poll, and the Liberal primary would go up and down by five; the two-party preferred vote went from 55–45 to 50–50 to 54–46 to 50–50 in four fortnights. Landslide–dead heat–landslide–dead heat. The PM's personal popularity recovered very strongly through spring as she went from being behind Abbott by two on the preferred prime minister measure to leading him by nine points. The picture steadied through November: Labor's primary vote was at 36 for another two successive surveys – not long before it had been at 30 per cent – and there were two 51–49 results head to head. Three months earlier, the two-party preferred vote had been 55–45 three polls in a row.

Political analysts who had rolled their eyes at our little 'social media fail' of mid-June when the government spent a few hours promoting the Schoolkids Bonus under the twitter handle #cashforyou – sure, it was a bit crass and was considered counterproductive – had failed to notice that the Schoolkids Bonus meant actual people received support for their living standards from the Gillard government. After a few months of this, along with the tax cuts, family payments and pension increases that accompanied the carbon price, some of those people were deciding that they preferred the Gillard government to the Abbott opposition, which opposed that support for their living standards.

It was a difficult period for those who had written Gillard off. The PM's furious counterattack on Tony Abbott's crazy accusation that she shielded misogyny had plainly lifted her standing, not only among women but among men as well; not just among female police in India and White House staffers but among ordinary people in Australia, who were sick of the insults that stuck to every woman in the country, or for that matter who were just sick of bullshit. The decision of the Liberals in October to bring the farrago of AWU claims into the Parliament reflected their obvious concern at the PM's personal recovery and the government's renewed standing. This hadn't worked; in fact it might even have reinforced the sense that their attack relied on insults and lies, and it might have solidified undecided Labor-leaning voters into our column; the recovery inched on.

—

At the end of 2012 we shared one last long Friday afternoon on her lawn. (The lodge repairs that Crabb had been amazed the PM was prepared to proceed with, even though everyone knew they were needed? Deferred. Actually too tricky for the public service, not for the politicians, after all.) We had fought and survived in government, again; had been a government worth fighting for, again; we even went to the break with the faintest whisper of a fighting chance in 2013.

Sean Kelly was leaving after five years of service as press secretary to two prime ministers and more with Nicola Roxon before that. He just didn't have it in him to front up for yet another campaign, and had the character to know it himself and call time. He'd earned it. I have a nice picture taken as the PM came to sit with a few of us and said, 'Right, I'm on in ten minutes and I need dirt on Kelly NOW.' Her eyes are wide and our mouths are open as we dish anecdotes that she remembered perfectly and delivered flawlessly in a farewell demolition a few minutes later. There was no greater sign of her affection for Sean than this.

My other warm memory of that day is the staff taking time to have a chat with the PM, but being conscious not to monopolise her. I sat nearby with the PM's parliamentary adviser Jo Haylen, who was telling all the best Rob Oakeshott and Tony Windsor stories, while the PM chatted to the cleaners about her nieces and their kids and while the advancers, the advisers who set up picture opportunities on the road, stood further off telling complicated and obscene jokes with the cops. (There's another photo of me searching for my phone in the bushes outside the front doors, taken while the fool who threw it in the bushes yelled at me, 'The cab's coming, quick! We're leaving!' and cackled with delight.) Later that evening in town, I saw a one-legged man dance salsa, something I won't soon forget.

In the unbearable phases of a 27-point primary vote in September 2011 and a 30-point primary vote in May 2012, or when NSW and Queensland Labor were wiped out, proving polls don't just evaporate in a campaign, we had been stoic but not stupid. We never doubted how much trouble we were in. Just so, in November 2012 we had no illusions at all that we were winning. But it was the third quarter of the game and we had halved the lead; governing well was almost enough in itself, and now it looked like it might be working in the community as well. If the carbon tax hadn't wiped Whyalla off the map, maybe it wouldn't wipe us off the map either. The Gillard project had restored purpose and respect to Labor at great cost in public support; but now it was eliminating the prospect of a wipe-out and just possibly creating the faintest prospect of a win.

For so long, we'd been outfought by our insurgent opponent. At last, at least, we were outgoverning him.

# INTERLUDE:
# the shy child

*They knew his limitations as well as his strengths and honoured him for all and despite all.*

FIN CRISP, ON CHIFLEY'S COLLEAGUES

You go to a function in your first summer as an adviser to the prime minister. You sit down next to a bloke you've sort of heard of, who's heard of you, but you don't think you've met before. You say cagey things like, 'It's good to meet you properly,' so if you have shaken hands before you're covered, and he says cagey things like, 'What are you reading over the break?' to start conversation – and when you say, 'Oh, a biography of TJ Ryan,' his eyes widen before you can explain who Ryan is – and he leans in and says, 'Really? Do you know much about Hugh Mahon? I'm researching a monograph' – and you smile and lean back a bit and you say, 'Oh, we're going to need another bottle of red on the table,' and you set your phone alarm so you won't miss the plane.

The Earl of Arran once mock-apologetically began one of his 'I know famous people' society newspaper columns with 'here is another Royal story'. Oh, well.

In January 2011, I hatched a plan to come off leave for a day while the PM was in Sydney to meet her and talk about some forums which we were planning, three events at which the PM would speak without notes and explain the government's approach for the year on climate, the economy and schools before taking questions from citizens. (As it happened, the floods in Queensland and around the country intervened and the events were largely modified and deferred.) She was in Sydney in order to host a reception for the Ashes teams at Kirribilli and to attend the third day of the Test match at the SCG, which doubles as a major fundraising day for the McGrath Foundation.

So I had a cunning thought: clock back on to work, fly to Sydney in the morning, meet her in the offices in the city and brief her early in the day. Do half a day's work, then go with the press secs in the staff car behind C1 to the cricket ground, where I'd accepted an invitation to the SCG Trust lunch from a friend in the law. I'd also get an introduction to a couple of key stakeholders who would be at lunch at the ground.

Unfortunately the PM took a look at her diary, said, 'That's silly, don't bring Michael off leave all the way from Melbourne to talk to me for an hour – I'll just read the material on the plane and if I need him to explain anything I'll call him on the phone.'

The acting chief of staff did his best, but without selling me out on my cricket plans he couldn't convince the PM to keep my meeting in the diary. He rang me the night before: 'No meeting, mate, sorry – what do you want to do?'

The flights were already booked and I had work to do in the Sydney office anyway (sort of), and I'd promised to be introduced to Cardinal Pell at the lunch in my role as the PM's contact for faith groups (not even sort of; really, I had), so I said, 'Look, mate, I'll just come up; what's the worst that can happen. See you in the Phillip Street office before nine.'

Well, the worst that can happen is the PM can spend the morning at Kirribilli reading up, then come into the Trust lunch at the

SCG, instantly spot her speechwriter about eighty metres away hiding behind a brimming glass of club red, a dubious pink tie and a seriously unkempt Christmas beard, and shout at him across the dining room that it was suddenly clear why he had said he needed an urgent meeting in Sydney and not to think she'd forget this outrageous abuse of her diary time.

At this point, Joe Hockey, Dyson Heydon, Kerry Chikarovski, Steve Waugh, Sir Michael Parkinson and – oh God, I've only just as I write this story realised probably the cardinal too – all sitting between me and the PM, are asking each other, 'Who's the bloke in the corner with a beard?' The next volley over their heads from the PM? 'What's with the beard, anyway!? I'm not sure I want anyone on my staff who looks like a terrorist!' (They were happier days.)

That's basically the worst that can happen. Oh, and Australia can lose the Test. But the Hugh Mahon conversation was a ripper.

She paid me out for months about both the beard and the cricket freebies (and gave a fair bit of proxy stick to the MPs and journalists who presented for Parliament in February with beards too – sorry Denis, Phil and Rob, it was mostly my fault) and in the end I really had no choice but to get drunk at a reception in Washington DC to give her a new subject to mock me about. She loved it; and as far as I could tell, she was like that with just about everyone she knew.

People ask me: what is Julia Gillard really like? As a person, she is resilient, game, proud, yes; she has character to burn. Above all, though, Julia Gillard is funny and fun. Humour is at the core of her character and at the heart of her personal style.

When Ben Hubbard, her chief of staff when she was deputy PM, returned to her office as chief of staff in the PMO, she told quite a few of us that she was disappointed that as prime minister she didn't go through airport security with him any more, because in the good old days he'd fairly regularly had to take his artificial leg off at X-ray machines, and it always brightened her day to see a grown man hop through a checkpoint before breakfast. He loved hearing this.

She gave people animal nicknames, like Monkey and Komodo, and joked about the 'jazz hands' she used as a protective barrier in press conferences and in doorways; and in morning press conferences she kept Matthew Franklin (then with *The Australian*, later a Rudd press secretary) at bay by regularly inquiring after his mood and whether he'd had his coffee. She was a practised observer of the people around her and kept an eye on all of us for material to work us over with. When staff (or officials, or MPs) were talking at morning meetings around Parliament House or on the road, you could see her scanning for who was tired and who was bright so she could pay them out about it; and she could always tell if one of the office units had been out late on the tiles or if a staff romance was heating up (or cooling off).

So when I think about Julia Gillard, the first thing I think about, even before her resilience, is her laughter.

I see her at the Lodge with staff for the last of her first chief of staff Amanda Lampe's farewells early in 2011. Laughing at me for talking to US diplomats at Jimmy Watson's, back when I was working for Per Capita, and laughing about this being news in light of Wikileaks; then laughing at the nervous legal adviser (Komodo), who said I really should stop doing that; then laughing again when Richard Maude exploded and said, 'That's just bullshit, of course he should keep talking to our friends!'

I see her watching Lodge cricket at the office Christmas party at the end of the same year and laughing as I dismissed Ben Hubbard with my first and last ball of the game (flight, drift, turn, edge... catch it, Matty Jose! Got him! Oh, YES YES YES!) and roared down the wicket in triumph to embrace a terrified media assistant standing at silly point while the wicketkeeper, staffer-for-life Matt Jose, mopped his brow with the ball. Laughing a few minutes later as I attempted a slog sweep, and the bat flew out of my hand and straight at Ben's head at square leg, where he was checking his phone, heedless of impending doom; laughing again when it hit him flat on the chest and my possibly Freudian attempts to kill him and ruin Christmas failed.

Each of her laughs was inflected with the slightest of variations, like a Fred Williams series. And those are only my stories; everyone who knew her has their own.

I see her laughing at all of us the year after, at our last Lodge Christmas; we were outside drinking on the lawns when a helicopter flew overhead and we spontaneously hid our faces, as if we were rugby league players on Mad Monday being filmed by Channel 7. Or at our very first Lodge Christmas, laughing and shaking her head as Carl sat by the pool and solemnly asked what it was like to sleep in the room next to where Curtin died.

If you don't have a sense of the ridiculous in that job, you'll go mad (it's happened), and the PM had the most wonderful way of widening her eyes when people said odd things, as people do from time to time to prime ministers, or when she related the tale afterwards ('and then Sarkozy said to me, "After all, there were no Chinese at Villers-Bretonneux" – right there at the table!'); either because she was listening carefully, or because she was trying not to raise her eyebrows or laugh.

God, she laughed and made us laugh, and I think most of the people who worked closely with her over the years miss that the most. At the same time I marvel at her ability to remain in command while employing that bantering style, to never betray the authority of her position in the process. David Marr identified this with her professional background:

> Her measured aggression, the professional poise she brings to the most brutal contest, the lacerating tongue and the disarming jokes are a style perfected years ago by woman lawyers. What seems exceptional in parliament has long been familiar in the courts.

She had a sense of humour and a sense of the ridiculous, and yet at the same time she had complete control of a room; she could put you in your place and give you a story to tell your grandkids all at once. But she'd pat you on the arm long before she'd kiss you on the cheek. Her humour wasn't simply a tool, not quite a shield between her and others, it was genuine and a part of her – but it's true that it did form a protective outer layer, and was part of the reserve of her nature.

Maybe this is why I remember a funny boss and many people remember a dour prime minister.

You have to see reserve as part of the Gillard personality. Her reserve was a way of maintaining her strength. (It was also exaggerated by a natural if excessive reaction to Rudd's enfeebling populism, and I am sure it contributed to the perception that she could be mechanical or wooden in her public performances. She was not always an engaging actor.) Naturally enough, she didn't often expand upon the origins of her reserve, but she has discussed it.

In that Adelaide speech to introduce herself, in her first weeks in office in 2010, she had briefly spoken about her upbringing as 'a shy child'. In a *Women's Weekly* interview in her final weeks in office in 2013, the PM told Caroline Overington that whenever her prime ministership ended and however her legacy was considered, her sister Alison would still be amazed that it was Julia who rose to become PM: Julia, the 'shy one', the 'one who was less forthcoming'. And on a famous occasion at the National Press Club, on 14 July 2011, the PM spoke at greater length about the connection between this aspect of her personality and the leadership she tried to give the country.

> I was the shy girl who studied and worked hard . . . and it took time and effort but I got from Unley High to the law and as far as here, where I am today. I've brought a sense of personal reserve to this, the most public of professions. And the rigours of politics have reinforced my innate style of holding a fair bit back in order to hang pretty tough. If that means people's image of me is one of steely determination, I understand why.

But I don't forget where I come from, why I'm here, or what I've learned along the way.

I don't forget Unley High, where I saw kids who sat at the back of the room and did 'make work' and were left behind. I don't forget how I felt at Slaters when I won my first case on behalf of an outworker. I got her paid what she deserved, and she just said, quietly, 'Thanks'. I don't forget September 2008 when the world stood on the brink of economic disaster and it took a Labor government and urgent action, decisions right in the moment, to save jobs and businesses.

As she spoke, I was watching from a lunch table a few feet away, with a copy of the speech in my hand, checking against delivery. I never found watching major speeches particularly easy, especially on a table with strangers at a function; having the text to look down to at hand gave me something to concentrate on. I needed it. When she came to speak about Unley and the kids left behind – something she'd done often in the past – she was brought near to tears.

Gillard's reserve was a necessary professional protection in the immediate circumstances of dealings with colleagues, opponents and reporters. Obviously her reserve had its origins in her personal essence, and was present in her own shyness as a child. But what I thought I saw that day was how her reserve was also a kind of bridge between the way she viewed her background and the way she viewed her purpose. It was intimately connected to the difficulty of the things she wanted to achieve. By that I mean that I think that day she could see how little separated her father's life, the life of the kids in the Unley back row, and her own – and how much more separated her from the kind of people who go to see a prime minister speak at a press club lunch. She wasn't just reserved among the people she dealt with as prime minister, because opening up was exhausting or they might judge her harshly; she was reserved among them because with many of them she had little in common, and with many of them she shared no common cause. Looking out at a room like that one, at all the established and complacent faces, didn't just reinforce how far she'd come herself – it reinforced how far she'd left the back-row kids behind, how great her responsibility was to them, and how alone she was in the politics of getting it done.

Don Watson later wrote in *The Monthly* that at the press club that day, the 'Oprahisation' of Australian politics was completed; that those tears were a surrender to 'the maw of magazine culture and afternoon television, and taking the office with her'. There was a high price to pay for letting the visor up.

So the personal reserve and the Labor purpose were inseparable. The background brought forth the purpose, each brought forth the reserve, and in some ways the legendary resilience was just an outward expression of all three. But they had their cost.

Shakespeare's Coriolanus was prepared to serve: 'I do owe them still/My life and services.' But when his friend Menenius begged him to show the people the wounds he won fighting for them at the gate of Corioli, he feared he'd blush.

> Let me o'erleap that custom, for I cannot
> Put on the gown, stand naked and entreat them.

Coriolanus was already elected consul – no one doubted he'd fought and won in war. The tribunes and the people knew that he'd bled for Rome. What they were looking for wasn't proof of his war record, it was proof that he wanted their support.

Gillard's reserve was a heavy barrier to the wider task of communicating with Australians who could never know her privately and relied on her media performances to understand her leadership. It made it hard for her to humble herself before the people; to tell them they were right and she wanted their support to deliver for them. Without being silly about it, if you keep telling people popularity doesn't matter to you, they can be inclined to reward you by agreeing that you don't need to be popular. People do want their leaders to be strong – and

Gillard was strong. She had a will 'like a dividing spear'. (There's a slender irony that in this, as in so much, she far more closely resembled Hugh Gaitskell than Aneurin Bevan.) But that doesn't mean they want you to be strong enough to use the forces of government to do things they don't want you to do. It means they want you to be strong enough to overcome all the countervailing forces of the economy and society that stop you using the forces of government to do things they do want you to do, things the public knows its nation needs. And the handy thing is, if you're a progressive, you'll believe that what is good for the great mass of the people is precisely what is good for the nation because they *are* the nation; and you don't even have to be progressive, you just have to be a democrat, to believe that the public *does* know what it needs, when it expresses itself deliberately in elections, and so delivering for them turns out to be the right thing to do as well.

And sometimes, you just have to make them smile; to say something they like hearing. In the film of *Primary Colors*, presidential candidate Jack Stanton lectures his staff:

> You don't think that Abraham Lincoln was a whore before he was president? He had to tell his little stories and smile his shit-eating backcountry grin.

Most of the days she was in office, giving the people everything of her 'life and services', Julia Gillard just couldn't give them that.

Funny; reserved and resilient, even to her cost. And she's so unmistakably Australian.

As a small boy I thought 'bird' was simply the feminine form of 'bloke' (thanks, Dad) and it took me a while to work out that not all Australian women see it that way. (Maybe it's just that I can't get away with it; maybe I'm just no Michael Caine.) So, look, if there's a better word, let me know and I'll use it. Til then, for me, Julia Gillard is a great Aussie bird.

To me this always was (is now) one of the most attractive parts of her personality and it was good gear for a speechwriter too. I could mine the Labor-friendly end of the Australian legends of fairness and solidarity and what John Hirst calls our 'egalitarianism of manners' — here Jack's as good as his master, blokes like Jack stick together, they get their fair share. I loved knowing that Gillard believed what D H Lawrence wrote about Australia many decades ago should always be true: 'Nobody felt BETTER than anybody else, or higher; only better-off.' It also meant I could mine her interviews and the speeches she had given before my time for statements about Australia and put them up in drafts to be repeated as often as I dared.

Both her strengths and weaknesses were in some way characteristic of the people she led. She meant it when she said her parents had taught her it was wrong to view yourself as better than the person who waits on you in a restaurant. (At Adelaide Town Hall she once added 'or at a flash town hall lunch'.) She meant it when she spoke of 'the snobbishness and expectations of obsequiousness that infect other societies' and she smiled when she compared this to the warm informalities she experienced as prime minister.

—

That egalitarianism of manners does mean Australians have a bit of trouble accepting help. We like to carry our own bags; this doesn't always make sense.

John McTernan wrote in a fond column after Gillard's defeat that as education minister she had liked to type up the communiqués which were the final record of decision for education ministerial councils. Her typing was accurate and fast and I think she enjoyed looking down to earth. I can picture it too; to be honest, I don't smile. For a long time I had used Julia's fast typing as my preferred example of the difference between relative and comparative advantage; it still isn't rational for a principal decision-maker to type even if she *is* the fastest typist in the office.

On one appalling occasion during our time in opposition I walked over to her suite from the leader's office to negotiate some minor late changes to a speech she was to give to the National Press Club in a few hours' time. She wasn't happy about it, but righto, let's do it, and we went through to her desk. Not long after, her press sec called out from the other room, 'Cameras!' and a crew from *Australian Story* walked into her office to find the shadow minister for health typing and some bloke leaning over her shoulder pointing to bits on the screen he wanted her to edit. God knows how bad this footage actually looked — fortunately the producers evidently didn't, and it never went to air.

She got better at accepting help and letting people fill in the details in the prime ministership. But the 'finisher' in Gillard still liked to sign off the details, to dot the i's and cross the t's herself, and remove the Oxford commas. (They were her only apparent neurosis.) The public service installed the first ever computer on a prime minister's desk when Julia Gillard became PM. Astonishing.

And overall, office didn't change her much, in any sense. She was a bit more careful, because mistakes hurt more and when she wasn't careful she sometimes made some; she did some new things, because she had a new job. Some people (especially Canberra journalists) thought Julia Gillard 'changed' in office — became more cautious, spoke less engagingly — and it's a generous explanation in some ways, explaining away a political weakness, but I'm not sure it's right. The same Gillard had been there all along, even the caution; what changed most of all was that everyone looked at her differently after 24 June 2010.

The PM's most formal expression of her Australian sentiment as it connected to the purpose of her politics was to cite historian Gavan Daws on Changi and mateship. I first saw her speak about this in a speech in opposition in the early 2000s; while in office, she sometimes returned to it in interviews with overseas magazines and in other remarks. She made a particular point of it at that 'flash town hall lunch' in Adelaide, in the weeks after Queensland and so much of the rest of the country flooded, during that first summer of her prime ministership, at that Adelaide Australia Day address.

> When things get hard, Australians stick together. We just do. I've long admired what historian Gavan Daws said about the Allied prisoners of war under the Japanese in places like Changi:
>
> '. . . all the way down to starvation rations, to a hundred pounds of body weight and less, to the extremities of degradation – all the way to death – the prisoners of the Japanese remained inextinguishably American, Australian, British. The Americans were the great individualists of the camps. The British hung on to their class structure like bulldogs.
>
> And the Australians kept trying to construct little male-bonded welfare states.'
>
> While time has moved on, and today we have moved beyond simply 'male bonding' and 'welfare states', when things are tough . . . Australian mateship comes through. Over this devastating summer, Australians have reached out to each other with the hand of mateship and we haven't let go. The force of the story about Aussies in Changi isn't the mateship that was shown on the first day of imprisonment, it is that the mateship endured through the continuing hell.

That's Julia Gillard: an Australian who passionately believed that the harder things get, the more like ourselves we should become ('Don't let go', she said in the same speech – don't let go of each other, don't let go of our own best selves); and that means sharing. So yes, Julia Gillard delivered a flood levy that year; and people who were better-off paid a lot more than people who weren't.

Tom Keneally spoke about Gillard's utopian Australianism at the University of Melbourne five months after that Australia Day address. He compassed some of the inevitable liberal cosmopolitan scepticism that patriotism can ever be a progressive force, or that the idea

Australia is unusually egalitarian is anything more than a myth – but in defence of Julia Gillard (and Russel Ward) he reflected:

> In this century, though, is the invocation of utopian brotherhood a delusion to be pitied? Is it mere mythology (if mythology can be mere), is it mythology in the modern and regrettable misusage by which the word is a synonym for a lie? I believe that the utopian myths can be a positive force in Australia, especially now, to help guarantee some minimum standards of dignity . . . as frequently as that expectation of the fair go might have been thwarted in this century, do we want it to vanish?

I know Julia Gillard didn't. Referring to the very floods that had prompted her speech, Keneally gave a striking example. A man whose house was ruined and whose insurance policy failed 'through a technicality' to protect him told the ABC, 'I mean, this is Australia, isn't it?' Keneally concluded:

> He, like the rest of us, assumes that special arrangements of fairness, and treatment along sensible, practical, fraternal lines, are part of the Australian fabric and inheritance. He is no doubt cruelly cured of that illusion now.

Gillard's utopian Australianism wasn't only expressed in speeches. She (and her responsible minister, Bill Shorten) made the insurance companies change those technicalities after they were revealed by the floods.

—

And every summer that she spent as prime minister, Gillard came closer to mastering that very Australian accomplishment of maintaining a polite interest in cricket with people around you who are obsessed with it. She hosted receptions at Kirribilli for the Test teams and at the Lodge for her own XI, supported the McGrath Foundation at Sydney in January each year, and, of course, half-listened to her bloke's reflections on pitch conditions and selections of teams. It was part of the job. It also meant that for her speeches on cricket occasions I had an outlet for all the cricket trivia stored up in my brain (and so did Carl) because we certainly weren't competing with her favourite childhood cricket tales.

You could also always suggest a self-deprecating story to Julia Gillard without fear she'd be offended. For her first PM's XI, with the help of the journalist Greg Growden, I dug up an anecdote that played nicely on the occasional commentary about her 'broad' accent and whether this was quite prime ministerial, comments which always annoyed me because I knew her voice was hardly without precedent. (The great Fin Crisp's loyal and fond Chifley biography has an entire index entry for that 'harsh and hacking' instrument. 'CHIFLEY, J. B.: – his Voice, 29–30, 34, 99, 286n, 410'.) Well, in 1950, the Canberra journalist and former Australian opener Jack Fingleton helped the English fast bowler Harold Larwood settle in Australia. On short notice, it was Fingleton who asked Ben Chifley, by then opposition leader, to help find Larwood housing. (Chifley was happy to help, later saying of the English, 'I think that Larwood was too good for you chaps.') A house was no easy thing to find in times of shortage and Fingleton later arranged a meeting for Larwood to say thank you. As Gillard told it, Fingleton recalled:

> I told Larwood when he arrived he should come to Canberra and thank Mr Chifley. He was delighted to do so. I took him in and Larwood, in his thick Notts accent, thanked Mr Chifley. Chif, as he was known, looked in some amazement at me.
> 'What did he say, Jack?' he asked. I interpreted. Then Mr Chifley, in his nasal Australian tones, said some nice words

about Larwood, who looked at me.

'What did he say, Jack?' asked Larwood.

The Gillard punchline to that story?

And you all thought I was unique.

The two PMs, Gillard and Chifley, shared a bit.

When I think about some of Gillard's bravest policy decisions, above all to price carbon pollution, and reflect on our failures to campaign for them successfully in government, I think of Crisp's description of Saturday 16 August 1947: a day of wonder. As Chifley walked out of the cabinet room in the old Parliament House, he was doorstopped by 'pressmen' (Crisp's word) asking for news of any decisions, and replied, 'Oh, Don [Rodgers, his press secretary] may have a little piece in there that'll interest you.' It was a forty-two-word announcement that there would be legislation to nationalise the banks. Supposedly one of the 'pressmen' bit right through his own pipe, which fell on the parquetry floor. Nationalisation had been in Labor's platform for twenty-seven years and through three terms of federal Labor government; the private banks had been given their chance to work with Labor to modernise monetary policy under the 1945 banking bills and they'd blown it; eleven months after being re-elected, Chifley just wasn't going to kick the can down the road any more. Over the next two years, he lost the argument, in a 'nationwide furore'.

(Chifley was also the subject of fantastical attacks on his private finances from former colleagues, especially the gang who hung around former NSW premier Jack Lang; claims forgotten in the years except as a reflection on his accusers.)

And Crisp records that when Chifley gave a warm fighting speech in Brisbane, a supporter interjected: 'Why didn't you give us a speech like that over the wireless the other night?' Ah well. I suppose Chifley was more at ease without notes than he was reading a script. Certainly Gillard was.

What is Julia Gillard really like?

She isn't perfect. She has a few of Ben Chifley's weaknesses and some all her own.

She is also smart and tough, proud of her origins. A woman of immense purpose and enormous will. A great Aussie bird, a person with a hinterland, a humble person who sometimes doesn't like help. She has an accent.

She was a shy child. She is the Labor Party's loyal daughter.

# PART FOUR

# SMALL HAMMERS

# 12.

# Now or never

*For the information of the house, I have determined that there will be a ballot for the leadership and deputy leadership of the Labor Party at four-thirty today. In the meantime, take your best shot.*

PRIME MINISTER JULIA GILLARD

We believed we'd ended 2012 outgoverning our opponent. We knew 2013 was an election year and if we wanted to keep governing, we had to do more. We had to win some politics now, right now, or the Gillard government was gone. Now or never.

The PM's last weekend at work in 2012 was the real start of 2013. She was in Canberra, and on Sunday 16 December, she met the deputy PM and treasurer Wayne Swan at the Lodge for two hours in the afternoon. They were preparing for yet another press conference at which Wayne would take one for the team. He'd been doing it for years.

Way back on 28 May 2008, Wayne and his then assistant Chris Bowen had fronted a mid-evening press conference to respond to what was, in some respects, the Rudd government's first crisis: the leaking of cabinet advice against the proposed Fuelwatch scheme, which was designed to help consumers compare petrol prices. In

2008 I was still in the woods of exile (or more precisely, on the couch of exile) and I happened to be watching TV that Wednesday night. The leak was particularly damaging because it was assumed by many outside observers who thought they had some insight (people like me) to have come from the minister for resources, Martin Ferguson, a fully enrolled member of Club Sensible and a seriously sincere advocate for the interests of the industry sector within his administrative responsibility (though the passage of the years leaves one to wonder if Godwin Grech, later of Utegate notoriety, didn't have a role to play). Regardless of where the leak came from, and no matter what else you say about Wayne, you certainly can't deny his preparedness to throw himself on a hand grenade. If his (and Chris's) performance that night didn't defuse the controversy, it certainly contained the blast.

Four and half years later and Wayne had more than a hand grenade to throw himself on: he was sitting on a million pounds of ammonium nitrate under the Messines Ridge. Revenue had gone down for the third time and the surplus we had promised for three years, and announced on budget night 2012, was gone. Finance Minister Penny Wong would soon have to release financial statements for October showing the revenue shortfall already outdid our $1.1 billion projected surplus. Wayne would follow this with a statement that surplus was now unlikely, and that the government would not make further cuts to achieve it. All this was to happen this coming week, while the PM was on leave.

So on 20 December, Wayne squared his shoulders, walked into the 'blue room' for the press conference, and told them we weren't going to get a surplus, because we weren't going to keep cutting spending: 'It's not because the Government is spending too much, it's because we didn't collect the amount of taxes that we expected to collect.' The fiscal breastplate of the 2010 campaign, the promise of a surplus as stimulus wound down, had become the 'other lie', to go with the carbon tax.

Political commentary fell into two camps – those who misunderstood the economy and those who ignored it. The conservatives said it proved we had mismanaged the economy, while liberal critics said it proved we had mismanaged the politics. Other critics further to Labor's left focused on renewing individual spending proposals like lifting the unemployment benefit – with the surplus now gone, what was another billion or two on the spending side?

Economic commentary was kinder. Few disputed the actual decision, to stop cutting as revenue drained away; economists were also humbler about making hindsight judgements of the plans of 2010, knowing the price we had paid for accepting their profession's best advice in forecast.

Yes, from the start, right back in 2010, we should have retained a forecast of a surplus without turning it into a commitment and then into a guarantee. The overall scale of spending constraint and fiscal consolidation was vital, but the eventual moment of moving from deficit to surplus was just a politically symbolic point on that journey not an economically important goal. Those with sufficient understanding and moderation to make the critique in this version also usually had sufficient proportion and experience to know that, in substance, it was a pretty fine set of distinctions to make about two-year-old political language that had served its purpose at the time. (And that the theoretical distinction between 'forecast' and 'guarantee' only became a practical difference because the forecasts turned out to be wrong.)

This was also a commentary on the political decision to adopt the surplus target 'in three years' time, three years ahead of schedule' back in 2010, not on the economic decision of 2012 to stop cutting while revenue fell. The decision was right, which was why neither the facts nor the ratings agencies deserted us: the day Wayne Swan said that we weren't spending too much, government spending as a proportion of the economy was still lower than its average over the life of the Howard government; and the day Wayne Swan said we wouldn't reach a budget surplus, we had triple-A credit ratings from the three major agencies, something the Howard government never achieved.

—

Over summer, my great mate Jim Chalmers left the government. On my first day back, two and half years earlier, I'd turned up with a pie and a can of Coke like we used to share at uni, saying, 'Sorry I'm three years late, are there any Tories left to beat?' I made a habit of watching my one game of rugby league a year in his office with pizza, when Origin was on a sitting night. In November, in a few minutes away from drafting the UN General Assembly speech, I'd lit a candle in St Patrick's Cathedral New York and sent him a photo captioned, 'For you in Rankin.' Now he was off to to lock himself up to write a book; and hopefully win federal preselection sooner or later in Logan City, where he had lived most of his life. It wasn't going to be easy not seeing him around, but I was looking forward to reading his work.

Summer took Jim, but it brought back my old staff buddy Jo Fox from London and from the staff past, to have dinner at social researcher (and former adviser) Rebecca Huntley's place in Balmain, with Keating minister Michael Lavarch and Annabel Crabb and a few others. I feel quite the country cousin on these occasions. Fox laughed about her London television channel PR staff winning over broadcast boffins ('I unleashed my crack team of eyelashes'). Crabb laughed about some terrible book, and wondered whether anyone wrote good female characters anyway, and I triumphantly offered up Frank Moorhouse. Mmm, they said, Edith Campbell-Berry, true. I knew there was a reason I'd read *Grand Days*. Huntley and Lavarch debated the surplus – Huntley reminding us that no one raises the surplus in social-research group discussions; Lavarch countering that while that was, of course, true, the abandonment of the commitment hurts as a symbol of competence, as well as of trust. After dinner, he and I talked ourselves into an optimism of the will: we've got all year, Abbott's still really unpopular, the worst of carbon is behind us, and Liberal premier Campbell Newman is going bonkers with cuts in Queensland; you have to give us some chance. Lavarch's parting words were something like, 'She's a rather strong figure, your boss.'

It was a serendipitous summer of cricket against Sri Lanka – it was, and felt like it was, an interregnum between big tours. Matthew Wade was picked, a fresh face from Victoria who faded on the fans over time, and in Sydney he nearly won the Test on his own with the batting gloves and nearly lost it on his own with the keeper's gloves. Having bowled an over on the final day in Hobart with no impact, within three Tests he'd achieved all possible outcomes in all possible disciplines, which is more than I can say in any field, cricket above all. While the PM marked the third day of the Test with her customary attendance and support for a range of functions, I'd finally worn out my welcome on the Trust (Cavalier definitely read the McGregor book). I watched from the Ladies Stand with the PM's parliamentary adviser Jo Haylen and my old Per Capita mate David Hetherington and made Ashes plans. Haylen had some stupid inner-west dinner party to go to after the cricket; I had a message from Damian Kassabgi saying we were meeting for a swim with Ben Buckler, who I didn't know, and to come to the Rocks at North Bondi. The next few hours redeemed Bondi for me, and almost made Sydney a place I look forward to visiting.

It didn't sound all that promising. I don't really get beaches in the city – for me, a beach is supposed to be like Guerilla Bay on the NSW South Coast. And Bondi had traumatic overtones. The worst Sunday morning of my life had been spent there only two months earlier, trapped in Kassabgi's kitchen making late changes to the Asian Century speech. (This still gave me flashbacks two years later when I went to make a cup of coffee in that kitchen and had a shiver run right up my spine.)

So my prejudices and I got in a cab together at the SCG and read the instructions off my phone to the driver – this street, that street, and then I'm going to the Rocks at North Bondi. I was expecting some appalling Sydney casual dining venue with a pointless postcard view. When I got there, I discovered it was the actual rocks.

And I walked onto the rocks and around the corner of this apartment block that was seriously almost in the ocean, and there were all these staffers and friends, Sean Kelly and Lachlan Harris, and Jim Chalmers ('Mate! Where have you been!') and Laura Anderson and Maggie Lloyd, and seriously twenty other people I knew and hadn't expected to see, all bobbing up and down in the water drinking beer while dogs swam around them and hipster weightlifters strolled past. It was just heaven. I borrowed Harris's spare swimmers and we cooled off in the ocean for an hour, and then the troupe walked back round the beach, bumping into more friends on the way – at this point I told Kassabgi it was a bit like a dream – and got fish and chips and riesling and all the pale ale in the world and went back up the hill to DK's place. Amit Singh arrived and Chalmers and I told him he was never allowed to leave – not this night, not staff work, nothing. Stay.

There were Rudd staff and Gillard staff and people who'd worked for both and for neither, and we told stories and made animated argument into the night. Granted, I woke up on a couch with salt water in my beard and Lachlan Harris's swimmers on, disturbing details at any time. But finally, Mum and Dad weren't there, and the kids didn't have to take sides. We should have filmed it and screened it at a meeting of our sullen, divided caucus, and made the poor bastards write a short essay about what they saw and whether they were jealous of our unity. I'll never forget it.

—

While we enjoyed this Christmas truce for staff on the second front, the PM had her mind on the contest with the Libs. She'd taken the time over the break to develop in writing her thoughts on the essential political argument for the election year, 2013. It was time well spent.

The eighteen-hundred-word 'open letter to the nation' she drafted herself over the break was released on the second Sunday in January; it was a cracker, and for the speechwriters we knew our job was going to be a lot easier. We'd just need some elegant variation on this text: it was a stump speech for the whole year. It had some personal reflections; a strong statement that we could never go back to easier times; a strong statement of optimism in our capacity to succeed in these times. Then a fresh characterisation of Australia as 'strong, fair and smart': economically strong; fair – in a characteristically social democratic way; but also smart – with the stimulus, 1980s reform and Medicare offered as examples both of Australian policy ingenuity and political maturity. Then the plan – reflections on the achievements of 2011 and 2012, and the priorities for 2013: jobs, school improvement, disability insurance. It was striking to hear schools and disability characterised as strengthening our society and families in challenging times, and as smart solutions for a complicated challenge, not just as big fairness projects. And she wrote briefly – movingly – about 'the benefits of being my father's daughter': the man who fired her passion for education and taught her 'it is important to have people you look up to but you must never look down on anyone'. This work, and a series of meetings in the final week of January, was preparation for opening the political year at the National Press Club, in a speech to be given after the Australia Day weekend.

For the press club I ground out a draft based on her open letter, top-and-tailed with some 'how we live now' facts and a bit more of a 'plan for the year' expressed as a determined timetable (budget, the Council of Australian Governments, the introduction of the national disability insurance scheme [NDIS] on 1 July).

This was interesting on its own terms – and the economic analysis of cost of living, the phases of the mining boom, the high dollar and the revenue pressures on the budget were described as 'tough and correct' by economic commentator Ross Gittins – but there wasn't a clear call to action; it was all good prose, without an ending or an announcement. But the PM seemed relaxed. At our meeting a few days before the speech, I pressed about the ending and the PM said, 'Oh, look I'll work on the conclusion myself a bit,' and my spidey sense really tingled. I actually wondered if she might be going to call the election in the speech. Instead, the PM announced the election date, for 14 September.

The PM briefed us on this the following day, making it clear the intention was a surprise announcement at the press club, and I loved it because I am biased in favour of anything bold. She hoped to end early election speculation in the following six months, which was growing despite the fact we were never going to go to an election early when we were well behind, in order to create space in the news for her own campaign priorities. In reality, 14 September was also one of only about three genuine options separated by a matter of one or two weeks – we weren't losing flexibility by picking the date when we did.

The other blokes were a bit wide-eyed, but I was grinning my head off. I am clearly an idiot. The announcement was widely ridiculed.

The rehabilitated former Labor Party official Graham Richardson unloaded with a withering, albeit rather self-conscious column in *The Australian* ('I am obviously past it because I simply don't understand Labor politics any more. Given that greater minds than mine were no doubt applied to the announcement of an election date eight months in advance . . .') and when the following days brought the announcement that Attorney-General Nicola Roxon and Senate leader Chris Evans would depart the cabinet now and not seek re-election in September, we were declared a club-in-crisis, again, and having to defend her judgement, again. Right or wrong, once a politician is having to defend their political judgement against critics, they are in an unwinnable, circular argument in which if you disagree with the collective judgement of commentators, your judgement is wrong by definition, because you've mismanaged media perceptions. (A small case study in gallery management for future operators, but hardly a matter for history.) In this respect, I came to wonder if tactical surprise in a big announcement is any advantage now; at times I felt commentators resented being out of the loop (Richardson certainly did) and reporters felt rushed to respond to actual breaking news, and they all punished us for catching them out. (An alternative explanation for their criticism is that the decision was just as mad as everyone said. It's a logical possibility.) Finally, we found out after the speech that 14 September was Yom Kippur. *Mazel tov.*

Between the last caucus meeting of 2012 and the first caucus meeting of 2013, we'd lost the surplus, lost two ministers, and been slaughtered on our first big announcement of the year. (At least the PM's cricket team had won its match.)

I hadn't had time to find out (or possibly hadn't been silly enough to ask) what she thought of the negative commentary on all this. But the day after caucus met, 5 February, Michelle Grattan left *The Age*, a funny moment of parochial-historical significance, a bit like John Kennedy leaving Hawthorn. The PM acknowledged this in Parliament, recalling that before there was a female governor-general, prime minister or Speaker, there was 'Cobber'; and in a wry take on the negative reaction to the election announcement and reshuffle asked the House:

> What explains the timing of this announcement? Who spoke to who about this announcement? Who was consulted about this announcement? And how long can this chaos in the press gallery go on? I do ask myself these questions.

In my three years of working for the prime minister there were elements of growth and progress, and elements of repetition and regeneration. It is fair to say the basic January experience – cricket days, Australia Day, natural disaster site visit, agenda-setting speech for year, prepare for February political crisis – was in the latter category. Through those three Januarys we would make our own history, but not as we pleased; in February, the facts would repeat, but as farce every time. I told you it almost made me a Marxist.

This was now or never time. But February was a curate's egg; not just because it was 'good in parts', but because when you are talking about an egg, or about the beginning of an election year, 'good in parts' means bad. To have any chance of continuing our end-2012 progress in cutting into the Coalition's lead we had to make every post a winner – instead, we were clipping every peg. Mid-month, we launched years of work on industry, innovation, clean energy and new technology – the serious policy challenge of future economic and employment growth in a high-dollar mining-boom economy – and morphed it into a crude 'plan for Aussie jobs' Sunday tabloid sell, on purpose. It was immediately written off as a concession to the PM's union supporters and a reflection of our political connections to the old economy.

Then at the end of the month, we campaigned in Sydney's west and south-west for a few days, with the PM staying in a hotel next to the licensed club at Rooty Hill; we made a complete circus of ourselves in the process. From the room I stayed in I could look out at a car park where outside broadcast vans had set up for days, alongside a variety of protesters and campaigns. In the bistro of the club itself, we had to dine with half the Canberra press gallery and anyone else who wandered in with something to share about how the country could run (hint: if you are a journalist trapped in conversation with 'Lord' Christopher Monckton, don't try to change the subject by mentioning the weather – #thisactuallyhappened).

I'll never forget Jo Haylen in an early meeting, asking the only question that mattered: 'So are we looking for a local campaign effect where we just do some things in the seats, or a national campaign effect where we get a big story out of being in Sydney's west?' and our directing staff not being able to answer her. We had evidently got to a point where our operation as a whole, and by this I mean not just the PMO but plenty of our other campaign operators and a few members of Club Sensible advising them from the background, forgot that you don't announce where a prime minister would be staying in advance, or stay in one place for five days. That is where car parks full of protesters and distractions come from. A week in which you find yourself measuring success by whether you can avoid the PM getting photographed next to Mark Latham or a poker machine, and whether you can avoid people finding out you are actually having meetings at your office in the CBD when you are supposed to be 'in the west', is not a week in which you are winning.

There's an enormous industry of myth and counter-myth dedicated to the politics of 'western Sydney', out of all proportion to its significance in our national politics – this is true even of the contrarians who assert that the region doesn't matter as much as people say, but who think that assertion itself is more important than it really is. As usual, if you start with the politics and the commentary, and try to build a freeway from there to the facts on the ground, you get lost. It seems to me that if you want an understanding of federal politics in Sydney's west and south-west, you start with jobs. Under Labor, there were a million new jobs created in Australia. About 135 000 were in Sydney – roughly proportionate to its share of the population and economy. But of these, barely *ten thousand* were created in Sydney's west and south-west regions.

That's effectively zero jobs growth in a region home to two million Australians for five whole years. No wonder they are grumpy and no wonder it's tough territory in which to campaign: it's the economy, stupid. Yet political commentators and advisers on all sides of the debate think you go to Melbourne to talk about a plan for jobs and to Sydney to talk about roads and boats and guns. I do not understand.

—

One of the things I've learned in my long experience of buggering up important political decisions is that 'now or never' doesn't necessarily mean 'now'.

I'm very fond of Stephen Conroy. Steve is a really unusual blend of charisma, pragmatism, conviction and fixity. He'd hate it being said, but in the famous Tony Benn taxonomy of 'fixers, straight men, and maddies', Steve is right in there with Keating as a maddie. His former mentor Robert Ray called him a 'factional Dalek' in 2006 (at the Fabians! In Sydney! A big call from the Big Indian) but I see a policy wonk. No other person would have had the determination and contrarianism to keep the NBN alive through nearly a decade, from conception to delivery, through an enormous conservative and commercial campaign against it. He took the project from something people didn't understand to something people thought might be a white elephant to something which sealed victory in 2010 to something which even the man appointed to destroy it, Malcolm Turnbull, had to promise he would build sooner and cheaper, not rip up out of the ground. The bloke is a lion.

And no other person would have risked introducing a package of media reforms designed to break the irresponsible, politicised editorial culture of News Limited. The ludicrous and grotesque campaign against Stephen and against those laws was the ultimate proof that those laws were needed. There was criticism from other media organisations, of course; but the News Limited front pages became ridiculous, disgraceful pamphlets – the worst, the *Daily Telegraph* on 13 March ran pictures of Stalin, Mao, Castro, Kim Jong-un, Mugabe and Ahmadinejad, headed, *These despots believe in controlling the press*, and then over a picture of the minister, *Conroy joins them*. All because of a proposed public-interest test for media-company mergers.

If you remember there was still an election to win, then taking on this virtual monopoly on popular print news was irresponsible. If you remember that by February we were cooked, and had one last chance to strike a blow for progress, then maybe it was worth a try. I change my mind on this every day. You can only be sure of this: independent MP Rob Oakeshott was 100 per cent wrong when he said, on 20 March, the day he pulled the pin on the legislation, 'Let's take some deep breaths, and if we really do want good policy in media laws in this country, time is a friend not an enemy.' Now or never didn't have to mean now, but it couldn't mean next year. (How the independent member for Lyne, of all people, who was probably more likely to lose his seat than the most marginal Labor MP, could think there would be a next year I really couldn't understand.) Time was our enemy, and as a result of not acting in 2013 we will all simply have to wait for technology or succession to fix the News Corp problem – the community has been denied another opportunity to make a democratic decision on this. And whatever else it was, the public (and parliamentary) debate of March on these laws wasn't the reason for the leadership spill of 21 March 2013.

Here I am, seventy-five thousand words into a book with the working title 'We weren't as bad as we seemed at the time', and I have to confess, recalling and describing the events of that March shake my conviction a little. It was pretty bad. The reality of a government divided into two leadership camps for years of its life was exhausting the limits of cabinet decision-making. The new ministerial appointments in February brought Mark Dreyfus to replace Roxon as attorney-general while Chris Bowen was finally released from immigration into Chris Evans's vacated higher-education post, with Brendan O'Connor taking Bowen's old place. In a particular sign of hope, Bill Shorten had been given workplace relations – giving us a real chance to open up a new front against the conservatives in a key portfolio while maintaining reasonable relations with reasonable business. But this didn't change the underlying dynamic. Despite the PM's efforts over two and a half years to restore good cabinet process to Labor in government, the divisions among the individuals themselves and the consequent lack of trust were now so entrenched that it was clear that no genuinely sensitive political decision could be left to sit in cabinet for days, for fear it would leak. The group had just lost the discipline or solidarity to hold their tongues through the conversation, much less after it. You could only take a decision to cabinet on the day you intended to announce it. All this isn't the same as saying our attempt to bang media laws through cabinet and the parliament in a month was necessarily right or wise (or successful) — just that it was the only method that created the possibility to get it done. The alternative wasn't 'a proper cabinet process': the alternative was not to proceed.

This was the immediate context for the farcical leadership spill of 21 March 2013. In the eight-week period where we just had to win some politics, we had fumbled constantly. It was hopeless and even I could see why people whose only calculus was which leader could win the election were giving up on the PM.

So, in events since described in great detail by others, during the final week of the March sittings, Simon Crean went to the PM and asked her to call a leadership spill in order to resolve the question over Labor's leadership. It took some front to propose this a week after his quarter-of-a-billion-dollar arts policy — one of the most fiscally and politically indulgent decisions in our whole period in office — had been pushed through cabinet by the PM. They met on the Wednesday and again on the Thursday. The PM declined to spill her own leadership, and naturally enough told Crean he'd have to think about his position. He did not. Instead, without resigning, he publicly called for the PM to spill the leadership and offered himself for deputy to an incoming prime minister Rudd. Or at least he tried to, in a mid-morning press conference that caused genuine confusion as to his meaning. Crean reconvened two hours later on the same spot (nice continuity direction, though I presume this was a happy accident) to spit it out properly. So the PM sacked Crean as minister.

While we had fought like bastards for jobs and growth right to the end of the year, and paid the price, the second front hadn't gone away. That precious Bondi night of unity was just that — one night — and of course, there were only staff there. In the end, we were spectators in caucus's decisions about the leadership, as was right. Six years earlier, back in 2006, challenger Kevin Rudd had been a very reluctant mover against Kim Beazley, arguing with his backers for more time. The deadline of December 2006 had to be set, and enforced, by both his running mate Julia Gillard and his supporters in the NSW Right; there's no doubt if they hadn't said now or never, he would have delayed into 2007. This pattern of indecision and delay would be seen many times, both as prime minister and as leadership challenger; early 2013 was no exception, and his indecision, combined with the press gallery's horror at missing the emerging yarn in 2010 and the mathematical possibility of a change of government in the house, created an atmosphere of rumour that felt like a black satire of the Elizabethan court.

Stories flew around the building. Could Crean really have not checked his text messages from Rudd saying, *Don't call for a spill*, before he called for a spill? Had Bowen and Albo really had to hide in a cupboard in Rudd's office when Faulkner had walked in demanding to know what the hell was going on? Was Robert McClelland really about to take a judicial appointment in New South Wales and force a by-election in a seat we could lose? You couldn't make this crap up.

The PM and Carl Green had worked together on a truly beautiful speech for a very important national occasion, the national apology for forced adoptions. No one who heard it will forget it. It is a document worth reading today, and it defies quotation. This long-hoped-for event took place in Parliament House on 21 March. The prime minister's grace and consideration of other people on this day, when other politicians paraded their self-indulgence and self-importance is hard to describe. For everyone who was part of it, this was a draining and emotional event. Then she had to come back to the office, sack Simon Crean as a minister, walk into the house for question time, tell the house about Crean, announce a spill of her leadership – and when that was done, she told the opposition leader: 'In the meantime, take your best shot.'

Rudd walked into caucus at four-thirty p.m. and, as he had done even when he was actually prime minister in June 2010, didn't nominate for the leadership. Among other consequences, this left his supporters out to dry – those who walked to caucus with him and those who felt they had to resign as ministers the following day. After a five-minute meeting, the PM came back to the office, where we were all waiting; we did not expect her to lose, but of course it was tense while she was away, and then there was an element of hysterical relief when she returned. Caterina and Emma had put up a poster that quoted the cult television serial *Game of Thrones*, 'What do we say to the god of death? Not today.' Which was grim and funny and precise.

We hadn't said 'no'; we'd said 'not today'. Out-governing our opponent wasn't enough. By the following Monday, the Coalition primary vote would be measured at 50 per cent and they would have a 16-point lead in the two-party preferred vote. We knew the Rudd challenge was finally over, but we also knew that so was even a mathematical chance of Labor winning in 2013.

# 13.
# The last grand days

*Is there a way to fix the damage that you see that's been done here?*

ABC JOURNALIST TONY JONES ASKING PAUL KEATING
ABOUT AUSTRALIA–CHINA RELATIONS, FOLLOWING
PRESIDENT OBAMA'S SPEECH IN AUSTRALIA,
23 NOVEMBER 2011

---

I have spent years of my life trying to get that T S Eliot quote about April being the cruellest month into a pre-budget speech. Even with Sean Kelly out of my hair at last, I didn't succeed in 2013; not because I'd finally accepted that the purpose of the PM's remarks wasn't to make me look clever (what speechwriter ever really accepts that?), but because April 2013 was anything but cruel. In fact it was much more Geoffrey Chaucer than TS Eliot: bringing sweet showers after the drought of March. Julia Gillard mustered the last of her strength as a negotiator – and advocate to drive home the last victories of her prime ministership.

—

The PM visited China from the fifth to the tenth of the month. As I recall her time in office, I have to notice that a lot of the highlights were outside Australia. In part that is a reflection on the government's policy successes on the international stage; in part also on the government's political failings at home. In another sign of the divergence of politics and policy, the substance of governing greatly intertwined domestic and global issues, while the accumulation of public impressions illustrated the two spheres with very contrasting images and pictures. (In part, travelling on your own plane, even a smallish one, is just a lot of fun.)

The visit began on that plane with the usual meeting between the PM, her staff and officials; it went for hours. Richard Maude, in his last trip with the PM before he would return to the public service, was made to wear a Mao cap for a bit of fun; eventually he said, 'I think I'm going to faint,' and took the cap off, revealing an enormous red ring around his forehead. Heaven knows how he'd kept the thing on when it was clearly three sizes too small. What a stoic.

I was relieved to be in the travelling group; two years earlier, on the long trip to north-east Asia over Easter 2010, we'd attempted to do the speeches from Australia. It was too hard, and the policy advisers on the road ended up having to do all the final versions, which was too much for them to do and compromised the speeches too. (The nadir was when they realised about midnight before ANZAC Day that the sun wouldn't be rising during the South Korean dawn service – at the latitude, it would have been up for hours – and the whole conceit of the speech needed a rewrite. Poor Maude.) In that trip, on this trip, always, Richard had powered on; the outcomes of this journey would be worthy reward.

We landed on the charmless island of Hainan, at the southernmost tip of China, and drove for an hour up the highway to something called the Bo'ao Forum. This is a sort of Peking-line Davos splinter: a residential love-in for the bit of Club Sensible (journalist Jennifer Hewitt, magnate Andrew Forrest, politician Julie Bishop) that does business in the People's Republic, added to a leader-level political dialogue that actually matters. It's quite a strange event. There, on 7 April, the PM met the new Chinese president Xi Jinping – it was on the way into this meeting that she and Christine Lagarde exchanged that droll corridor high-five – and there, she made final progress on the deal of a lifetime. The announcement would come two days later.

Even by the standards of prime ministerial travel, this visit was weird. The public focus was very strongly on investment and trade, rather than diplomacy and security, which gave all the speeches and meetings a character more akin to a multilateral summit. The 'billionaires staying at the Bates Motel' feel of Bo'ao was just the beginning of business oddness, as we then drove and flew CEOs Gail Kelly of Westpac and Mike Smith of ANZ and their staff with us from the forum through to Shanghai. (This included a sixty-minute minibus ride from the Bo'ao resort back to Hainan airport, during which the two beers for the road I'd pinched from the photographer Andrew Meares served a happy dual purpose of dulling the pain and unnerving Smith. My beard was really wild by this time.) Bill Shorten brought a delegation of superannuation industry leaders on to Beijing.

The PM stopped in Shanghai for less than twenty-four hours, arriving so late that the lights had gone out on the Pearl Tower, which took some of the edge off the view from the piano bar we improvised in the hotel. (Don't ask, I've already said too much.) In the morning, the PM announced that our dollar and the Chinese renminbi would be traded directly onshore in China for the first time, joining only the US dollar and the yen as directly convertible currencies; and announced that the People's Bank of China had approved licences for ANZ and Westpac to act as market makers for direct trading on the Chinese foreign-exchange system. These were big deals, announced in a major press conference with leading Australian bankers – though Mike Smith's watch seemed to stop during the press conference to announce this, requiring his repeated attention while the PM spoke. He wasn't typical of Australian business; at least Gail Kelly, standing on the other side of the PM, didn't think she'd spoken too long. We were on a serious roll.

Beijing was next. At the Australia-China Chamber of Commerce, the Perth businessman sitting on my right turned and said, 'This is much better than her last speech to this audience two years ago'; when I told Maude this afterwards, I was merciless, and he gracious. He had reason to think speeches weren't the main game. There, following her meeting with Premier Li Keqiang, the PM announced a new annual leader-to-leader meeting between Australia's prime minister and China's president – only the UK prime minister, the German chancellor and the Russian president have a comparable arrangement. This was backed by an annual foreign and strategic dialogue between the respective ministers for foreign affairs, and an annual strategic economic dialogue between our treasurer and minister for trade and their Chinese counterparts.

Just like that, it was accomplished: the signature foreign-policy achievement of the Gillard prime ministership. We had stepped on the plane knowing this was the intended outcome, but barely wanting to breathe lest we disturb it somehow. The announcement made, we all exhaled.

That week in China was weird because we did three cities in five days, because it was mercantile, because the best (and the worst) of business people travelled with us – and weird because it went well. Genuinely non-partisan commentators were sincerely confused; they appeared to share the disorientation you'd feel if the car you were in was moving smoothly while images of turbulence were projected onto the windows. Having been so suavely assured since at least November 2011 that we had buggered everything up with China because we didn't understand the 'realities' at stake, it took some work for many to adjust their commentary to the reality of our success. John Garnaut, who had started the week telling the *Sydney Morning Herald*'s readers, 'It is not too late for Gillard to find redemption in China, if only she can find the confidence to squarely talk about the subject . . .' found the confidence to dig himself out of the hole and acknowledge the week's outcomes as 'unprecedented'. Even the poor old *Oz* called it a 'foreign policy coup' and 'the cornerstone of Julia Gillard's Asian Century'. And not a hint of protest from Club Sensible this time.

Hawke refounded the US alliance as a bipartisan touchstone, Keating had the APEC Leaders' Forum and Rudd the G20; Gillard secured the China strategic partnership.

Two years in the making, this had its conception in leader-level discussions in 2011. In April 2012, with her new foreign minister in harness, the PM had written to President Hu to propose the next steps. The week after the 2012 budget, while the PM had spent Mother's Day at a marginal-seat barbecue in Redcliffe in Brisbane's suburbs, Bob Carr had travelled to Beijing and met Li Keqiang (then the vice-premier) as well as the foreign minister. In 2012, while the PM prepared to travel to the UN General Assembly and the opposition leader polished his cherished 'Jakarta versus Geneva' grab, Dennis Richardson had travelled to Beijing as her special envoy and further advanced the deal. Through this period, many were arguing that Australia faced a looming 'choice' between our alliance with the United States and our trading relationship with China. On 19 September, between returning from Beijing and departing with the PM for New York, Richardson gave the Michael Hintze lecture at Sydney University's Centre for International Security Studies, with a moderate and modulated but unmistakable rejection of that 'choice' argument:

> That is not a basis for the execution of a country's foreign policy . . . Interests may sometimes be able to be expressed in stark and unambiguous terms but the conduct of foreign policy is, inevitably in my view, pursued more often in colours of grey, than in black and white . . .

Remarkably, our officials (and China's) were able to keep the discussion moving through the Chinese leadership transition that occurred between October 2012 to March 2013. Just weeks after the new president and premier took office, Australia had achieved this grand result. There's plenty of credit to be shared on a big job like this; above all it's a tribute to Australia's status as a big country that the Chinese saw the importance of striking a deal. I believe it's also a tribute to Julia Gillard's status as a big leader that they also saw the urgency of striking a deal with Australia in April 2013. This was the moment in which Gillard both reached a high point for our biggest economic relationship and locked that high point in for the future.

The China work sounded intense harmonies with the government's domestic project – this was a week of integration. It's no accident, for instance, that we were talking with the Chinese about currency trading, financial services and carbon market design at the same time – after 1 July 2012 these had become the same conversation. It's no accident either that we were talking about human rights, consular cases, property law and business cooperation – after Stern Hu and Matthew Ng, these had become the same conversation as well. Just so, it's no coincidence that in the margins of the visit, the PM was setting time for phone calls home to oversee final preparations for the school improvement plan; this was an Asian Century policy too. As she said in the same final press conference, Australia needed to 'embed' Asian languages in school funding.

Beijing was tremendously professionally satisfying for the PM, her staff and officials, and a serious achievement for Australia; it brought wonderful backstage moments as well. At the final public engagement of the visit, an education-sector dinner on the last night, press secretary Eamonn Fitzpatrick and I snuck in late and found a table right up the back next to the translator's booth. When the PM had finished speaking, we introduced ourselves to our neighbour. She was Linda Chan; a very successful businesswoman in Australia and China, her partner is Eric Walsh, who as press secretary to Gough Whitlam had travelled to China forty years earlier on that first prime ministerial visit. Linda couldn't have made a bigger fuss over Eamonn and me if she'd had musical instruments on hand.

The Whitlam staff who travelled to China with Gough must have felt like the first men on the moon; at that dinner, for a moment, we felt like we were at least part of the Apollo program. Labor staff, like Labor's caucus and leaders, live and work with the icons of the past still very present to us – present in the public debate and in our private minds. This wasn't one of the nights where our predecessors made us feel unequal to their legacy; Mum and Dad didn't feel ashamed.

We survived a fair bit of cabin fever that week. Travelling in China is exhilarating, but it's not easy. When the air conditioning gets too much in Beijing, you don't pop down to the street to get some fresh air and a Lebanese roll the way you do in New York; when you have a meeting, you don't head in with your phone in your pocket the way you do in Washington: you lock your phone outside the swept room, and indeed you take temporary phones with you for the trip and throw them away when you return. We have two friends, but one ally, and we know what that means.

But despite the lock-in element to the final days of the visit, we'd had a big win for Australia, and were in a good mood, even if we were climbing the walls a bit. Even when Maude found out that the PM's PA had a good university degree, and expressed his astonishment that she had gone into mere staff work a little more forcefully and in front of a slightly larger group of people than strict good manners would require, no one got slapped and no one cried. I saved the day by reminding Richard that if Caterina had gone as a graduate to his former department, foreign affairs, she probably would have been translating our room-service orders at that moment. (The DFAT graduate translating our room-service orders at that moment was good enough to laugh.)

How well did the visit go? The first question at the final press conference was:

> Prime Minister, the whole world is focusing on China and wants to strike up relationships with the new Chinese

leadership. You've beaten the rest of Asia to the punch by getting the strategic dialogue that only a couple of other countries of the world have. How does it feel to have scored that sort of coup and put Australia right in the forefront of this relationship?

Not the hardest question she was ever asked.

Our officials stood at the back of the press conference with the staff and we all grinned like schoolkids – Trade Minister Craig Emerson was on camera and he grinned like a schoolkid too – while the PM replied it was a good week for Australia. The final words of the press conference were from Bob Carr – who deserved plenty of credit for the diplomacy of that week himself, and hadn't been asked a question until right at the end – and who just laughed, smiled and said, 'I don't want to add to what the prime minister said,' with drollery and good grace. You don't hear a politician say that very often. That's how well the visit went.

How much strife were we still in back home? The only question to still our laughter was, 'Will this be a fairly important legacy of your prime ministership?'

—

Gillard could negotiate even when there was no time for negotiations – and often that is what the prime ministership looked like in April 2013. I don't know when the 'rest day' after intercontinental travel disappeared. The morning after the all-day flight from Beijing to Sydney (via Darwin to refuel and offload Canberra-bound staff), the PM had her first engagement (a telephone conference) at eight a.m., left Kirribilli House half an hour later, and returned to the house at four-thirty p.m. for a meeting with the immigration minister, a reception with editors of ethnic community newspapers, an interview with the editor of the *Sunday Telegraph* and a briefing on the negotiations for her school plans with the states and the Catholic and independent sectors. It went on; the second morning, the PM had her first engagement at seven a.m. She was then driven an hour from Kirribilli House to Macquarie Fields to visit a youth centre; back to Kirribilli House for a meeting; then to the airport and was flown (over Macquarie Fields) to Canberra, where she had cabinet at three-thirty, followed by meetings with her department head, then the secretary-general of the Commonwealth – then she cut the cake for a staff member's birthday! – then she met with senior executives of the oil and gas company BG Group at five-thirty that Friday afternoon. Gas was big, man.

I still say giving the woman that schedule and a knife to cut cake took guts. But she had what Crisp saw in Chifley, the 'unfailing capacity to be refreshingly, recreatively alone', and a Saturday at the Lodge with an iPad full of briefs seemed to reload her with all the fuel she needed. It was just as well: that Saturday as she rested up, the Council of Australian Governments meeting, with the mostly Liberal premiers and chief ministers, was six days away.

They would come to Canberra on 19 April to meet a Labor prime minister who was personally unpopular and who was clearly facing likely electoral defeat within months. But they also faced a prime minister whose proposals on school improvement and disability insurance had been campaigned on for years and had been developed as policy for nearly as long. This would be hard to resist. They also faced Julia Gillard.

Many see in Gillard a poor advocate but a great negotiator, but this was a moment in which both were required, and she delivered in every measure. The whole next week, she drove the game home. She knew the education story inside out – she'd written it – and from the windowless room I watched on TV as she told it in numbers and words and pictures all week, through radio blitzes, expenditure review committees and cabinet; in visits to schools in Melbourne's suburbs and in the Australian Capital Territory. (And of course, she did the right thing and went and signed one of those ludicrous *I give a Gonski* placards from the Australian Education Union. It was like the UK Hospital and Welfare Services' Union demanding Nye Bevan sign up to the NHS in the 1940s under the banner *I want a Beveridge*. Some days the teachers' union is like a high-school branch of the Greens.) And the DisabilityCare story hardly needed us to tell it: a campaign of great community depth and great professionalism had run for years and was yet to reach its peak. (When Kevin Rudd had appointed Bill Shorten as parliamentary secretary for disabilities and children's services in 2007 it wasn't regarded as a political opportunity for Bill – it was barely considered a promotion. His advocacy transformed the politics of disability in Australia and by 2013 the issue was central in Australian life.)

Had the government been in front and cruising to victory in 2013, our 'future conditionals' – in other words, uncompleted Labor work to offer as a pledge card for a third term – would have been a great tactical strength and a triumph of long-term governing strategy. Instead, with the clear evidence that we were in deep strife, there was great private frustration that we were running out of time to get things done. No one really thought Tony Abbott wouldn't be prime minister at COAG 2014. Only Gillard could turn that lack of confidence in our future to our advantage: she recognised that no one even dreamed a Prime Minister Abbott would come to COAG 2014 with thorough reform of school funding or a major extension of the social safety net. So the premiers had only one opportunity to get funding from a prime minister – and surely they knew it. If you wanted it done, you had to get it done now; was anyone going to make Rob Oakeshott's media-policy mistake and wait for time to solve it? If not now, then never. The storm was coming and everyone needed the storm windows finished now.

Going into COAG on Friday, the PM was outnumbered on the conservative vs Labor head count, but had the advantages of her recent strong campaigning performance, her ability as a negotiator, the urgency on the states to agree, the merits of the proposals (not a small point) and the progress she'd already made. On schools, South Australia had already signed up in-principle in 2012. We had legislation in the house. We were making huge progress towards agreement with the Catholic school system – it wasn't in the bag in April but it was coming, you could just feel it, and so could the premiers; Barry O'Farrell in New South Wales was already preparing to agree at the right moment. On disability, New South Wales had long agreed to launch the scheme. The federal Parliament had legislated for the scheme in March. And the Australian Capital Territory and South Australia had already signed up to run a transition to a full NDIS. By Friday afternoon, after a night and a day of jaw-jaw in Canberra, we had something which politically was probably even better than complete agreement with the states – we had big progress on schools, plus a fight with conservative premiers over something that was popular, DisabilityCare.

Gillard was a realist; she knew where we were at. When she flew to Melbourne and went to Moonee Valley racecourse to address the Victorian ALP conference on 20 April, the day after COAG, she told the delegates:

> I so vividly remember this state conference in May 2008: our first since taking office in October the previous year. We all met in hope and expectation for the achievements which still lay ahead. Today those achievements and these plans are the substance of our governing record.
>
> I know we meet today in a different mood. Ours is the determination of seasoned soldiers, not the enthusiasm of raw recruits... I know you are ready for the campaign to come.

I sat on the steps leading out of the auditorium listening, while fiddling with my footy scarf – I was staying for the Collingwood–Richmond match that afternoon – and thinking about everything that had happened since 2008. But Gillard also had a message for the Victorian premier on disability: 'Make a decision, Denis. Sign up to

DisabilityCare today.' And the same message on education to the rest: 'Do the right thing by Australia. Sign up for better schools.'

Both approaches worked.

By Tuesday 23 April, much as they'd planned all along, the PM and the NSW premier gave a joint press conference in Sydney announcing the country's biggest Liberal government and biggest education system had just signed up to the Gillard education funding reforms. I remember sitting in the car with the PM, driving out to the airport, while she spoke to O'Farrell on the phone with satisfaction about the outcome, and expressing some droll sympathy about his phone call with the federal opposition leader's office following the press conference.

By contrast, on DisabilityCare Napthine wasn't so much trapped in a corner as in a wet paper bag. It's crazy how often politicians find themselves unable to say the popular thing even when it's right. On 30 April, fully eleven days after COAG, with the public pressure raining down on him to support the scheme, he was still arguing about 'clarity' over funding as if he was a state treasury official making co-ord comments on a cabsub, not the political leader of a moderate state. It would have been horrible to watch if it had been us.

We were running out of time in office and Gillard had turned this to her advantage; we were running out of cash, with the surplus now a memory, and Gillard turned this to her advantage as well. Come 1 May, just nine days before the budget, the PM took a huge political risk, raising the stakes on the future of funding for DisabilityCare. After a night and morning of phone calls to premiers to inform them of what was coming, she made a morning announcement alongside Wayne Swan and Jenny Macklin in Melbourne's Treasury Gardens: Labor would go to the election promising to lift the Medicare levy by 0.5 per cent to fund DisabilityCare Australia. Her position?

> The Gillard government will offer this choice to the Australian people, by asking them to endorse this decision at the next

election. If re-elected, the government will bring legislation for this increased Medicare levy to the 44th Parliament.

If Abbott said no, it was a campaign trump card; if Abbott said yes, it was a policy triumph. She then flew to Tasmania to campaign, and a dramatic ping-pong on tax policy followed. The opposition leader saw the political threat of an election campaign fought on the NDIS and immediately demanded she bring the legislation into the Parliament following the budget. But he couldn't say how he'd vote – lacking either the authority or the wit to say he would support the tax increase to fund an extension of the safety net, he reserved his position. So down at Wynyard, where the PM was inspecting how the Fonterra milk and cheese plant was spending clean-energy grants (ah, that diary process), she shot back:

> The leader of the opposition has called on me to bring the legislation forward but has been unable or unwilling to say whether or not he would support a half a per cent increase in the Medicare levy to fund DisabilityCare . . .
>
> If the leader of the opposition is prepared to support this half a per cent increase in the Medicare levy to fund DisabilityCare, then I will bring the legislation into the Parliament immediately.
>
> If the leader of the opposition is unable to answer the question, what he believes in about this matter, or wants to oppose this increase to the Medicare levy, then I will take it to the Australian people in September.

We'd lost everything over two years through our inability to manage the politics of a big new tax and yet somehow this was working. It was unbelievable to witness, terrifying and magnificent. I was glued to the TV screen in Canberra, desperately trying to write yet another horror economic speech about revenue falling, and just wanting to stop everything and shout like a barracker during the news.

Abbott was now stuck in the same paper bag that had enclosed Napthine for days. By the evening the PM was still punching on TV, telling Ten's *The Project,* 'I'm very happy to bring the legislation to increase the Medicare levy to the parliament; if the opposition is going to vote for it, then we know it will go through.' I'd love to have sat with the Libs after the TV news that night and seen them scramble. I wonder if anybody piped up to say, 'This NDIS is actually a good thing we've said we support . . . right?' If so, they didn't pipe up loudly. The television news smashed Abbott – the tabloid front pages the next morning did their best for him, God love them, with the *Herald Sun* 'paraphrasing' the PM in its headline, *Vote for my tax.* By Thursday morning things were going so well that Jon Faine of ABC 774 Melbourne asked the PM on air why she was making this a challenge for Tony Abbott instead of just getting on with nation-building. It had been a while since we'd managed the politics of something well enough to be accused of putting policy considerations second. And then the most amazing thing happened: Tony Abbott said yes.

So when the PM stood up, in Tasmania with Premier Lara Giddings, to announce a new funding agreement with the state to launch and implement the NDIS from 1 July, she could claim victory, because the 'change of mind by the Leader of the Opposition' meant she could bring to the Parliament the legislation to increase the Medicare levy by half a per cent.

DisabiltyCare Australia had a launch date, a permanent funding stream and a naturally temporary but nevertheless important status as a bipartisan achievement for Australia; Napthine collapsed and Victoria would formally sign up in two more days. New South Wales, South Australia, Tasmania and the ACT were now in for the National School Improvement Plan and the new school funding arrangements – and the Catholics would follow for certain now. The budget would bring ten-year estimates for the cost and ten-year proposals for the funding.

You can win everything you wanted, but you can't convince everyone you've won – the *Sydney Morning Herald*'s analysis was 'a political wedge on Mr Abbott, over increasing the Medicare levy to fund disability insurance, failed when he agreed to back the 0.5 per cent rise' – yes, we failed because we succeeded – but April was sweet.

They weren't the last good days, but they were the last grand days. Autumn sates, winter kills.

# 14.
# Drafting the B speech

*This soul now free from prison and passion*
*Hath yet a little indignation*
*That so small hammers should so down beat*
*So great a castle*

JOHN DONNE, 'THE PROGRESS OF THE SOUL', FIRST SONG, XXXVIII

The ancient Christian tradition of *quo vadis*, fairly faithfully represented in novels and the famous Hollywood movie of the same name, sees St Peter in old age, on the Appian Way, with his back to Rome, fleeing likely crucifixion in the persecutions of Nero. He has a vision of his Lord, Jesus Christ, walking towards him, and Peter asks, '*Quo vadis?*' (Where are you going?) Jesus replies, '*Romam vado iterum crucifigi.*' (To Rome, to be crucified again.)

Unlike much Apocrypha, this has the ring of truth to it. The cryptic, ironic, almost sarcastic words of this Christ – you can see him shrug as he thinks, *Where do you reckon I'm going? Where are you going, more to the point? Someone has to die and if you're walking that way it looks like it's got to be me* – fit so neatly with what the gospels reveal of the personality of the Man who walked out of the Herodian Temple to curse a barren fig tree.

Shamed, St Peter turns around and returns to Rome, and to his death.

The worst hangover I ever had in my life was the day after the party at my house to celebrate the election of Joseph Ratzinger as 264th successor to St Peter in 2005. This occasion went down in family lore as the night of the 'miracle of the reds' – I genuinely do not know where all that wine came from – and finished with someone saying, 'Grab your pitchforks, we march on the archbishop's house this night!' My mates in the Macklin office summarised the situation as, 'The Pope made it to work the next day, but Michael Cooney didn't.' Possibly not my finest hour.

As Pope, Ratzinger scandalised the world in many ways; it's in the job description. I know he wasn't popular. One of my favourite Ratzinger scandals was his article on Europe and its discontents in the conservative American journal *First Things,* published in 2006, in which he wrote:

> In Europe, in the nineteenth century . . . democratic socialism managed to fit within the two existing models as a welcome counterweight to the radical liberal positions, which it developed and corrected. It also managed to appeal to various denominations. In England it became the political party of the Catholics, who had never felt at home among either the Protestant conservatives or the liberals. In Wilhelmine Germany, too, Catholic groups felt closer to democratic socialism than to the rigidly Prussian and Protestant conservative forces.
>
> In many respects, democratic socialism was and is close to Catholic social doctrine and has in any case made a remarkable contribution to the formation of a social consciousness.

The most traditionalist pope in sixty years had all but come out as a social democrat. You could hear the rending of pinstripes all over conservative DC.

On 11 February 2013, Pope Benedict XVI, who on inaugurating

his pontificate had said to the faithful, 'Pray for me, that I may not flee for fear of the wolves,' resigned his ministry, citing old age and the possibility of future incapacity. In his final sermon, he preached against disunity:

> We can reveal the face of the Church and how this face is at times disfigured. I am thinking in particular about sins against the unity of the Church, the divisions in the ecclesial body . . . overcoming individualism and rivalry, is a humble and precious sign for those who are far from the faith or indifferent.

I had some mates around (a few of them had been present at the Miracle of the Reds) and we fried up some boxty pancakes; then I watched *Quo Vadis* and I cried. I knew my prime minister would never, never resign, but I knew it was time to start drafting the B speech.

---

Time in office brings great personal pleasures and good fortune. You meet famous and fascinating people and see extraordinary things with all kinds of levels of seriousness. I walked past Christopher Lawford, a nephew of John F. Kennedy, one day waiting in our office's outer foyer – he really looks like a Kennedy too; I walked past Ben Roberts-Smith, who was about to be awarded the VC, coming out of the PM's suite; I had a beer with Peter Hudson after the 2010 grand final.

I tried to savour the good things.

In 2013 my beloved ACT Brumbies became the only Australian state team in my lifetime to beat the legendary British and Irish Lions rugby team. I had been waiting for this all my life. When they toured in 1989, I took the afternoon off school to see the Lions play a team of Canberra and district amateurs in Queanbeyan and blow them off the park. When they came again in 2001 we had a little baby and I couldn't go to see the ACT Brumbies' brave, narrow, late loss. Now I was working for the prime minister; through a mate I was invited to a Parliament House dinner the night before the game with a panel of Brumby legends; I scored brilliant tickets to the match itself on the night of 18 June; a front row of local club players held up a front row of England internationals and little Colby Fainga'a stood up off the back to clear the last scrum. He used to catch the bus to school with my kids. I swapped texts with the Brumbies CEO after the game, tweeted about Max Boyce ('I was there!') and walked out of the ground with a press gallery reporter who people around us recognised.

Seriously, if you didn't follow Thomas More's example and wear some kind of hair shirt at court, you'd go mad with pride.

---

The most usefully humbling thing that happened to me in my years with the PM was reading *Five Days in London*, John Lukacs' amazing history of the 'fight or deal' debate in the UK war cabinet in May 1940, in which Churchill stared down the establishment and the conservative right to take the prime ministership and fight on, not negotiating with the Nazis. One reason it changed my life was that it really steeled my spine against the idiotic blimps who cry appeasement whenever a progressive tries not to start a war out of nothing, utterly ignorant that at every dinner party and in every university college in England for nearly ten years and in the end in the cabinet itself it was the *right* arguing for appeasement, it was the Tories who wanted to give Mr Hitler his way. The other reason it changed my life was that I was reading it in bed one Sunday morning in 2011, feeling very very very very important, noticing little staff cameos in this cabinet-centric book and picturing myself and my mates in various roles, and planning which anecdotes I would harvest to drop into conversation with the PM at the right moment, and thinking maybe I wouldn't finish it, maybe I'd lend it to the PM; that'd be a good move. God forgive me, I was even listening to ABC Classic FM during this ludicrous self-adoring reverie.

Then I turned a page and a salacious hand-drawn cartoon fell in my lap. It was in pink ink, dedicated to the mate who had lent me the book from the woman who had given him the book, and had clearly been left in there as a bookmark and forgotten. It was like finding a note from my younger self saying, '*Sic transit gloria mundi*, dickhead.' So passes the glory of the world, indeed. I honestly try not to forget this. (And oh, yes, *wow,* I'm glad I didn't lend that book to the PM.)

So look, obviously the main thing is you've got to laugh, which keeps you both sane and Australian; enjoy the good things, savour the moment, don't get up yourself. But on the other hand, you have to take your boss and the job seriously. And then, you try to remember that all this will pass – *sic transit*; that's where the B speech comes in.

Working on what your advice will be for the final remarks given in defeat is more than a scapular, more than a salutary spiritual discipline; it is the perfect memento mori of politics, the skull in Holbein's *Ambassadors*, the rotting apple in the drawer.

Thinking about the B speech is also a practical necessity: unprepared and ungracious speeches in defeat can damage a politician's legacy greatly, while a good final effort can serve a politician well. For the people who work on it, there's some grim satisfaction in serving to the final hour. Mark Latham on election night 2004 had given a fine concession speech. There were a handful of advisers contributing – I offered only a few lines – and he was well served. Before my staff time, Kim Beazley had spoken beautifully on the bitterest of election nights, 10 November 2001, when he'd 'looked down through the fog of war to the kitchen table' and hoped that Australians would 'turn to each other and not against each other'.

I can't say the thought of an election night B speech never occurred to me in 2011 or 2012. But it was after March 2013 that I started occasionally opening up my notes and updating them in an idle moment or when an inspiration came.

Budget week in May captured the politics of the two fronts, the culture of the period – and our prime minister's governing power.

The cover article of *The Monthly* magazine had reopened the second front, which, would you believe it, hadn't gone away, even after the debacle of March. The article summarised everything that had happened in the Rudd camp in that mad non-challenge, and laid out what they were doing now. It was a kind of postmodern version of the famous May 1989 *Four Corners* appearance by Andrew Peacock's supporters to boast about their leadership challenge success – but politics had changed a bit. This was anonymous (or sort of – attributed to members of a group of named individuals, 'the cardinals', a nickname inspired by March's papal conclave), and different too in that it boasted about a leadership challenge debacle, and contained unflattering statements by the plotters about their own candidate ('When Rudd dropped by, he was furious. Four-letter words were sprayed around the room . . .').

In what in some sense was now the fourth year of a permanent Labor leadership crisis, I think every participant and close spectator had lost all perspective on the scale of the problem. Take this paragraph for example:

> Their new destabilisation will be no destabilisation, so that Gillard's low ratings can't be blamed on them. 'She needs to wear every bad poll,' says one of the cardinals. 'It's a waiting game. People like me have deliberately gone to ground. Being quiet is the hardest thing I've had to do.

You have to have a sense of humour about this – a comment for the record, attributed to one of an identified group of four or five people, in a cover article of the country's most influential magazine. I cite it not as an act of particular bastardry – indeed it's quite the contrary.

Comment of this kind was now absolutely routine on both sides of the leadership fight, and neither the Labor MP quoted nor perhaps even the journalist reporting it appeared to think a person publicly explaining the difficulty of his current policy of shutting up was utterly ludicrous.

You had to have a sense of humour about the general political culture by that time too. Misogyny hadn't gone out of fashion. Plenty of people remember the foul Mal Brough fundraising menu that came out on 12 June 2013 – the same day the pioneering feminist Eva Cox wrote on *Crikey*:

> Prime Minister Julia Gillard's appeal for women to vote for Labor – most notably through the Women for Gillard group, launched yesterday – is a rather desperate attempt to exploit the gender tensions that exist in our society.

Some remember the mad questions about Tim Mathieson that shock jock Howard Sattler asked the PM on Perth radio, which led to his sacking the same month. But it wasn't really that Mal Brough had got even crasser or Eva Cox had become a worse contrarian or Howard Sattler had lost his mind – it was that they'd held their respective positions on the bell curve while the *mean* went mad, leaving outliers having to go crazy-ape bonkers to be heard at all. *The Monthly* article cited Peter Hartcher in his *Sydney Morning Herald* column two months earlier, on 16 March, drawing an analogy between the Labor leadership contest and a 1964 New York rape and murder, a comparison that made no impression on me at the time but which, almost two years later, is unbelievable to read, let alone imagine edited or published. I have no doubt that no one at the time gave it a second's thought. It was what self-consciously serious, senior correspondents considered normal in 2013.

—

And of course, you have to lose sight of how mad your environment is if you are going to stay sane and persist in the work that matters. So she did; and so did we. She was still governing.

On Monday 4 May, the government put amendments into the House to include the details of school-funding changes into the Australian Education Bill she had introduced the previous year. It legislated detail of the structure of funding, with a general per-student amount, loading amounts for disadvantaged schools and students, and taking into account the capacity of parents to contribute in non-government schools, based on what the Gonski review had found an effective school education costs. The legislation also detailed the implementation of the National Plan for School Improvement – in short, how the money should be spent. The PM wouldn't tip cash into the states to be blown on cutting class sizes or to backfill for state Liberal cuts. The model allowed the Catholic systems to sign up before 1 July, which they duly did. These changes would pass both houses in just twenty-two days.

Tuesday 14 May brought the last Swan budget speech. He told the Parliament about an Australia 'where our prosperity spreads opportunity to every postcode in our nation'. You can draw a line through Wayne Swan's career from its first day to today and on to the last, whenever that comes.

His sixth budget, like his first, put jobs and growth first. It included ten-year estimates on the cost of school improvement and disability insurance and details of how these would be funded. (Within a year, we would see a Liberal treasurer forecast higher unemployment in a global recovery than Labor delivered in a global recession, and abandon many of the savings decisions designed to fund these programs.) And the conservatives who spent the vast proceeds of the first phase of the mining boom on nothing better than super concessions for their wives crowed that we couldn't bring down a surplus with the lowest revenue results in twenty years.

The Medicare Levy Amendment (DisabilityCare Australia) Bill

2013 was introduced to the House on the day after the budget and passed the Senate the day of the budget reply. Done.

—

And yes, the budget reply encapsulated the first front: the contest with the conservative. The opposition leader's speech told the nation he was wearing RM Williams boots and that he still had a wife named Margie:

> Margie and I know the pressure that every Australian – that each one of you – is under. We're not crying poor but we run a household with power bills, rates, health and education costs to be paid all the time.

Sure, he'd taken his time signing up to the NDIS, but funding would be fine under an Abbott government; after all, he reminded viewers at home, he'd ridden a thousand kilometres the week before last to raise money for Carers Australia – would he do that if he was 'half-hearted about the NDIS'? But this didn't forbid him from attacking the government for 'massive new programs in areas that are the states' responsibility':

> It's no way to run the country and it's no way for adult leaders to behave . . .
> You want a grown-up government like the ones that John Howard and – yes – Bob Hawke too used to run.

It was no point us sneering at this mélange of populist contradictions and Club Sensible clichés. We'd had our chance to tell our story, and could hardly roll our eyes at other people who were doing it better than us. All we could do was to keep delivering in our final days and work on the B speech at night.

On 9 June, my friend and my first editor Christopher Pearson died. Thank God I had found time for a phone call to him a few months earlier; I had last seen him in person three and a half years before, at a wedding in January 2010 when he told me that Abbott had Rudd on the ropes, to which I replied he was wilfully blind. The worst of it for Christopher was that he was months, perhaps weeks, from seeing Tony Abbott as prime minister, something which would have given him all the happiness available to him on this earth. He was sixty-two years old and had lived a bizarre and fascinating and prolific life: he had his prayers for the grace of tears answered many times; he spent a short period on John Howard's staff from 1995 and contributed occasionally in the years that followed, and was obituarised as 'Adelaide journalist and former John Howard speechwriter'. If I'd ever doubted that this job I was clearly in the last weeks of was life-defining, not just career-defining, then no more.

As if I needed another memento mori, journalist Guy Rundle 'outed' me as one of the young men Christopher had savoured a crush on over the years, in a droll *Crikey* corrective to the many over-the-top and/or discreetly partial public encomiums to Christopher's character. A bit weird, but it gave me a chance to say something fond about CP on the record, and with my chief of staff's generous permission, I wrote to *Crikey* the following week:

> Every 10 years or so *Crikey* gives me a passing mention eccentric enough to merit a response. I enjoyed Guy Rundle's Friday thoughts – even the reference to me raised a smile.
>
> To quote one of the great Catholic sybarites and rogues of the last century, 'There are some incidents in my career, as you doubtless know, which are very easily capable of misinterpretation.'
>
> Perhaps Christopher had a crush on me – my wife certainly

thinks he did, and he was only human, after all – but if so, he expressed it chastely. His charity, if often counter-productive, seemed always pure; and his contrition seemed always perfect. Our last conversation was about an interview with Graham Greene in *The Paris Review*, of course. I am really sad that we won't speak again in this life.

God knows he's not the only one who hopes to spend a millennium or two in purgatory. That's what it's there for, after all. May he rest in peace.

Here I was, genuinely too busy to go to the funeral (even though I was actually in Adelaide that day, travelling with the boss); instead, I was writing jokes.

It was now becoming clear that *The Monthly* in May was no last gasp. We were seriously being hunted and people were seriously changing sides. There might not be much more time.

Wednesday 19 June was the second-last sitting week of winter – and the second last of the electoral term, with the election date now set – and that brought the press gallery ball, an annual highlight for many journalists, politicians, staffers and lobbyists alike. The ball has been attacked sometimes, by misanthropists like Gerard Henderson and sanctimoans like Bob Brown and even the faux outsiders of Holt Street. In reality the ball is no more indulgent or cliquish than any other industry or charity night in the country. I've worked with some of the charities that have been beneficiaries and they couldn't care less if it's a clique or an in-crowd. Or that on the day of the ball in 2012 some dim journalist asked Tony Abbott at a press conference concerning an asylum-seeker boat smash if, under the circumstances, the night's fun should go ahead. They didn't even mind Kevin Rudd's inexplicable copulating-rodent gag of 2010 – although if Joseph Furphy had been there he would have found a home for his grand phrase, 'the painful constraint induced by this unfathomable joke'. The charities just appreciated the financial support.

So the PM fronted up yet again, under pressure yet again to be a good sport and make the mob laugh. I told you life with the prime minister contained elements of repetition. We even got the same 'tough act to follow' reply from the opposition leader and the same probably overgenerous reviews in print as the previous two years. The PM threw out all my Skywhale jokes in perhaps understandable bewilderment (she kept my jokes about News Corp lecturing Labor about inherited privilege and Fairfax lecturing Labor about structural decline) and then wowed them, again; in 2011 it had been her reshuffle gags; in 2012 she'd started by asking if they wanted the funny speech or the serious speech, in 2013 it was *Game of Thrones*. These nights didn't matter; they don't mitigate any of her, or our, mistakes; but they said, and say, something about the prime minister's patience and courtesy. And you do have to laugh.

That night I got a message from the PM's PA, Caterina Giugovaz, who was sick in bed, saying that if we were going to lose office I had to call her; she couldn't be left at home.

On Saturday 22 June the PM flew to the Atherton Tablelands to honour our thirty-nine Afghanistan dead. Gordon and Susan Chuck, parents of commando Ben, worked for three years to create a memorial for the Australian soldiers killed in Afghanistan. Ben Chuck had died on 21 June 2010, his funeral the first Julia Gillard attended as prime minister. Three years after Ben's death, the PM was there again to speak on the shores of Lake Tinaroo near Yungaburra, as the Avenue of Honour was opened.

While she was there, Corporal Cameron Baird was fighting and dying in Ghawchak village, Uruzgan, Afghanistan, in an action which earned him the Victoria Cross for Australia. He was the fortieth Australian to die in Afghanistan: 'at the front, giving it his all, without any indecision'.

—

In Canberra, we were losing. The final sitting week was about to begin and that meant if there was a challenge, it was going to happen now.

At the start of the week, I was as crook with a cold as I'd been on a workday for a long time. But there was a minerals council speech to finish (more repetition, if not quite regeneration) and the PM was going to speak at the Tasmanian state conference on Saturday. Work to do. And a fair few reasons not to be away from my desk.

Wednesday 26 June started at home with Codral and oranges in a sunny chair. I came in to work that day honestly not certain we were gone. The election date was fixed, and there had to be some chance we would get through these last two days before the winter recess. I had some hope; I wish I hadn't – 'where no hope is left, is left no fear'. I parked outside the building in the car park reserved for ministerial staff and trotted up the stairs. People who had only worked in government often just walked in under the car park on the southern side of Parliament House; I found staff who had spent years of their lives coming in the Senate and reps entrances in opposition never missed a day of walking in the big ministerial entrance doors. Whenever I went up those stairs at pace, I thought of my old boss Latham talking about the young Lyndon Johnson as a staffer running up the steps of the Capitol building, because he just wanted to get in there as soon as he could. This morning, when I got in and walked the corridor to the side entrance to PMO, I saw Stephen Smith, walking with his shirt out as always early in the day (so it didn't crease) and Kim Beazley, visiting the capital on his ambassadorial duties. The big bloke shouted out, 'It's the speechwriter,' and I got a bear hug to start the day. I am still smiling about it nearly two years later.

In my eleven years as a staffer, seemingly spent mostly in the final weeks before a leadership challenge – I directly worked through six, saw my closest mates through a seventh, and was there when a few more came within days of materialising before fading away temporarily – I came to recognise many of the signs. The two things that happen right at the end are that the caucus and party stop calling, deferring anything until after the change; and then a sliver of 'chin up' messages start coming through from distant parts. One year I even got a text from someone on holiday in Vietnam saying, *I hope you're hanging in there*, which really did tell me we were in strife. In memory, it is all one long challenge now, and one of the strangest things is it feels like there's literally no one who was on the same side with me in every one of them. But up to that day, I'd never lost one where I'd been on the same side as Gillard.

About the same time as the Australian Education Bill passed the Parliament that lunchtime I got a 'how are you holding up?' email from Joanna Brent, an old staffmate in Beijing. I really was not making very much progress on this Tasmanian conference speech. Five years earlier she'd rung me in tears from her first proper Canberra night out in government to say it wasn't fair that I wasn't there. Now it was the last day. News websites were reporting that a petition for a spill was circulating among Labor MPs. Rudd himself wouldn't challenge – an important point of pride for him, given the strong previous statements he'd made that he would not – and this was proposed as an alternative; a petition offered a front to say that Rudd was being drafted, albeit with some loss of face on Rudd's part at not saying, 'I want the job.' It was a bit ridiculous, but they were just doing what they had to do.

At the other end of the PMO, my new mates, Michael Carey and Jess Loefstedt, who'd joined our office from other ministers during 2013, were sitting at their desks near the side door. As one supportive senior player after another walked past them to the PM's office, Carey turned to Loefstedt and said, 'Does it strike you not enough people are walking past us right now?' In other offices there were staff who would have died for Julia Gillard whose bosses were turning, and who didn't even know where to sit and hide from the news.

When Chifley gave Nugget Coombs advice about his future as a senior public servant, he said, 'Oh, Doc, never, never resign.' Gillard was from the Chifley school. She also believed she was the better person for the job and given that, believed this was the right course. It's the prime ministership; you don't resign for someone you honestly lack confidence in. In this, the PM was also offering Rudd the opportunity to gain a clear mandate in the caucus, and offering her remaining supporters the chance to cast their vote in good faith; this was a far better path to settling the personal differences that existed and giving the caucus a chance to reunify in the years ahead.

It really was the last day. The PM, miraculous to the last, called the spill in a television interview mid-afternoon, committed to stand down from Parliament if she lost, and asked that Kevin Rudd agree to do the same.

I watched the last episode of *Blackadder* and the final scenes of Butch and Sundance on YouTube alone at my desk. I emailed my predecessor, Tim Dixon, and asked him to refresh my memory on a quote from Peggy Noonan's book that I wanted to use in a speech of my own, to staff when we went to the bar for the last time, as now seemed inevitable. He came back to me immediately; he was watching online in New York, where more than two years earlier I'd kept him up til dawn telling yarns after the Congress speech.

An adviser's husband rang with genuinely decent and helpful advice, something we'd never have thought of in our bubble: if the PM did by some miracle win, she shouldn't talk too long: State of Origin rugby league coverage could begin once her press conference stopped.

Bruce Wolpe, the PM's business adviser and long-term friend, and almost the nicest bloke I know, passed the final hours fidgeting with the A speech; that's the difference between a sanguine and a melancholic. Neither Carl or I really thought it needed a lot of attention and we were sure it would help Bruce get through the afternoon.

My contribution to the B speech was now done, and sitting on my desktop, as well as in a draft email saved in my BlackBerry, in case I was away from my desk when the balloon went up. (I did love the qwerty keyboard on the BlackBerry.) Once the PM had gone to caucus with her supporters, I fired it in to her email and Ben Hubbard's, and put a printed copy in Ben's hand too. He was stoic and responsible and worked solely for her interests to the very last hour.

I went and sat with Carey and Loefstedt; the room filled up with mates; we cheered the PM when her face appeared on TV and argued about what music to listen to, and when we asked, 'Why isn't she back yet?' were agog at the news that a ballot was underway for the deputy leadership between Albanese, who was the victorious Rudd's running mate, and Crean, whose position had seemed so absurd since March. You couldn't make it up. We told travel stories and had a few drinks while we waited for her to come back to us one last time.

My notes for the B speech tried to claim sensible credit for the good things: half a million jobs, higher living standards, better universities, the NBN, carbon, the NDIS, and, above all, school education. She had a right to look gracious by taking responsibility for the mistakes and missteps, and by sharing the credit for the successes with all those who had worked with and for her to get that done. The speech had to deal with some specific business — to clarify her own intention to advise the governor-general to appoint Kevin Rudd PM, and to confirm her position on leaving the Parliament; and the necessary thank-yous.

In writing the speech I imagined Australians would be wondering, again, what had happened to the political stability they had taken for granted for thirty-five years; and that this might leave them vulnerable to the strongman of the right, who wanted them to choose between national unity and their own wellbeing. I offered up some of Gillard's own words over the years about our strong, fair, smart country: unpretentious, united, good at policy, good at care. It wouldn't persuade, but it might show others what could. In some ways, these lines were just a précis of our writing together over nearly three years, on two of the big subjects we had tackled: her project; our country.

I also thought it was a moment in which we should speak to the Labor Party and movement as a whole, in all its moral and political disappointment — in her and Kevin, and the cabinet, and the caucus – and say something that could be remembered as a hopeful characterisation in what were surely very difficult times ahead. And in turn, this was really just a chance for me to write about my one true subject – Julia Gillard – and to tell her what I thought of her by putting it in a draft.

If I couldn't twine her a bower, at least it allowed me to fashion her a wreath.

So I had her saying:

> I want to speak to the members and supporters of the Australian Labor Party and of the union movement. I came to this country as a small girl with nothing but family. Everything I have achieved in life – in education, in the law, in Parliament, as prime minister – has been because of the movement you serve, the movement our forebears built. Ours is still the great party of initiative in Australian life.
>
> These are not easy days for the Labor family. I am the Labor Party's loyal daughter. I know we will go on.

The PM didn't use a word of my B speech. It had served its spiritual and political purpose for me throughout the months of 2013, but she didn't need it at all. She had her own magnificent words; she is quotable today from that night; and my White House counterpart sent me the same one-word email he'd sent me after the misogyny speech – *WOW*.

And in the most authentically Gillard moment of all, she came back to the office to find us all with glasses in our hands and said, 'Cooney! Sorry I didn't use any of your lovely speech!'

And we both laughed.

# Endnotes

Note: on the many occasions where the date and context for a statement on the public record is clearly stated in the text I haven't repeated this in an endnote, particularly for speeches or remarks by the PM Julia Gillard.

The PM's public remarks are widely available in newspaper records and in an official archive at http://pmtranscripts.dpmc.gov.au/ covering prime ministers back to 1940.

PREFACE

1   **'Writing a speech'**: *Death of a President*, 2006, directed by Gabriel Range

    **He would not 'desert his side'**: Philip M. Williams, *Hugh Gaitskell: A Political Biography*, Jonathan Cape, London 1979, pp. 17–18

2   **'collective memory in action'**: see for instance Graham Freudenberg, *Cause for Power*, NSW Labor Party and Pluto Press, Sydney, 1991

    **'true believers'**: see television series *True Believers*, 1988, directed by Peter Fisk

    **'grand old party'**: see for instance Senator Bob Carr (NSW), first speech to Australian Parliament, 21 March 2012

    **'party of initiative' and 'party of resistance'**: see Keith Hancock, *Australia*, Ernest Benn, London, 1930

    **'impatient for the coming fight'**: the Irish national anthem

4   **'We all get taken out in a box, love'**: see interview with Ray Martin, 'Julia Gillard – the Whole Truth', Channel Nine, September 2014

'a man-killing job': Ben Chifley, 'Light on the hill' speech, NSW Labor conference, 12 June 1949

5    **she wouldn't 'lie down and die'**: Tony Abbott, remarks to Coalition party room, 29 May 2012

**'strong and fair but also smart'**: Julia Gillard, letter to Australians, 13 January 2013

6    **'If we want things to stay as they are, things will have to change'**: Guiseppe Tomasi di Lampedusa, *The Leopard*, first published in Italian 1958; translation by Archibald Colquhoun, Pantheon, 1960

**'you will pardon some obscurities'**: Henry David Thoreau, *Walden*, first published 1854

# PART ONE

9    **'The crown in the bush'**: the anecdotal end of the reign of Richard III at Bosworth Field

## CHAPTER 1

11    **'In the plants and mines'**: Julia Gillard, address to Australia Day luncheon, Adelaide, 21 January 2011

17    **'struggling with the perception'**: Senator John Faulkner launching Rodney Cavalier's *Power Crisis* (Cambridge University Press, Sydney, 2010), 13 October 2010

## CHAPTER 2

20    **'That first fine'**: 'Home thoughts from abroad', Robert Browning

**'Can I say'**: Julia Gillard, joint press conference with Deputy Prime Minister Wayne Swan, Parliament House, Canberra, 24 June 2010

21    **'within the limits of nihilism' and 'to live and create'**: Albert Camus, preface to *The Myth of Sisyphus*, Hamish Hamilton, London, 1955

22    **'back on track', 'believe that a good', 'a responsibility to step up', 'people who play by the rules', 're-prosecute the case'**: Julia Gillard, joint press conference with Deputy Prime Minister Wayne Swan, Parliament House, Canberra, 24 June 2010

23    **'through some shopping centres'**: Paul Keating, 'Placido Domingo' speech, National Press Club, Canberra, 7 December 1990

**'She's not a real Australian'**: Phil Coorey, 'Shoppers check out the red-hot special', the *Sydney Morning Herald*, 29 June 2010

24    **'It honestly looked like'**: Paul Toohey, 'Julia Gillard's technicolour coat shows Prime Minister needs an allowance', the *Daily Telegraph*, 6 July 2010

**'Bye, Julia!'**: Samantha Maiden, 'Queen Julia's got the right touch', *The Australian*, 29 June 2010

'a very safe pair', 'a strong and safe pair', 'welcome him into':
Julia Gillard, press conference, Parliament House, Canberra, 28 June 2010

'We campaign in poetry': Mario Cuomo, speech at Yale University,
15 February 1985

26 **Graves and Sassoon**: see Robert Graves, *Goodbye to All That*, first published 1929

28 **'new humanitarianism'**: Robert Manne, 'Comment', *The Monthly*, September 2010

32 **'I am still worried'**: author's private papers

33 **'Today I seek a mandate'**: Julia Gillard, press conference, Parliament House, Canberra 17 July 2010

36 **'rusted-on Bulldogs member'**: Chip le Grand, 'First kick straight between the posts', *The Australian*, 4 August 2010

'the only thing I wouldn't do': see for instance Misha Schubert, 'The day Abbott bared his soul', the *Sydney Morning Herald*, 28 August 2011

## CHAPTER 3

41 **'We have outlived'**: Julia Gillard, remarks for Proclamation Day, Holdfast Bay Glenelg, 28 December 2010

43 **'there will be no carbon tax'**: Julia Gillard, interview with Network Ten, 16 August 2010

'I don't rule out the possibility': Paul Kelly and Dennis Shanahan, 'Julia Gillard's carbon price promise', *The Australian*, 20 August 2010

49 **'they also serve'**: 'On His Blindness', John Milton

**'The Ascent of Heracles'**: retyping from the book's pages, I committed the PM to a typo – this should have read 'in fear', not 'with fear'. John Kinsella was 'nettled' by martial use of even McAuley's poetry ('Leaders scale poetry's register', *The Australian*, 20 October 2010); the author Peter Coleman himself ('Australian Notes', *The Spectator*, 29 October 2010) doubted Gillard comprehended McAuley's theme of a stoic courage insufficient to save a dying secular civilisation.

51 **'indelible rhetoric' and 'Does Gillard grasp'**: Paul Kelly, 'New talk, old story', *The Australian*, 27 October 2010

## INTERLUDE: THE STAFF LIFE

54 **'a wreath for Nye'**: it's also said that the portfolio Lee accepted, arts, was the 'wreath for Nye' and that this was a remark made by critics of the offer, and her acceptance; I prefer the other version of events.

58 **'perfection of the life'**: 'The Choice', William Butler Yeats

**'it yet again'**: Bernard Keane, 'Is Julia Gillard terminal', *Crikey*, 23 May 2011

59 **Sophie Morris and *The West Wing***: Sophie Morris, 'Federal Labor's next generation', *The Saturday Paper*, 12 April 2014

**Peter Hendy and** *The West Wing*: see for instance Chris Johnston, Daniel Flitton and Martin Daly, 'It was West Wing night but this was not make-believe', the *Sydney Morning Herald,* 10 September 2011. Deputy PM John Anderson's adviser Paul Chamberlin was watching too: see Annabel Crabb and Louise Dodson, 'How nation's leaders reacted', *The Age*, 7 September 2002.

63   **'banking is the artery of the economy'**: Paul Keating, remarks to Australian Labor Party national conference, Canberra, 9 July 1984

**'Howard will wear his leadership'**: Paul Keating, remarks to reporters, Parliament House, Canberra, 18 February 1986

64   **The woman on the Gold Coast**: see David Marr with Aban Contractor and Tony Stephens, 'Fall of a knuckleman', the *Sydney Morning Herald*, 22 January 2005

66   **'hopes expire'**: 'September 1, 1939', W H Auden

**'a bowl of bitter tears'**: this is actually a misquote of *Ulysses*, by James Joyce, in which the correct line is 'a bowl of bitter waters'; the misquote was in my head from President Kennedy's address to the Dail, 28 June 1963

73   **'tear our pleasures'**: 'To His Coy Mistress', Andrew Marvell

**'The drift of'**: letter from Clancy Sigal, Los Angeles, the *London Review of Books*, Vol. 35 No. 6, 21 March 2013

# PART TWO

75   **'Sufficient to have stood'**: from Book Three of *Paradise Lost*, John Milton – God describes Satan and all the angels

## CHAPTER 4

77   **'Pivot'**: President Obama's characterisation of his turn to Asia. It's a basketball analogy.

79   **privy council**: television miniseries *Elizabeth R*, 1971

**the dignified part**: Walter Bagehot, *The English Constitution*, first published 1867

80   **'If I had a choice'**: Julia Gillard, interview with ABC's *The 7.30 Report*, 5 October 2010

**'I didn't run for office'**: President Obama, interview with David Remnick, 'Going the Distance', the *New Yorker,* 27 January 2014

83   **'Grant, how many wolves'**: Ulysses S. Grant, *The Personal Memoirs of Ulysses S Grant*, first published 1885–86

85   **'perhaps it was a tactic'**: Matt Buchanan and Leesha McKenny, 'PM engaged? No, it's a ring-in', the *Sydney Morning Herald*, 21 December 2010

**'performance'**: see for instance Susie O'Brien, 'Anna Bligh outperforms Julia Gillard in the greatest leadership test of all', the *Herald Sun*, 14 January 2011

**Hedley Thomas's deer-stalker**: see for instance Hedley Thomas, 'The great avoidable flood: an inquiry's challenge', *The Australian*, 22 January 2011

**National Party and dams**: see for instance Senator Barnaby Joyce in 'Bligh hoses down Abbott dam plan', the *Sydney Morning Herald*, 7 January 2011

86 **Liberal Party and aid to Islamic schools**: see for instance Michelle Grattan and Katharine Murphy, 'Libs would make Indonesian schools pay for floods', the *Sydney Morning Herald*, 9 February 2011

**'The majority of Australians'**: see for instance Dennis Shanahan, 'Voters back Julia Gillard's flood levy', *The Australian*, 7 February 2011

92 **Hasluck groaned inwardly**: see Paul Hasluck, *The Chance of Politics*, Text Publishing, Melbourne, 2000

97 **Bono and the moon landing**: see for instance Tony Wright, 'PM's over the moon. What about Bono?', *The Age*, 12 March 2011

**Lindsay Tanner's jeremiad**: see Lindsay Tanner, *Sideshow*, Scribe, Melbourne, 2012

# CHAPTER 5

99 **'Delivery and decision'**: Carl Green's phrase for the PM to describe the year 2012

**'Any government'**: Julia Gillard, address to Sydney Institute, 13 April 2011

109 **'powerful growing pains'**: Julia Gillard, address to Australia–Israel Chamber of Commerce, Melbourne, 1 February 2012

**Oskar**: see Gunter Grass, *The Tin Drum*, first published 1959

112 **Kennedy's scorn**: see Arthur Schlesinger Jr, *A Thousand Days*, first published 1965

113 **an 'idol to his niece and nephews'**: statement on behalf of Lieutenant Case's family released by Department of Defence

114 **'some businesses will'**: Julia Gillard, address to the nation, 10 July 2011

**'the carbon price is'**: Julia Gillard, address to the National Press Club, 14 July 2011

115 **'Ben Chifley, in this very hall'**: Julia Gillard, address to NSW Labor conference, 10 July 2011

**'lived experience'**: see for instance Phil Coorey, 'Judge me when you've lived the regime, Gillard tells voters', the *Sydney Morning Herald*, 14 July 2011

# CHAPTER 6

116 **'The shadow of the past'**: an early chapter in J R R Tolkien's *The Fellowship of Ring*, first published 1954

**'The responsibilities of government'**: Julia Gillard, 'we are us' speech, Australian Labor Party national conference Sydney, 2 December 2011

119 **'The men who were in the Labor Party now'**: *The Riverina Grazier*, 10 June 1921

120 **Chifley 'brought off the street'**: R G Casey to the House of Representatives, 20 April 1950

**Chifley 'opponent of freedom'**: cover title and illustrations, *IPA Review* January 2014

121 **'our dollar float'**: Julia Gillard, the National Press Club, 14 July 2011

**'a real white whale'**: Julia Gillard, address to Per Capita Reform Series, 4 August 2011

**'Australia looks to America'**: John Curtin, 'The task ahead', *The Herald* (Melbourne), 27 December 1941

122 **Libya**: see for instance Phillip Coorey and Jason Koutsoukis, 'Gillard in open conflict with Rudd', the *Sydney Morning Herald,* 11 March 2011

123 **Grattan and Occam**: see Michelle Grattan, 'Lessons of a campaign trail', the *Sydney Morning Herald*, 17 July 2010

## CHAPTER 7

131 **'Delegates. Australia is a special country'**: author's private papers

135 **Kevin Rudd 'Toys'R'Us' and 'Fuck the future!'**: see for instance www.independent.co.uk/news/world/australasia/gillard-shuffles-the-deckchairs-to-ward-off-rudd-rebellion-6276165.html

138 **1987 'no child' and 1990 staff blue**: see for instance Blanche d'Alpuget, *Hawke the Prime Minister*, MUP, Melbourne, 2010; Graham Freudenberg, *A Figure of Speech*, Wiley, Sydney, 2011

## INTERLUDE: THE MOVEMENT

148 **'we've got your back'**: Ewin Hannan, 'Julia Gillard's parallel universe', *The Australian*, 22 February 2013

149 **'standard stump address'**: Ibid.

**Bowen, Kelly, Van Onselen and the spade**: interview, SKY News Australia Agenda, 3 March 2013

150 **Critics on the left**: Tim Soutphommasane, 'How "Chicken Kev" has left Labor on its knees', *The Age*, 25 March 2013; Geoff Robinson, 'Spectres of Labourism', *Overland*, Summer 2013; Dennis Altman,' What class war? Searching for Labor values in the Labor party', *The Conversation*, 26 March 2013

**Serious critics**: Geoff Kitney, 'Unions' choice: dump Gillard or get Abbott', the *Australian Financial Review*, 23 February 2013; Denis Glover, 'Gillard spells the end of the big left project', the *Australian Financial Review*, 1 March 2013

155 **'we were and are a pluralist party'**: Paul Keating, Australian Labor Party Gala Federation Dinner, 8 May 2001

'**preserve at all costs the union links**': Neville Wran, address to NSW Labor conference, 7 June 1986

'**Labor people weighed**': Bede Nairn, *Civilising Capitalism*, Australian National University Press, Canberra, 1973

157 '**a tribal chief**': see for instance Tony Abbott, address to National Press Club, Canberra, 31 January 2013

160 '**hyper-bowl**': Julia Gillard, interview with ABC's *The 7.30 Report*, 6 April 2011

'**steering from the steerage**': widely attributed to Sir George Reid

'**wouldn't know a bank**': R G Casey to the House of Representatives, 20 April 1950

'**the Hawke–Keating socialist government**': famously associated with Michael Hodgman, Liberal MP for the Tasmanian electorate of Denison, 1975–1987. Geoff Townshend once described Hodgman as the 'last Regency buck of the old House'.

# PART THREE

161 '**Raining stones**': see *Raining Stones*, 1993, directed by Ken Loach.

## CHAPTER 8

163 '**the measure is in the years**': several speeches of Julia Gillard's about governing. The second volume of Robert Menzies' memoir is titled *The Measure of the Years*.

'**It's the economy, stupid**': see *The War Room*, 1993, directed by Chris Hegedus and D A Pennebaker

165 '**in three years, three years ahead of schedule**': Treasurer Wayne Swan, budget speech, 11 May 2010

169 '**the government had accepted**': Ross Garnaut, *Dog Days*, Black Inc., Melbourne 2013

171 '**time to move on**': Tony Abbott, remarks to journalists, Sydney, 26 January 2012

178 **Toorak and Cessnock**: or perhaps it was John Howard, saying Canberra looks like Killara and votes like Cessnock

181 '**lacerating tongue**': David Marr, 'Born to run', the *Sydney Morning Herald* 24 August 2010

## CHAPTER 9

183 '**Basest things**': one of Satan's many fine speeches in John Milton's *Paradise Lost*

191 '**Oh, of course**': Mitch Hooke, ABC AM radio, 31 May 2012

## CHAPTER 10

194 '**I will not**': Julia Gillard, 'the misogyny speech', House of Representatives, 9 October 2012

196 **'First woman, first redhead'**: Julia Gillard, joint press conference with Deputy Prime Minister Wayne Swan, Parliament House, Canberra, 24 June 2010

**'ribald texts'**: Jessica Wright, 'Ashby files ribald texts with Slipper', the *Sydney Morning Herald*, 7 October 2012

197 **'make an honest woman'**: Tony Abbott, press conference in Brisbane, 24 February 2011

**'when she said no'**: Tony Abbott, press conference, 3 August 2010. Full quote:

Are you suggesting to me that when it comes from Julia, 'no' doesn't mean 'no'? When she said 'no', I thought she meant 'no'. I believed her. You can't change the rules just because you are in trouble. She's surely not trying to say to us that 'no doesn't mean no', because that's what she said, 'no', repeatedly. And when she said 'no' I believed her.

**'meowing'**: Liberal Senator David Bushby, Senate economics committee, 31 May 2011

## CHAPTER 11

208 **'forget the spin'**: Greg Sheridan, 'Forget the spin: the gig is in the bag', *The Australian*, 27 September 2012

**'Bloomingdales'**: Tony Walker, 'Obama's strong hint of harder line on Iran', the *Australian Financial Review*, 29 September 2012

209 **'in Jakarta not in New York'**: Tony Abbott, 2GB radio, 24 September 2012

211 **'unremitting', 'jejune', 'real', 'hard', 'understanding', 'courage', 'privately', 'Washington', 'Canberra', 'in denial'**: Hugh White, 'White Papering the Cracks', *The Monthly,* December 2012–January 2013

217 **'selfishness'**: Bob Carr, *Diary of a Foreign Minister*, NewSouth Press, Sydney, 2014

218 **'nothing hard ever gets easier'**: Julia Gillard, address to the National Press Club, Canberra, 14 July 2011

## INTERLUDE: THE SHY CHILD

227 **'Her measured aggression'**: David Marr, 'Born to run', the *Sydney Morning Herald,* 24 August 2010

230 **'the maw of magazine culture'**: Don Watson, 'Comment: political leadership in Australia', *The Monthly*, August 2011

231 **will 'like a dividing spear'**: John Strachey, UK Labour Minister, speaking to Aneurin Bevan about Hugh Gaitskell

**Abraham Lincoln**: see *Primary Colours*, 1998, directed by Mike Nichols

232 **'nobody felt BETTER'**: D H Lawrence, *Kangaroo*, first published 1923

**'or at a flash town hall lunch' and 'the snobbishness'**: Julia Gillard, address to Australia Day luncheon, Adelaide, 21 January 2011

232 **Gillard typing**: John McTernan, 'The Julia I know and love but you never really met', the *Sunday Telegraph*, 21 July 2013

235 **'In this century'**: Thomas Keneally, 'Australian Identity in the 21st Century', keynote lecture to the Festival of Ideas, University of Melbourne, 16 June 2011

237 **Chifley's days of wonder**: Leslie Finlay Crisp, *Ben Chifley*, Longmans Green and Co, London, 1960

# PART FOUR

239 **'Small hammers'**: John Donne on the regicide of Charles, in 'The Progress of the Soule', first song XXXVIII

## CHAPTER 12

247 **'tough and correct'**: Ross Gittins, 'Gillard's reality check tough and correct', the *Sydney Morning Herald*, 2 February 2013

248 **'I am obviously past it'**: Graham Richardson, 'Gillard heads into dangerous waters', *The Australian*, 31 January 2013

## CHAPTER 13

257 **'the last grand days'**: see Frank Moorhouse, *Grand Days*, Random House, Melbourne, 1994

260 **'It is not too late'**: John Garnaut, 'Gillard's turn to put China back in the frame', the *Sydney Morning Herald*, 29 March 2013

**'unprecedented'**: John Garnaut, 'Arm in arm with Xi', the *Sydney Morning Herald*, 8 April 2013

261 **'foreign policy coup' and 'the cornerstone'**: 'China deal the cornerstone of Julia Gillard's Asian Century', *The Australian*, 10 April 2013

271 **the wedge that failed**: Mark Kenny, '$100bn Budget trap', the *Sydney Morning Herald*, 14 May 2013

## CHAPTER 14

272 **'Man reaches'**: John Steinbeck, *The Grapes of Wrath*, first published 1939

**Quo vadis**: see for example *Quo Vadis*, 1951, directed by Mervin Le Roy

282 **'this unfathomable joke'**: Joseph Furphy, *Such is Life*, first published 1903

283 **'at the front'**: personal details of Corporal Baird, released by Department of Defence

284 **'where no hope is left, is left no fear'**: Paradise Lost, John Milton

285 **'never, never resign'**: Coombs interview with Robin Hughes, 23 January 1992

288 **'I want to speak to the members and supporters'**: author's private papers

# Acknowledgements

I can't deny my faith or my Church. These acknowledgements would be false without a sincere thanks to God and in particular an offering to the Sacred Heart. *Cordi Jesu.*

I am certain there is nothing I could say about my wife and children, my daughters' partners or my grandson, without being trite or ridiculous; and I promised I wouldn't be trite or ridiculous. So enough of that.

My mum taught me to read, drove me to the library, took me to children's book week, joined me up for the Puffin Club, bought me Roald Dahl, gave me the dream. Thanks, Mum.

I thank my dad in the text.

Many friends said to me over the years I should write a book and I am so grateful for all those kind words. Two people really insisted: Gerard McManus told me I simply must and made me feel a responsibility to get it done; George Megalogenis amazed me with his total confidence in my ability and by introducing me to Penguin. Jamie Button was also marvelously supportive and his introductions gave me great heart. Chris Feik at Quarterly Essay and Nick Feik at *The Monthly* both took for granted that I could write in periods when I wasn't taking it absolutely for granted. Two people actually made it real: my publisher Ben Ball and my editor Arwen Summers, who were completely perfect. Josh Bornstein and Tony Hodges provided invaluable background. Amit Singh and Jim Chalmers gave up precious personal time in desperately busy lives to read and comment on the draft. I could not have done it without you. (Any remaining errors are my own.)

The long gestation of this book took in many years among the Per Capita circle. David Hetherington, Denis Glover and Tony Kitchener – and more recently, Emily Millane – each found completely different ways to inspire me over and over again, in good times and bad. On the very edge of the Per Capita circle, while I was in Melbourne and since, John Roskam has never failed to make me smile. Andrew Barr threw me a lifeline to come home.

Right at the start, Mark Latham gave me a chance, and then Kim Beazley gave me a second chance, and I would never have worked in Government or had anything to say remotely worth putting in a book without those two bosses.

While I was writing this book I had enormous support from the Chifley Research Centre: our chair Nick Martin and directors, our financial supporters – and especially my remarkable colleague Jane Austen, who has an amazing future in our movement. I had absolutely essential support from Federal Labor leader Bill Shorten, MPs Jim Chalmers and Andrew Leigh and NSW General Secretary Jamie Clements; Professor Tom Kompas at the ANU's Crawford School, David Pembroke at contentgroup, Jo Scard at Fifty Acres and Rowena O'Neill at Global Shapers; the Chief Minister of the ACT Andrew Barr and Meegan Fitzharris MLA.

Carl Green and I had a lot of help writing for Julia Gillard, and I especially thank Virginia Cook, Penelope Layland, Julianne Stewart, James Newton and Corinne Grant.

So many current and former staffers, dear mates and beloved friends, are not named in this book, for all sorts of reasons. You all know who you are. I loved your work.

When he told her she should hire me as her speechwriter, Tim

Dixon said to Julia Gillard 'Michael Cooney would rip the heart out of his chest for you'. Still true.

Thank you all.

—

Grateful acknowledgement is made to the following sources for extracts reprinted in this book:

Speeches and parliamentary transcripts licensed from the Commonwealth of Australia under a Creative Commons Attribution 3.0 Australia License. The Commonwealth of Australia does not necessarily endorse the content of this publication. Paul Hasluck, *The Chance of Politics*, Text Publishing, 2000, reproduced with permission from The Text Publishing Company Pty Ltd; full acknowledgement is made to Robert Graves, *Goodbye to All That*, and Carcanet Press Limited, 2007; Thomas Keneally, 'Australian Identity in the 21st Century', the Festival of Ideas, University of Melbourne, 16 June 2011, by arrangement with the Licensor, Thomas Keneally, c/- Curtis Brown (Aust) Pty Ltd; John Hirst, 'Labor's Part in Australian History: A Lament', Allan Martin Lecture at the Australian National University, 2006, reproduced with permission from the author; Erik Jensen, 'Kevin Rudd's Unrelenting Campaign to Regain Power', *The Monthly*, March 2013, reproduced with permission from the author; Annabel Crabb, 'Damn the Torpedoes. PM puts pedal to the metal', ABC *The Drum*, 12 October 2011, reproduced by permission of the Australian Broadcasting Corporation and ABC Online © 2011 ABC, all rights reserved; letter from Clancy Sigal in the *London Review of Books*, 21 March 2013, reproduced with permission from the *London Review of Books*; Brian Brivati, *Hugh Gaitskell*, Hushion House Publishing, 1997, reproduced with permission of the author; lines from *Primary Colours* reproduced with permission from Universal Films; Laurie Oakes, 'Like concrete, like could sink Gillard', the *Daily Telegraph*, 12 March 2011 and Paul Kelly, 'Labor's tragedy: a lack of strategy to govern for all', *The Australian*, 30 March 2013 have been licensed by Copyright Agency Limited (CAL) — except as permitted by the Copyright Act, you must not re-use this work without the permission of the copyright owner or CAL; the Pogues, 'Thousands Are Sailing', reprinted with permission from Hal Leonard Australia; 'The Ascent of Heracles' from Peter Coleman, *The Heart of James McAuley*, Connor Court Publishing, 2006, reproduced with permission from Connor Court Publishing; Ross Garnaut, *Dog Days*, Black Inc., 2013, reproduced with permission from Black Inc. Publishing; Leslie Finlay Crisp, *Ben Chifley*, Longmans, Green & Co, 1961, reproduced with permission from Pearson; Gavan Daws, *Prisoners of the Japanese*, William Morrow, 1994, reproduced with permission from the author; Joseph Ratzinger and Marcello Pera, *Without Roots*, Basic Books, 2006, reproduced with permission from Basic Books; lines from *The Leopard* by Giuseppe Tomasi di Lampedusa, translated by Archibald Colquhoun, published by Harvill and reproduced by permission of The Random House Group Ltd.

Every effort has been made to trace and acknowledge copyright material, and the author and publisher would be pleased to hear from anyone in this regard.

# Index

Abbott, Tony
    Aboriginal Tent Embassy 171
    Afghanistan war 49, 88–9
    Beazley on 69
    budget reply speeches 112, 280
    carbon pricing 126
    characterised as 'Mr No' 136
    'convoy of no confidence' 113–14
    'debt and deficit' 164
    election campaign 2010 37
    on Gillard 5, 157
    Gillard on 58
    'grown-up government' 210, 280
    'Jakarta versus Geneva' 261
    national disability insurance scheme 269–71, 280
    opinion polls 32, 220
    opposition leader 118
    personality 36
    public opinion 15
    quoting Chifley 119–20
    replaces Turnbull 33, 44
    Safe Rates 147
    seen as next prime minister 266
    sexism and 198–9
    unsupportive of UN Security Council bid 209
ABC 124, 270
Aboriginal Tent Embassy 171–2
Afghanistan war
    Australian casualties 21–2, 37, 47, 49, 88–90, 112–13, 191, 193, 211, 213, 283
    Australian involvement 46–9, 87–9, 206, 211–12
*Age, The* 109, 123, 150, 199, 201–2, 249
Albanese, Anthony
    adviser Loefstedt 56
    background 146, 192
    leader of the House 114, 140, 144–5
    rumour 255
    speech after personal attack 114
    speech after Safe Rates passed 146
    stands for deputy leadership 287
    support for Rudd 178–9
Al-Qaeda 47
Altmann, Dennis 150
Anderson, Laura 72, 246
Aplin, Timothy 21
Arbib, Mark 180
Ashby, James 184, 186–7, 196–7
Asia Society 206
Asian Century White Paper 93, 118, 204, 206, 213–16, 219
Asian tsunami 2004 64–5
Association of Southeast Asian Nations (ASEAN) 205, 216
asylum-seeker policy 21–3, 27–8, 84
asylum seekers
    *SIEV-221* 84–5
    Sri Lankan 27
Atkinson, Richard 89
Aubin, Tracey 71
Australian Agricultural Company 195
Australian Chamber of Commerce and Industry 145

303

Australian Council of Trade Unions
  (ACTU) 151, 159
Australian Education Bill 279, 285
Australian Education Union 266
*Australian Financial Review* 208
Australian Industry Group 50–1
Australian Labor Party (ALP)
  difference from other parties 1–3
  laborism 149, 154–5
  'Laborites' 62
  National Conference 2009 133–4
  National Conference 2011 134–9
  NSW Conference 2011 115
  NSW Conference 2012 136, 192
  opposing forces 3
  'party of initiative' 2–4
  past identities 118–22, 143
  'progressives' 62
  staff life 54–74
  union movement and 143–60
  Victorian Conference 2013 267
  victory 2007 124
  victory 2010 124
Australian League of Rights 113
*Australian Moment, The* (Megalogenis) 180
*Australian Story* 233
*Australian, The* 36, 43, 46, 51, 55, 59, 72, 85, 119, 149, 152, 184–5, 201, 208, 210, 248, 260–1
Australian Workers Union (AWU) 148, 200–3, 221

Bagehot, Walter 79
Baird, Cameron 283
Baker, Mark 201–2
Baker, Steven 39
balance of trade 108
Band, The 64
Bandt, Adam 140
Barr, Andrew 26, 37–8
Batchelor, Ryan 35
Bayley, Adrian Ernest 194
Beazley, David 69
Beazley, Kim
  adviser Cooney 25, 27, 66–9
  ambassador to the US 83, 96–7, 130
  Cooney and 284
  defeat 2001 276
  defeat 2006 25, 69–70

Dixon and 38
  Labor leadership 66–8
  Rudd and 254–5
  Young and 16
Belloc, Hilaire 158
Benn, Tony 252
Berger, Simon 195
Bevan, Aneurin 'Nye' 231, 266
Bewes, Nathan 22
Birt, Ashley 191
Bishop, Bronwyn 184
Bishop, Julie 197–8, 258
Bleich, Jeff 21
Bligh, Anna 100
Bloomberg, Michael 21
Boeing Business Jet (BBJ) 77–8
Bolt, Andrew 172
Bouvier, Jacqueline 95
Bowen, Chris 37–8, 141, 149, 241, 253, 255
Boyce, Max 275
Bramston, Troy 127
Brandis, George 185
Brent, Joanna 285
British American Tobacco 101
Brough, Mal 184, 186, 196, 278
Brown, Bob 45, 282
Brown, Jason 37
Bruce, Stanley 14
Buchanan, Matt 85
Burke, Tony 24, 128
Burton, John 57
Bush, Kate 64
Business Council of Australia 145
Butler, Mark 128

Calwell, Arthur 69, 117, 156
Cameron, David 21
Cameron, Tom 103–4
Campbell, Colin 70
carbon pricing
  abatement schemes 86
  accompanying welfare increases 220
  capture and storage 44
  carbon tax 87, 104–5, 113, 125–6, 176–7, 242
  clean energy funded by 164
  Clean Energy Future 113
  failures of 2009 43
  fixed price 84, 87, 105, 125

Gillard achievement 6, 14, 107, 111, 126, 178–9, 217–19, 237
Gillard agenda 22–3, 46, 121, 206, 287
negotiations with China 262
'no carbon tax' 43, 87, 105
not household budget disaster 193
pollution permits 87, 114
pollution reduction scheme 43, 45
unpopular 125, 183
Carey, Michael 285, 287
*Caring for Older Australians* (Productivity Commission) 128
Carr, Bob
    China visit 261
    Cooney and 98
    Gillard and 217, 264
    McGregor and 60
    Senator NSW 179–80
    stand-in for Gillard in US 207–8
    UN Security Council bid 212
Carr, Kim 111, 141
Carville, James 163, 167
Case, Marcus 112–13
Casey, R G 213
Cassidy, Barrie 33
*Catcher in the Rye, The* (Salinger) 58
Cater, Nick 119
Cavalier, Rodney 61, 115
Centre for International Security Studies 261
Chalmers, Jim 18, 59, 72, 244, 246
Chan, Linda 262
Channel Ten 21
Chaucer, Geoffrey 257
Chifley, Ben
    biography 236–8, 265
    criticisms of 120, 160
    death 5
    Gillard on 116–18
    Larwood and 236–7
    'never, never resign' 285
    on party leadership 4
    statue 116
    'the light on the hill' 119, 154
    'things worth fighting for' 115
Chikarovski, Kerry 225
China
    Australian relations with 6, 14, 130, 216
    growth 93–4, 97, 181
    resources boom 108

2013 agreements with Australia 259–64
'upstage issue' 80
Christmas Island 84–5
Chuck, Benjamin 21, 283
Chuck, Gordon 283
Chuck, Susan 283
Churchill, Winston 275
cigarette plain packaging 101–2, 105
Clare, Jason 141
Clarke, Michael 61
Clean Energy Future 113
climate change 44–6, 50, 87, 107–8, 141, 160
Clinton, Bill 59, 163
Closing the Gap campaign 174
'Club Sensible' 210, 242, 250, 258, 280
Cohen, Barry 210
Cohen, Eliot 71–2
Coleman, Peter 49
Combet, Greg 37, 45, 141
Commonwealth Heads of Government Meeting 118
Commonwealth Parliamentary Offices, Sydney 11–12
company tax 189
Conroy, Stephen 117, 185, 252
*Conversation, The* 150
Coombs, Nugget 285
Cooney, Brian 49
Cooney, Frank 49
Cooney, Michael
    Beazley's adviser 25, 27, 66–9
    becomes Gillard's speechwriter 39–40
    Howard and 71–2
    Labor 'lifer' 63–73
    Latham's adviser 13, 25, 27, 64–6, 68
    'look West' 82, 97
    on 'moving forward' 32
    Per Capita 26, 226
    on political style 165–7
    regrets over national conference speech 135–9
    relationship with Gillard 6, 13–14, 19, 67–8, 225–7, 233, 288
    staff work 14, 54–74
    US House of Representatives 96
Cooney, Paul 49
Coorey, Phil 23, 46
Corlett, Peter 116

Council of Australian Governments 247, 265–8
*Courier-Mail* 64
Cowan, Eddie 56
Cox, Eva 278
Crabb, Annabel 217–18, 221, 244
Crean, Simon
    arts funding plans 111, 254
    leadership ballot March 2013 254–5
    ministry 24, 38
    press secretary Spencer 59
    Rudd and 175
    sacked by Gillard 254–5
    stands for deputy leadership 287
credit rating, Australian 181
Creighton, James 88
*Crikey* 58, 278, 281
Crisp, Fin 223, 236–7, 265
Crook, Tony 146–7
Cuchulain 58
Cummings, Bart 18–19
Cuomo, Mario 24–5
*Current Affair, A* 21
Curtin, John
    on Calwell 117
    Gillard on 117–18
    respect for 4
    Rodgers on 121
    social-democratic ideals 96
    statue 116
cyclone Yasi 86

*Daily Telegraph* 105, 192, 252
Dale, Tomas 37
Dastyari, Sam 104
David, Larry 35
Davidoff, Ian 35, 72, 99–100, 171
Daws, Gavan 233–4
de Beer, Suzanne 146
Demetriou, Andrew 40
Diddams, Blaine 191
DisabilityCare Australia, 5, 218–19, 266–70, 279–80 *see also* national disability insurance scheme
Dixon, Tim 26, 31, 38–9, 72, 98, 180, 286
*Dog Days* (Garnaut) 108, 111
Doha Round 93
Donaldson, Mark 130
Dowdell, Kevin 97

Downes, Andrew 61
Dravid, Rahul 60
Dreyfus, Mark 253
drought 2008–2010 107
*Drum, The* (ABC) 217
Duffy, Bryce 191
Durban, Alan 166

Economic Club of New York 206
economic policy
    budget 2011-12 110–12
    budget 2012-13 188–9
    budget 2013-14 279
    commitment to future surplus 30, 50, 110, 165, 168–9
    deficit 2012 242–3
    difficulties 108–9, 164
    economic reform 51
    flood levy 86–7, 102, 105, 110, 141, 187, 234
    funding for education reform 270
    growth 167–9
    international agenda 93
    Medicare levy 268–71, 279–80
    micro-economic reform 31
    revenue writedowns 183
    spending cuts 86, 110–11, 243
    tax cuts 114, 220
economy, Australian 204–5, 216, 244
education reform 14, 187–8, 206, 218–19, 265–8, 270, 279
e-health 34
e-learning 34
Eliot, T S 257
Ellis, Bob 2, 15
Emerson, Craig 18, 202, 264
emissions trading 43–5, 87, 125
Epstein, David 15
equal-pay case 160, 175, 192
Evans, Chris 38, 248, 253
Evatt, H V (Doc) 57

Faine, Jon 270
Fainga'a, Colby 275
Fair Work Australia 160
Fairfax 68, 124, 201
Fall, Bernard 106
Farley, David 195
Faulkner, John 13, 17, 255
Ferguson, Martin 38, 141, 242

Fingleton, Jack 236
*First Things* 273
Fisher, Andrew 4
Fitch Ratings 181
Fitzpatrick, Eamonn 262
*Five Days in London* (Lukacs) 275
flood levy 86–7, 102, 105, 110, 141, 187, 234
foreign policy
 conservative 209–10
 Labor (*see* China; Indonesia; UN Security Council; United States of America)
Forrest, Andrew 258
*Four Corners* 277
Fox, Jo 72, 244
Franklin, Matthew 226
Fraser, Malcolm 42
Freudenberg, Graham 2, 15, 98, 136, 138, 157
Frey, James 97
Frey, Rob 97
Fuller, Sir George 119
Furphy, Joseph 282

Gabriel, Peter 64
Gaddafi, Muammar 122–3
Gaitskell, Hugh 1, 231
Galagher, Nathanael 193, 211
Garnaut, John 260
Garnaut, Ross 108, 111, 169
Garrett, Peter 141
Gavin, Luke 191
GetUp 174
Giddings, Lara 270
Gillard, Julia
 activism and optimism 30, 99
 agenda 5, 22, 25, 111, 127, 219
 attacks on 23, 114, 195, 200–1
 Australia Day footpath fall 171–2, 174, 181–2
 bid for seat on UN Security Council 98
 call for spill June 2013 286
 on Chifley 117–18
 cricket 236
 on Curtin 117–18
 defeated by Rudd 2013 287
 elected leader 20
 election campaign 2010 32–5

 election date 2013 announced 248
 election victory 2010 34–7, 42–3
 family 30, 192–3
 flight to Washington 2011 77–83
 Gandhi memorial fall 212
 'got it done' 86, 178, 182, 217–18, 230
 'great nation progressive' 5–6, 205, 216
 'I will not lie down and die' 136, 153, 192
 leadership ballot March 2013 241, 253–6, 277
 legacy 287
 on Megalogenis 181
 ministries 24, 37–8, 141, 253
 misogyny speech 194, 198–200
 'moving forward' 33
 Obama and 21, 80, 92, 96
 'party called the Labor Party' 149, 160
 personality 5, 11, 18, 20, 22, 29–30, 36, 217–19, 225–38, 283
 Prime Minister's Office (PMO) 14
 public appearances 23–4, 106
 public opinion 25
 relations with China 130, 182, 259–64
 relations with independents and minor parties 35–6, 43–5, 87
 Rudd and 20, 24, 122–5, 135, 143, 177–8, 286
 shadow minister for health 67
 on Swan 180
 US Alliance 80–2, 87, 90, 96, 216
 visit to China 2013 257–64
 Washington visits 2011 81, 83, 90–8
 working style with staff 78–82
 *see also* Afghanistan war; Asian Century White Paper; carbon pricing; economic policy; education reform; equal-pay case; national broadband network (NBN); national disability insurance scheme; Safe Rates; speeches; UN Security Council
Gittins, Ross 247
Giugovaz, Caterina 99, 256, 263, 283
*Global Mail* 185
Glover, Dennis 55
Gonski school funding review 219, 279
*Gorton Experiment, The* (Reid) 64
Gorton, John 64

*Grand Days* (Moorhouse) 244
Grant, Ulysses S. 83–4
Grattan, Michelle 123, 199, 249
Graves, Robert 27
Grech, Godwin 19, 242
Greece 168
Green, Carl 15–16, 18, 115, 129, 158, 170–1, 236, 255, 286
Greens, The
    Afghanistan war 48
    Bandt 140
    carbon pricing 87
    company tax 189
    election campaign 45
    emissions trading 44–5, 126
    mining tax 152–3
Greenspan, Alan 180
Greer, Germaine 15
Gregory, Lady 58
Growden, Greg 236
Guard, John 158
Gusmao, Xanana 28
Gyngell, Alan 47

Hadley, Ray 61, 144
Hall, Barry 36
Hannan, Ewin 149
Harper, Paul 21
Harradine, Brian 67
Harris, Lachlan 57, 139, 246
Hartcher, Peter 199, 210, 278
Hasluck, Paul 92, 213
Hawke, Bob
    adviser Walsh 57
    benefit from end of drought 107–8
    economic policy 121
    Gillard on 116
    hairstyle 19
    Indigenous affairs 174
    'no child' speech 138
    pro-market reformism 51
    retired statesman 5
    Telstra and 42
    US alliance 261
    Young and 16, 18
Hayden, Bill 63, 179
Haylen, Jo 222, 245, 250
health policy 43
*Heart of James McAuley, The* (Coleman) 49
Henderson, Gerard 282

Hendy, Peter 59–60
Henry, Ken 28, 128, 180
*Herald Sun* 105, 270
Hetherington, David 25–6, 245
Hewitt, Jennifer 258
Heydon, Dyson 210, 225
Hirst, John 157–8, 232
Hockey, Joe 34, 225
Hodges, Tony 172
Holt, Harold 92–3
Hooke, Mitch 191
Horta, Ramos 28
Howard, John
    address to US Congress 88
    asylum-seeker policy 28
    climate change 44
    Commonwealth Parliamentary Offices, Sydney 11–12
    Cooney and 71–2
    economic policy 110
    emissions trading 44
    Indigenous affairs 174
    interest rates 188
    Iraq war 47
    Pearson and 281
    private health insurance rebate 43
    re-elected 1998 34
    relations with China 130
    Vietnam war 90–1
Howes, Paul 148
Hu Jintao 261
Hu, Stern 262
Hubbard, Ben 128, 137, 199, 225–6, 287
Hudson, Peter 274
Hughes, Billy 4, 14
Hughes, Phil 60
Huntley, Rebecca 244

*Illawarra Mercury* 21
independent MPs 35–6, 43, 87, 102–3, 140
India 212
*Indian Summer of Cricket, An* (McGregor) 60–1
Indigenous constitutional recognition 173–4
Indonesia 27, 209
*Insiders* 52
Institute of Public Affairs 120

308

*Intellectual Life of the British Working Classes, The* (Rose, J) 30
Iraq war 47, 91, 102, 172, 179

Japanese tsunami 98, 100
Jenkins, Harry 184
Johns, Gary 210
Johnson, Lyndon 284
Johnston, David 88
Jones, Alan 113–14, 144, 194–6
Jones, Andrew 112
Jones, Barry 67
Jordan, Alister 57
Joyce, Barnaby 44, 51
Judd, Chris 173

Kaiser, Mike 15
Kassabgi, Damian 55–6, 215, 245–6
Katter, Bob 141
Keane, Bernard 58–9
Keating, Paul
   advice to Gillard 4
   on ALP 155, 157
   APEC Leaders' Forum 261
   Cooney and 63
   economic policy 121
   Gillard on 116
   on Howard 63
   Indigenous affairs 174
   'maddie' 252
   pro-market reformism 51
   on public appearances 23
   *Recollections of a Bleeding Heart* 62
   relations with China 130
   retired statesman 5
   Telstra and 42
   'true believers' 2
Kelly, Gail 259
Kelly, Mike 20
Kelly, Paul 51, 143, 149
Kelly, Sean 139, 221–2, 246, 257
Kempton, Mark 100
Keneally, Tom 234–5
Kennedy, John (president) 94–5, 97, 112
Kennedy, John (football coach) 249
Kenny, Chris 59
Key, John 21, 100
Khawaja, Usman 60

Kilcullen, David 106
King, Catherine 58
Kirby, Grant 37
Klein, Joel 21
Knowledge Nation 67
Kramer, Kirk 94
Kyoto Protocol 179, 219

Lagan, Bernard 185
Lagarde, Christine 182, 259
Lake, Jack 73
Lakoff, George 167
Lambert, Matthew 191
Lampe, Amanda 226
Lang, Jack 237
Langley, Todd 113
Larcombe, Jamie 89–90
Larwood, Harold 236–7
*Last Waltz, The* [film] 64
Latham, Mark
   concession speech 276
   Cooney and 13, 25, 27, 64–6, 68, 71
   Labor leadership 64–6
   'Manboob Habib' 185
   *60 Minutes* 34
Lavarch, Michael 244–5
Lawrence, Carmen 72
Lawrence, D H 232
leaks 34, 123–5, 172, 241–2, 253
Lee, Jennie 54
Lewis, Duncan 95
Lewis, Steve 185–6, 196
Li Keqiang 260–1
Liberal Party
   Afghanistan war 88
   company tax 189
   differences from Labor 1–2
   fiscal policy 167–8
   in opposition 118
   poker machine reform 140
   Queensland floods 86
   Slipper case 184–5
   think tank 119, 195
Lloyd, Maggie 246
Loefstedt, Jessika 56, 58, 285, 287
*London Review of Books* 73
Lowy Institute 27–8, 30
Lukacs, John 275
Lyons, Joseph 14

Macklin, Jenny
    Cooney and 39–40, 66
    funding for DisabilityCare 268
    minister for Indigenous affairs 174
    poker machine reform 103
    staff 35
Mahon, Hugh 223, 225
'Malley, Ern' 132
Malouf, David 15
Malthouse, Mick 128
mandate, interpretation of 41
Manne, Robert 27
Maritime Union of Australia (MUA) 143–4
Marr, David 65, 175, 181, 227
Martin, James 211
Mathieson, Tim 18–19, 208, 215, 278
Mauboy, Jessica 131
Maude, Richard
    Cooney and 72–3, 226, 260
    on Giugovaz 263
    international adviser 47, 80, 82, 258
    not responsible for 'anonymous statement' 123
    Office of National Assessments 47
Maxwell, Nick 39
McAuley, James 49
McClelland, Robert 38, 141, 255
McDonald, Mervyn 193, 211
McGiveron, Jim 145
McGrath Foundation 224, 236
McGregor, Cate 60–2
McKenny, Leesha 85
McKew, Maxine 202
McKinney, Jared 37, 88
McKinnon, Michael 88
McTernan, John 137–9, 171–2, 232
Meagher, Jill 194
Meares, Andrew 259
media laws 252–4
Medicare levy 268–71, 279–80
Medicare Levy Amendment (DisabilityCare Australia) Bill 279–80
Megalogenis, George 33–4, 180–1
Menadue, John 57
Menzies, Robert 14
Mick Young Scholarship Trust 11
Mills, Stephen 138
Milne, Christine 45, 152
Milosevic, Stjepan 211

Milton, John 183
Minchin, Nick 44
Minerals Council of Australia 143, 190–1
Minerals Resource Rent Tax 179
mining tax 21–3, 29, 152–3, 190–1
Monckton, Christopher 250
Mondale, Walter 105
*Monthly, The* 211, 230, 277–8, 282
Moorhouse, Frank 244
Morris, Sophie 59
Multi-Party Committee on Climate Change 45–6, 107
Murdoch, Rupert 117
Murray-Darling Basin Plan 128
MV *Oceanic Viking* 27

Nairn, Bede 155–6
Napthine, Denis 267–8, 270
national broadband network (NBN) 34–5, 42, 111, 164, 179, 206, 219, 252
national disability insurance scheme, 14, 121, 188, 206, 266–71, 279–80
    *see also* DisabilityCare Australia
National Party 85–6
National Plan for School Improvement 218–19, 279
National Press Club 30–1, 86, 114, 121, 218, 228, 233, 247
National Transport Commission 144
National Union of Workers 59
Nelson, Brendan 44
*New Idea* 20
*New Yorker, the* 80
Newman, Campbell 193, 245
News Corp 253
News Limited 24, 45–6, 67, 105, 124, 172, 201, 252
Newspoll
    2010 June 21
    2010 July 32
    2011 February 86
    2011 July 113
    2011 September 123
    2012 September & October 220–1
Ng, Matthew 262
Nixon, Richard 112
Noonan, Peg 62, 286
Nutt, Tony 185

Oakes, Laurie 21, 105–6, 123
Oakeshott, Rob 140–1, 174, 222, 252, 266
Obama, Barack
    Afghanistan war 47
    Gillard and 21, 80, 92, 96
    opposition to 23
    visit to Australia 2011 118, 129–31
O'Brien, Flann 166
O'Connor, Brendan 253
O'Dwyer, Kelly 199
O'Farrell, Barry 219, 267–8
O'Leary, Tony 72
O'Loughlin, Fiona 18
One Nation 113
Overington, Caroline 228
*Overland* 150

Palmer, Scott 21
*Paradise Lost* (Milton) 183
Parenting Payment 189
Parkinson, Michael 225
Parnell, Charles Stewart 96
*Party Thieves* (Cassidy) 33
Peacock, Andrew 277
Pearce, David 47
Pearson, Christopher 210, 281–2
Pell, George 144, 210, 224
Penrose, Clare 113
Per Capita 25–6, 29
Pickering, Larry 200–1
Plenary 18
Plibersek, Tanya 102, 141
Poate, Robert 211
poker machine reform 102–5, 140
Pope Benedict XVI 273–4
population policy 27–8
Price, Matt 72, 186
*Primary Colors* [film] 59, 231
private health insurance rebate 43
Proclamation Day celebrations, Adelaide 52–3, 170
Productivity Commission 103, 128, 152
*Project, The* 270
public opinion polls
    2010 June 21
    2010 July 32
    2011 February 86
    2011 July 113
    2011 September 123–4

2012 September & October 220–1
2013 March 256

Queen's visit 129
Queensland floods 2011 85–7, 233, 235
Queensland Media Club 50
Quinlan, Gary 208

Ratzinger, Joseph 273
Ray, Robert 252
Razak, Najib 21
Reagan, Ronald 62, 95, 97
*Recollections of a Bleeding Heart* (Watson, D) 62
Reid, Alan 64–5, 178
Reith, Peter 60
'Remorse for Intemperate Speech' (Yeats) 72
Resource Super Profits Tax 21–2, 29
Rice, Condoleezza 68
Rice, Jordan 100
Richardson, Dennis 80, 82, 95, 138, 261
Richardson, Graham 248–9
Riley, Mark 88–9
Rio Summit 219
Rippingale, Sandy 63, 66
Robb, Andrew 37
Roberts-Smith, Ben 274
Robinson, Geoff 150
Robinson, Rowan 112
Robinson, Tracey 73
Rodgers, Don 121
Roosevelt, F D 96, 129
Rose, Campbell 36
Rose, Jonathan 30
Rotary Club of Adelaide 51
Roxon, Nicola 101–2, 141, 202, 221, 248, 253
royal commission into institutional responses to child sexual abuse 219–20
Rudd, Kevin
    adviser Kassabgi 55
    Afghanistan war 47
    anti-traditionalist 33
    asylum-seeker policy 27–8
    Beazley and 254–5
    challenge 2012 175–9

311

*Kevin Rudd (cont'd)*
    Cooney and 27
    defeat of Beazley 69
    Dixon and 38, 72
    economic policy 121
    emissions trading 44
    Foreign Minister 38, 122–3
    Fuelwatch scheme 241
    G20 261
    Gillard and 20–1, 24, 122–5, 135, 143, 177–8, 286
    Indigenous affairs 174
    Labor leadership 25
    leadership challenges 4, 255
    loses office 2010 122
    Mark Baker on 202
    media exposure 29
    'mining tax' 29
    National Conference 2009 133–4
    National Conference 2011 135
    not challenging Gillard 255–6, 285
    perceived legitimacy 50
    poker machines 103
    population policy 28
    populism 228
    preferred vocabulary 100
    Prime Minister's Office (PMO) 12–13, 27
    relations with China 130
    same-sex marriage 134
    Shorten and 266
    Slipper and 140
    speechwriter 26
    staff 57
    support for return of 118, 124, 141
    UN Security Council bid 213
    YouTube footage 174–5
Rundle, Guy 281
Russell, Andrew 47
Ryan, T J 154, 223

Safe Rates 144, 146–7, 160, 192
Saggers, Amber 72
Salinger, J D 58
same-sex marriage 134
Sassoon, Siegfried 26–7
Sattler, Howard 278
*Saturday Paper*, the 59
Save Our Shipping 144
Sawyer, Lisa 146–7

Schlesinger, Arthur 112
Schoolkids Bonus 220
Schubert, Misha 71
Scullin, James 4
September 11 2001 terrorist attacks 46, 67, 97
Seven Network 88
*7.30 Report, The* 21, 28
sexism 195–6, 198–200, 221, 278
Sheldon, Tony 146–7
Shepherd, Tony 39
Sheridan, Greg 208, 210–11
Sherry, Nick 72
Shorten, Bill
    cabinet position 141
    equal pay for community services workers 192
    Minister for Financial Services 235
    Minister for Workplace Relations 253
    parliamentary secretary for disabilities 266
    poker machines 103–4
    visit to China 2013 259
*SIEV-221* 84–5
Singh, Amit 18, 246
Sinodinos, Arthur 210
Slipper, Peter 118, 140–1, 184–7, 192, 196–9
Smith, Mike 201, 259
Smith, Scott 213
Smith, Stephen 24, 66, 193, 284
Snowden, Edward 172
Sorkin, Aaron 59
Soutphommasane, Tim 150
speech writing
    allocation of speeches 15–16
    comments and revisions 16–17, 81, 94–5, 136–8, 215
    first drafts 15–16, 131–3
    last minute edits 12–14
    *see also* speeches
speeches
    address to US Congress 88, 90, 94–8
    Afghanistan war 49
    apology for forced adoptions 255
    Asia Society and Economic Club of New York 206–8
    Asian Century White Paper 213–16
    Australia Day Adelaide 2011 232–4
    Australian Industry Group 50–1

    B speech (Cooney's draft) 286–8
    on Chifley and Curtin 117–18
    'cunning and courage' 17
    draft for National Conference 2011 131–3
    'I will not lie down and die' 136, 153, 192
    Industry and Innovation Statement 148–50
    Light on the Hill address 38
    Lincoln Memorial, USA 90–2
    Lowy Institute 2010 28, 30
    Minerals Council of Australia 143, 190–1
    misogyny speech 194, 198–200, 221
    'moving forward' 28–30, 33
    National Conference 2011 134–9
    National Press Club 2010 30–1, 121
    National Press Club 2011 86, 114, 218, 228–30
    National Press Club 2013 247–9
    NSW Labor conference 2011 115
    NSW Labor conference 2012 136, 192
    'party called the Labor Party' 149, 160
    Per Capita 26
    Per Capita 2010 29–30
    Proclamation Day celebrations, Adelaide 52–3
    Queensland Media Club 50
    Rotary Club of Adelaide 51
    on success of UN Security Council bid 213
    Sydney Institute 106, 112
    UN General Assembly 208
    US Chamber of Commerce 93–4
    Victorian Labor Conference 2013 267
    'we are us' 133, 135–6, 139, 191
    Western Australia speech 28
    *see also* speech writing
Spencer, Stephen 59
Stanhope, Jon 26
Sterle, Glenn 145–6
Summers, Anne 202
*Sunday Herald-Sun,* the 33
*Sunday Telegraph,* the 264
*Supreme Command* (Cohen) 72
Swan, Wayne
    budget 2011-12 110, 112
    budget 2012-13 188–9
    budget 2013-14 279
    Chalmers and 18
    funding for DisabilityCare Australia 268
    Greens and 45
    press conferences 241–4
    Rudd and 176
    Treasurer 163
    Young and 16
    YouTube footage 181
Sydney Institute 106, 112, 145
*Sydney Morning Herald,* the 23, 46, 85, 123, 199, 260, 271, 278
Sydney, western 251

Taleb, Nassim 132
Taliban 47
*Tampa* 67
Tanner, Lindsay 24, 37, 97
Telstra 42, 121, 178–9
Ten News 43
Tendulkar, Sachin 60–1
Textor, Mark 210
*Third Policeman, The* (O'Brien) 166
Thomas, Hedley 85, 201
Thompson, George 65, 68
Thoreau, Henry David 6
Timor Leste 28
*Tin Drum, The* (Grass) 109
*Today Tonight* 21
Toohey, Paul 24
trade unions 143–60
Trans-Pacific Partnership 81, 93
Transport Workers Union (TWU) 143–6
*Trivial Pursuit* (Megalogenis) 33
Tuckey, Wilson 171
Turnbull, Malcolm 33, 44, 160, 252

UN General Assembly 208
UN Security Council 81, 87, 98, 206, 208, 211–13
United States of America
    Australian US alliance 5, 48, 80–3, 87, 90, 92–3, 96, 129, 216
    marine training in Darwin 14, 118, 129–30
    security presence in Asia 97

uranium sales to India  134

van Onselen, Peter  149
Veness, Peter  170
Vietnam Veterans Education Centre (USA)  90
Vietnam war  90–2

Wade, Matthew  245
*Walden* (Thoreau)  6–7
Walker, Tony  59, 208
Walsh, Eric  262
Walsh, Geoff  15, 57
Walsh, Peter  210
Ward, Eddie  156
Ward, Russel  156, 235
Watson, Chris  4, 160
Watson, Don  15, 62, 137, 230
Waugh, Steve  225
*Weekend Today*  21
Weereratne, Jessica  58
welfare reform  111–12
*West Wing, The*  59–60
*What I Saw at the Revolution* (Noonan)  62
White, Hugh  130, 211
Whitlam, Gough
    exclusion from Kingston Hotel bar  69
    Gillard on  116
    Hayden and  179
    press secretary Walsh  262
    private secretary Menadue  57
    program for government  41
    retired statesman  5
    visit to China  262–3
Wikileaks  226
Wilkie, Andrew  36, 102–4, 140, 153, 172, 177
Wilson, Bruce  200
Wilson, Harold  54
Wilson, Ray  18
Windsor, Tony  36, 140, 222
Withers, Reg  17
Wolpe, Bruce  286
*Woman's Day*  20
*Women's Weekly*  21, 228
Wong, Penny  37, 72, 197, 242
Wood, Brett  112

Wran, Neville  155
Wright, Tony  59

Xi Jinping  182

Yeats, W B  72
Young, Mick  16–18
Yousafzai, Malala  197, 199
Yudhoyono, Susilo Bambang  21, 209